The Abingdon Creative Preaching Annual 2015

The Abingdon Creative Preaching Annual

Jenee Woodard
Editor of textweek.com

Abingdon Press™

Nashville

ISBN 978-1-4267-8026-4; ISSN 2326-9898

14 15 16 17 18 19 20 21 22 23—10 9 8 7 6 5 4 3 2 1

MANUFACTURED IN THE UNITED STATES OF AMERICA

In memory of the Reverend Timothy P. Boal, who lent me his books

How to Use This Book

The *Abingdon Creative Preaching Annual* gathers the best of the best ideas and resources for preachers and teachers. Use this book as a starting point for the preparation of weekly sermons or other lessons. This resource will spur your creativity, providing a rich assortment of reflections, commentary, ideas for worship elements, poetry and other artistic resources, and websites in conversation about the weekly lectionary. The *Annual* will not write sermons for you but it will save you time and energy required to comb through the overwhelming array of resources now available in print and online.

For Lectionary Preaching or Teaching

- Read the texts and the week's meditations, commentaries, and other offerings. What strikes you as relevant or important for the people in your setting? What ideas or illustrations arise in your own mind?

- Next, take a look at the websites, videos, songs, and other elements suggested for the week's worship. What might resonate in your congregation?

- Allow ideas to emerge from the conversation in the printed text and elements you review online and in other resources. What rises to the top of your mind? What nudges at your heart? What generates the most energy for you? What matters most for your congregation?

For Non-Lectionary Preaching or Teaching

- If you have a Scripture text in mind, consult the index of scriptures (p. 243) to determine if it's in this year's lectionary cycle.

- If the passage is in this year's cycle, you may explore it here by turning to the appropriate week's material. Not every lectionary text is explored each week. Knowing where the text appears in the lectionary, however, can lead you to additional resources online. Textweek.com is a great first stop for exploring any lectionary passage.

- If the passage is not in the cycle, or if you are starting your sermon prep with a theme rather than with scripture, review the index of themes (p. 247). There you will find topical listings from throughout the lectionary year, which you can use for thematic sermon or lesson preparation.

- Please see page 250 for instructions on how to access the online version of this resource.

Contents

April

May

June

July

August

September

October

November

December

Resources

Introduction

How do we communicate about Scripture, about ancient, living text, within current congregations and with people who may not be fully part of those congregations? How do we communicate at once with folks who have read the Bible all their lives and find something fulfilling and important about each text, with people who feel wounded by interpretations of certain passages, and with people who do not know Scripture well, or find Scripture merely irrelevant? How do we communicate about interpretations of Scripture throughout the ages that have led to evil, in an increasingly global world where people look at "religion" with more and more suspicion? How do we understand and communicate Scripture within our congregations, our communities, and the world where we who find deep meaning in the text may no longer be among the majority, even within our own congregations? And how do we understand and perform the task of preaching when we are often speaking to all of these audiences at once, perhaps no longer from a position of authority, and perhaps no longer with full attention, and perhaps no longer with the expectation that there is "something here" at all?

This is the very difficult task of preachers in our contemporary churches.

How do we keep from becoming a club where everyone thinks alike, pretending that this thinking is biblical and going about what we do without thinking much about whether or not that is true? How do we read the Bible in a way that leads to more unified community and to mission that has an actual effect on the world of our hearers, as individuals and as communities? How do we keep Scripture in any way central to our thinking as individuals and communities when programs, media, church-growth strategies, branding, and slogans all vie for our fear and attention? The Spirit moves among us and takes us into strange places, indeed!

Looking and Listening

I have been thinking a lot about a ministry of listening and looking, of being quiet and hearing the word of God through Scripture and through the world, and seeing the word of God in places I had not expected. This is hard work, but I believe it is a very important part of the work of the pastor. Pastors are increasingly pressed for time and attention in a world where denominations are divided or merely irrelevant, where hierarchies, congregations, and media watch ministry carefully; each looking for missteps as we seek to be in ministry to diverse populations within our communities and outside of them. The work of ministry—pastoral and preaching ministry—is rewarding, but it is very, very difficult. People and things clamor for our attention. Bible study attendance is either down or it is up, but it has become homogenous, leading our congregations to become every bit as homogenous as they were in the "dreaded" 1950s, only in different ways—around an issue, a political position, a moral stance. The Spirit moves through a congregation and something important is done, and then perhaps the Spirit moves on (or the congregation does), and the people are left thinking in old ways, which just yesterday were the new ways, and wondering what happened to the Spirit that was so immediate and present just a short time ago. So we seek to be creative, and somehow lose the whole thing.

I have been thinking a lot about a ministry of listening and looking, of being quiet and hearing and seeing the word of God in Scripture and in the world; finding it…living it inside myself and with the communities and relationships I share. It is difficult to look and to hear in our world; it is also dangerous in many ways. We do not necessarily score points with folks in our communities, hierarchies, and relationships by doing so. We don't necessarily gain members this way. More effective for all of that is probably thinking and listening less and coming up with what we think people want to hear on Sunday—what they want to listen to for how long and in what words, and even more, what they *don't* want to listen to or see or hear in the world, in their communities, in the world, and therefore from the pastor. So, we quickly whip up something that people will want to hear. Or we read a single commentary, or find a "good sermon" to preach. They are certainly out there, and this can be one way to provide a message that touches folks and helps them think about Scripture.

I wonder, though, about the discipline of the lectionary, and some of the wisdom there. I don't think I want to defend any particular lectionary too much. There are values and points of view in a pattern of reading, be it the *Revised Common Lectionary* (RCL) used here or another system. Scholars and well-meaning people created these systems for purposes that may not be currently helpful. There are problems with where the readings begin and end and which ones are skipped, and sometimes a system leaves out the "nasty bits" while including the parts that are "Rated Comfortable for All Audiences."

And yet, using a lectionary gets us all on one page, and in a way, gives us an opportunity (if we will take it) to actually listen. It presents us with a scripture to read carefully, individually and as communities. We take a week to look around us for that text and what it means. We take a week to really listen to others' understandings of that text, even when they speak in languages and concepts foreign to us or even abhorrent to us. We listen. We take our hands from our eyes and we look...for a week. We look and we listen. And then, only then, do we speak.

This volume is composed of images and stories, of exegesis and of liturgical material; all of it derived from looking at and listening to Scripture for a long time and then pared down to small glimpses. As I have read these contributions, I have considered them parables of a sort, how each participant experiences each text in his or her native way of understanding. The diversity here is not only that of race, country, and denominational and theological background but also of people who speak "in academic," who paint word pictures, who speak in poetry or song or prayer. We present here the works of teachers, preachers, church leaders, laypeople, poets, liturgists, and others as another way to look, and another way to listen carefully to Scripture.

Readers may use this volume in many ways. Topical preachers might browse and find topics that lead to texts that lead to deeper thought. Lectionary (and other scriptural) preachers might read little by little and learn to see and hear through different eyes and ears for a time. Nonpreachers might use the book to help them think about how various perspectives fit and don't fit their view of a text, and how struggling with this can lead to new interpretation and deeper understanding. Readers might use the book as an opportunity to spend time in and with Scripture through the perspectives of others who have also spent time with Scripture, in prayerful respect for how they have heard the Spirit moving. These parables of Scripture reading are short, diverse, and meant to be read throughout the week. Read easily, letting ideas flow back and forth, and then engage in conversation through the world of ministry as you seek to communicate the Spirit of God through the weekly text for your congregation in your setting.

I am very grateful for all of the people here who have shared their perspectives. They have taken large ideas and expressed them in very few words in order to allow you the room to think and listen and see through them and around them. Feel free to use these as starting places for your study and as thinking places—space within your busy lives and ministries. Spend time with Scripture, not just for your congregation and for the sake of a sermon, but for yourself and your relationships to God, Spirit, community, and self. I am grateful for Barbara A. Dick for compiling, editing, managing, and making this an especially useful volume by seeing to all of the things that make it so.

Take time. Read. Hear. See. May the peace of Christ be with you as you prayerfully immerse yourself in Scripture and emerge to communicate your particular experience to a community that is diverse and wary, but also very much in need of what you have found.

Jenee Woodard
Editor, *Abingdon Creative Preaching Annual 2015*
Curator, textweek.com

January 4, 2015

Epiphany (Year B)

Isaiah 60:1-6; Psalm 72:1-7, 10-14; Ephesians 3:1-12; Matthew 2:1-12

John Wesley

http://www.ccel.org/ccel/wesley/notes

Isaiah 60:1

"Arise"—A word of encouragement accommodated to the Jewish, or Hebrew style, wherein, as by lying down, is described a servile and calamitous condition, chap. xlvii, 1, so by rising, and standing up, a recovery out of it, into a free, and prosperous one, as may be seen frequently; Rouse up, intimating her deliverance to be at hand. Here under a type, of Jerusalem's restoration, is displayed the flourishing state of the Gentile—church, under the Messiah. Thy light—Thy flourishing and prosperous state.

Ephesians 3

This chapter consists of two parts. I. Of the account which Paul gives the Ephesians concerning himself, as he was appointed by God to be the apostle of the Gentiles, ver. 1-13. II. Of his devout and affectionate prayer to God for the Ephesians, ver. 14-21. We may observe it to have been very much the practice of this apostle to intermix, with his instructions and counsels, intercessions and prayers to God for those to whom he wrote, as knowing that all his instructions and teachings would be useless and vain, except God did co-operate with them, and render them effectual. This is an example that all the ministers of Christ should copy after, praying earnestly that the efficacious operations of the divine Spirit may attend their ministrations, and crown them with success.

http://www.ccel.org/ccel/henry/mhc6.Eph.iv.html

Chuck Aaron

Isaiah 60, Ephesians 3; Matthew 2

The readings from Isaiah, Ephesians, and Matthew all proclaim a grand message with wide implications. Although Isaiah acknowledges the reality of the "darkness" and "gloom," he calls for the people to lift their eyes to see the far-reaching effects of the Lord's influence. First, the community itself will be reestablished as the sons and daughters return. Then, the nations, those at enmity with Judah, will bring gifts. The scene painted by the prophet is at once both worldly and otherworldly. The prophet assumes that this reconciliation will take place in this life, in this world, not in a resurrection scene. Nevertheless, the promised reconciliation seems impossible given human nature and international relations. The prophet still suggests an international influence for the people and the overcoming of barriers and animosity.

In the Ephesians passage, the Pauline voice reveals a cosmic dimension to the role of the church. God has had a hidden plan to include all people in the church. This diverse church now speaks to the cosmic forces of evil, revealing divine wisdom.

The well-known story of the visit of the magi displays the significance of the birth of Jesus for the wider world, beyond his role to his people, the Judeans. Does the story suggest that God can use even the Babylonian religion of astrology to bring Gentiles to an understanding of Jesus' significance? Just as the Isaiah passage acknowledges the darkness, so this charming story becomes the precursor to great horror, with the murder of the children.

In January, on Epiphany Sunday, these three passages recognize the evil in creation, yet promise reconciliation among people and the powers that hold creation in bondage. This promise offers hope, energy, and assurance as the church looks ahead to the challenges and opportunities of a new year.

Marci Auld Glass

http://www.marciglass.com

Matthew 2

The epiphany is only the beginning of the changes for the magi. And not all changes are easy. The epiphany of a child born as king in Bethlehem shakes the palace in Jerusalem. The world responds when God breaks into the world—and it is not always peaceful. I invite you to read ahead in Matthew this week and see how the powers of the world respond to the epiphany.

The magi are warned in a dream not to return to Herod, so they leave for their own country by another road. But Matthew doesn't say what happens next for the magi.

Do they make it home?

And if they do make it home, what is it like to return to their routine?

We don't know what happened with the magi, but we do know that once you encounter Jesus, you travel on different roads. Epiphany is about God coming to us in ways we would never have predicted on our own.

Because, really, if you can come up with the idea on your own, then what need do you have for Epiphany? And, post-Epiphany, you don't travel the same roads; you go home by another road.

What star will we follow as we journey? How will we prepare for this other road?

Minnie Louise Haskins put it well in her poem, "God Knows": "And I said to the man who stood at the gate of the year, / "Give me a light that I may tread safely into the unknown."

He replied, "Go out into the darkness and put your hand into the hand of God. That shall be to you better than a light and safer than the known way" (*The Desert, 1908*).

(Excerpt from http://marciglass.com/2009/01/08/home-by-another-way/)

Editor's Insights

Go Home Another Way (Matthew 2)

The wise men/astrologers/kings were told to look for one thing. They found another. They were sent to be part of the promotion of evil uses of power or at least to contribute to the wealth and power of a system that is pronounced evil by the writer of Matthew. They were sent as kings, as those who know what they are looking for and have an idea what must be done when they get there in order to further their self-interest in a world where they have precarious power. And they experience a conversion.

What changes their minds about who this is they seek? What changes *our* minds about our behavior in the world, from self-serving to giving ourselves away and putting ourselves in inconvenient and even dangerous places for the sake of God in Christ? How do we see in new ways what all of that means and become part of such change in our own communities, in situations that may turn us from people of respect and power into people who need to "go home another way"?

Conversions. Learning to see Christ anew. It's not always about becoming part of a social group that supports us and helps us feel good about our choices. Sometimes it's dangerous. Sometimes it's confusing. Sometimes we leave our greatest treasures at the feet of Jesus before we go on to our new, more precarious lives. This, too, can be gospel.

Eric D. Barreto

Matthew 2

In Latin America, January 6th marks the celebration of Three King's Day. On that day, children collect grass and water in a shoebox, which they leave under their beds. During the night the magi visit, taking the gathered supplies for their camels and leaving a present in their place. This joyous holiday, of course, relies on the story of the astrologers from the East who chase a mobile star in the heavens that leads to the doorstep of a toddler Jesus.

For me, there are at least two critical facets to this narrative. First, that the magi follow this star for some incredible distance is a sign of the expansive import of Jesus' birth; this was worldwide, breaking news. The indefatigability of the magi in chasing this star is an example of deep faithfulness as well as openness to see the signs of the time and follow them wherever they may lead. Second, this is also a frightening story. Herod's interest in this child is not the same as that of the magi. They come to worship a child in the shadow of his startled parents. They come to adorn him with extravagant gifts. Herod, however, sees in this child, and in the many others that populate his kingdom, a threat. Power is an addictive drug Herod is unwilling to relinquish. From the very first, therefore, Jesus' life is threatened by the political forces of his time. He represents a threat to their unchallenged reign and promises a world turned upside down.

At the same time, there are many who will see what Jesus' very presence means, even if it requires pursuing a star across the skies day after day. This is the very essence of faith on Epiphany.

Julie Craig

http://winsomelearnsome.com

Matthew 2

Led there by the star, they went home by another way. Possibly motivated by fear or perhaps by cunning, they eschewed the known route, and took off on an unknown path, carrying everything they had learned in Bethlehem with them.

Very early in my ministry, here in this river-and-railroad town, I did something kind of silly. I took an afternoon drive into the heart of town—famous for its one-way streets—for the sole purpose of getting lost and finding my way home again by different roads, but without a map. It's very easy to get lost in this town, but fortunately, there are many roads home.

As I drove, I found I had to rely on what I was able to perceive around me: Which side of the river was I on? How many times had I crossed the tracks? Were there any signs pointing me to the freeway? (This, technically, would have been cheating if I'd followed them.)

It was scary and exhilarating at the same time. It caused me to think: What if the church were to do this same thing? What if we went somewhere we had been before, but changed course and found ourselves going back home by another road?

What if continuing to do the same things over and over again and living our lives as if the act of kneeling at the manger changes nothing is our way of being complicit with the powers that be?

Two Bubbas and a Bible

http://lectionarylab.com

Matthew 2

Fear…joy—two fairly strongly contrasting emotions that dwell together in this text. Herod is "frightened" by the news of the magi who come in search of a king. By all accounts, he was a nervous fellow when it came to threats to his sovereignty. He "axed" several of his own family members when he thought they might be after his seat of power. He later orders the "Slaughter of the Innocents" in order to root out what was, in his mind, a pretender to his throne.

Okay, so much for fear; now we know why not only Herod but also "everyone in Jerusalem" was frightened.

The "wise men" from the East, despite Herod's best efforts, do find their way to the child, Jesus, and discover great joy.

They discover overwhelming joy, in fact. That's an interesting sensation to think about—when are the times you can remember being so happy that you were nearly overcome by it?

These guys aren't Jewish...and they probably don't fit anyone's definition of a Christian, either, at least not at this point in the story. We can't make them people of faith. But their response is instructive. They came a very long way to find this child, and when they met him, they knelt and offered him gifts.

I have an odd passion for what I call "Bumper Sticker Theology." I collect and remember pithy sayings about religious topics—most of which are pretty bad (think of the slogans you see on most church signs. Ouch!).

Occasionally, one will hit the mark. I think I once put a bright, pink bumper sticker on our family station wagon when I was young and enthusiastically evangelistic: *Wise Men Still Seek Him*!

Inclusive language issues aside, not a bad thought.

Carolyn Winfrey Gillette

http://www.carolynshymns.com/

Once Long Ago (Matthew 2)

SANDON 10.4.10.4.10.10 ("God of Our Life")

Once long ago, the wise men sought a king—a little child.
They brought him gifts so they could honor him; perhaps he smiled!
How can we honor Christ with what we bring?
How can we now give presents to our king?

We seek you, Christ, and far away we hear a child's small cry.
She lives with war, with constant daily fear, as loved ones die.
Christ, can we honor you with what we bring?
Can deeds for peace be gifts to you, our king?

We seek you, Christ, and close at home we see a child who's poor.
His family tries to pay for food and heat, but both cost more.
Christ, can we honor you with what we bring?
Can deeds of mercy make you smile, our king?

As we love neighbors, Christ, we also show our love for you.
When we serve those we may not even know, we serve you, too.
Now may we see what you would have us bring:
Our love for neighbors honors you, our king.

Biblical references: Matthew 2:1-12, 5:9, 25:31-46, 14:13-21; 22:34-40

Tune: Charles Henry Purday, 1860; Text: Copyright © 2008 Carolyn Winfrey Gillette. Email: bcgillette@comcast.net Web Site: www.carolynshymns.com

January 11, 2015
Baptism of the Lord

Genesis 1:1-5; Psalm 29; Acts 19:1-7; Mark 1:4-11

John Wesley

http://www.ccel.org/ccel/wesley/notes

Genesis 1:1

The holy scripture, being designed to maintain and improve natural religion, to repair the decays of it, and supply the defects of it, since the fall, lays down at first this principle of the unclouded light of nature: That this world was, in the beginning of time, created by a Being of infinite wisdom and power, who was himself before all time, and all worlds. And the first verse of the Bible gives us a surer and better, a more satisfying and useful knowledge of the origin of the universe, than all the volumes of the philosophers.

Acts 19:4

John baptized—That is, the whole baptism and preaching of John pointed at Christ. After this John is mentioned no more in the New Testament. Here he gives way to Christ altogether.

Sharron Blezard

Genesis 1; Psalm 29; Acts 19; Mark 1

Do you remember your baptism? If your parents brought you as an infant, you may remember the experience itself only through family story and image. If you were baptized as a teen or adult, your memory may be more vivid. Perhaps you recall the splash of water as it poured over your head or the feeling of being immersed beneath the water and then lifted up with a gasp for air. What you probably did not feel was that instant when the Spirit of God was gifted to you in the holy confluence of water and word. Most important, whether you remember the day or moment itself, your baptism changed you forever.

This Sunday's readings flow with water, word, and Spirit. God creates order from chaos in Genesis, making something new and good, bringing light that foreshadows the light that no darkness will ever quench. Psalm 29 praises God's majesty and creative power over the mighty waters, as well as mercy, grace, and blessing.

In Acts 19, Paul baptizes disciples in Ephesus in the name of Jesus, laying his hands on them and bestowing the gift of the Holy Spirit. Immediately, their lives are forever changed. Finally, in Mark's account of Jesus' baptism, the heavens are rent asunder, and the Spirit descends with power on the Son, and God is pleased.

These lessons flow with rich possibility, and no matter which way the Spirit guides and informs your proclamation this week, make sure to set a joyous tone where water is central to the sensory experience of worship. Do be attentive to those who may not yet have come to the living water. Welcome all to walk wet into a new reality as disciples of Christ, empowered and guided by the Holy Spirit, and made new each day.

5

Lowell E. Grisham

http://lowellsblog.blogspot.com/

Genesis 1; Psalm 29; Acts 19; Mark 1

Prayers of the People

Presider: Let us pray to our God, whose Spirit breathes life into being, that through baptism we may be empowered as God's beloved children to share in the healing and reconciling work of Christ, saying: God shall give strength to the people; God shall give us the blessing of peace.

Litanist: Fill your church with the power of your Holy Spirit, O God, that we may bring the light of your blessing to the whole world. God shall give strength to the people;

God shall give us the blessing of peace.

Let your gentle Spirit be upon this nation and upon all in authority, so that we may share in your work to bring forth justice upon the earth. God shall give strength to the people;

God shall give us the blessing of peace.

Let your prophets speak powerful words of repentance and transformation to the ends of the earth, so that the breath of your creative love and the sound of your blessing may go forth throughout the world. God shall give strength to the people;

God shall give us the blessing of peace.

Let your grace descend and dwell among the people of this community, that we may be united in love, abounding in compassion, and proactive in peace. God shall give strength to the people.

God shall give us the blessing of peace.

May your heavens open and your Spirit descend upon us,
    bringing your comfort and healing to all for whom we pray, especially ___.
Hear our grateful thanks and praise for your manifestation of presence and grace in our lives and in the lives of
    others, giving thanks especially for ___.
Welcome with your divine pleasure all who have died, especially ___, that they may have a place in your eternal
    domains.
God shall give strength to the people;

God shall give us the blessing of peace.

Presider: Gracious and loving God, you have anointed your people with the waters of baptism and have made us your beloved children: Let your Spirit spread mightily among us, that we may share in the work of your Son, bringing blessing and light to all the world in the power of the Holy Spirit, through Jesus Christ our Savior. Amen.

Teri Peterson

http://clevertitlehere.blogspot.com

Acts 19

We've not even heard that there is a Holy Spirit" (Acts 19:2b).

O Lord, how we have neglected your Spirit.

Though she is all over the Scripture, brooding over the waters and breathing life into creation and descending upon Jesus and enlivening the church, we forget that there's more to faith than an intellectual understanding of the One who is Three, more to who we are than created and redeemed, more to God than Word.

On this day when we remember Jesus' baptism, the Trinity comes into stark relief, but rather than seizing the opportunity of a new beginning, we're mostly relieved when it's over and we can go back to our comfortable and undisturbed blindness to the Holy Spirit. The Spirit changes things—brings life, but also chaos. There are cacophony and unmediated communication, breath and wind and flame and water, all of which both create and destroy.

This is what happens in baptism, of course. Gone is the predictable tradition we've carefully built up to control our experience of God, swept away in the water the Spirit has been carefully troubling for millennia. In its place is possibility, calling out in unexpected ways through strange voices. Water needs only the smallest crack to seep in, and the Spirit seeps in with those baptismal waters.

It's clear that baptism changes something—for Jesus and for the community we meet in Acts 19. Have we heard there is a Holy Spirit? How has that baptismal experience changed us?

Paul Bellan-Boyer

http://seedstuff.blogspot.com

Wading into the Water (Mark 1)

A friend of mine used to have a bumper sticker on his office door: "Faith = Risk."

It's true. If you ever try to do anything significant, anything that helps others, anything that can change the world, you step into troubled waters.

Stepping into the water is always a risk. We depend on water, yet from earliest times humans have that known water is dangerous, unpredictable. Storms and tsunamis cause the sea to break its bounds, rain causes rivers to rise and desert gullies to rage with flash floods. Even a wading pool is deep enough to drown in.

In the beginning, God wades into the water. In the Bible, creation happens when God steps into the disorder of the universe and begins to weave it into patterns of life, of justice, of love.

Unlike the other Gospels, Mark spends no time at all on Jesus' ancestry, birth, or youth. For Mark, the good news begins when Jesus steps into the water. The same is true of us. The good news begins when the water of Jesus washes over us, setting us free and setting us forth on a mission—albeit a risky one.

We should hear two things in this story of Jesus' baptism. First, he did not drown in the water. But it set him forth on a journey into the chaos of the human heart, with sufferings he could not imagine on that first day.

And second, that amazing word comes when Jesus steps into it: "Beloved." Weigh the risk of ministry against the reward. Wading into the water of life in Christ = risk. And it leads to the experience of God's favor, and the joy that comes when you hear that word, "Beloved," and share it with the world.

Suzanne Guthrie

http://www.edgeofenclosure.org

Mark 1

Love tore the heavens open and spoke. If Jesus didn't comprehend the fullness of his being before that moment, with the help of John the Baptist at the Jordan River, he understands now. And, as Gregory of Nyssa says, all these things are a figure (*typos*) of ourselves. The Voice tears open the heavens to declare us Beloved.

Long ago, the unborn infant John *recognizes* Jesus, unseen, womb to womb. The baby John leaps for joy as the two mothers, Elizabeth and Mary, *recognizing* one another, fill with the Holy Spirit (Luke 1:41-4). Amniotic water prefigures Jordan River water and rebirth.

Now the two grown men face each other, their grim destinies before them. Again the Spirit descends upon them and "The Lord's voice is over the waters" (Psalm 29:3). They recognize each other—the bridegroom and the bridegroom's friend—together, at the inauguration of this last, self-sacrificial era of their lives. Or, perhaps, as before, they recognize and dedicate themselves to something entirely new. They meet again over the waters of new birth.

To touch this water is to say yes to the movement of the Holy Spirit—to new life, to new birth, to the Something Unseen waiting for the yes—waiting for you and I to *recognize* that something that is strangely familiar, but absolutely new.

"Christ is bathed in light; let us also be bathed in light. Christ is baptized; let us also go down with him, and rise with him."*

* Gregory of Nazianzus, Oration 39, 14, *Sancta Lumina* at http://www.crossroadsinitiative.com/library_article/394/baptism_of_the_lord___st._gregory_nazianzen.html, accessed August 5, 2013. [trans. ICEL (The Roman Catholic Liturgy of the Hours, 1974); quoted from *Celebrating the Seasons: Daily Spiritual Readings for the Christian Year* (Morehouse Publishing)]

John Petty

http://progressiveinvolvement.com

Mark 1

"All" the region of Judea and "all" the people of Jerusalem went out to John in the wilderness. What does this mean?

Jerusalem was a company town. Some of the inhabitants literally lived in the shadow of the temple, and thousands worked there. The temple had its own tradition-approved mechanisms for repentance and dealing with sin. Institutional and traditional religion, always expert at sin, had sin covered.

The Lord God, however, was not operating through the existing institutional channel of the temple, but rather the "voice" directed the people to the uncharted territory of the wilderness. The people went there to confess their sins and not to the temple.

In other words, they walked right by where they were supposed to go and went instead to see a prophetic preacher out in the middle of nowhere. Mark's gospel has only just begun and already we see the outlines of the ensuing conflict: wilderness vs. temple, Jesus vs. Jerusalem.

Mark then calls attention to John's dress and behavior: "John wore clothes made of camel's hair, with a leather belt around his waist. He ate locusts and wild honey" (v. 6). Compare 2 Kings 1:8: "They said to him, 'He wore clothes made of hair with a leather belt around his waist.' [He] said, 'That was Elijah from Tishbe.'"

Mark is obviously drawing a parallel between Elijah and John. The book of Malachi—the last book of the Old Testament—ended with the promise of the coming of Elijah, who would bring in "the great and terrifying day of the Lord" (Malachi 4:5). For Mark, that day has now arrived. Moreover, the mention of Elijah had a political dimension. Elijah, after all, had plotted against the king.

January 18, 2015
2nd Sunday after Epiphany

1 Samuel 3:1-10, (11-20); Psalm 139:1-6, 13-18; 1 Corinthians 6:12-20; John 1:43-51

John Wesley

http://www.ccel.org/ccel/wesley/notes

1 Samuel 3:10

Came and stood—Before, he spake to him at a distance, even from the holy oracle between the cherubim: but now, to prevent all further mistake, the voice came near to him, as if the person speaking had been standing near him.

John 1:46

Can any good thing come out of Nazareth? How cautiously should we guard against popular prejudices? When these had once possessed so honest a heart as that of Nathanael, they led him to suspect the blessed Jesus himself for an impostor, because he had been brought up at Nazareth. But his integrity prevailed over that foolish bias, and laid him open to the force of evidence, which a candid inquirer will always be glad to admit, even when it brings the most unexpected discoveries.

Dan R. Dick

1 Samuel 3

We live in the age of "too much of a good thing." In Samuel's day, "the word of the Lord was rare," and "visions were not widespread" (v. 1 NRSV). It was difficult to know what God wanted or intended because the messages were few and far between. Ah, simpler days. In our modern world, words attributed to God are everywhere, and visions abound on street corners, television, the Internet, and in any of thousands and thousands of Christian churches. God's "word" comes in translations, versions, paraphrases, studies, commentaries, and even abysmally inaccurate fictional print, video, and digital formats. Religious pundits claim to know God's will for us all. Many assert an exclusive possession of "the Truth." It's interesting how rarely these interpretations agree. With Samuel, there was scarcity; with us, abundance. However, we both share a significant problem: when the word arrives, do we have the wisdom to listen and to understand? Samuel received one word echoing through a vacuum; we are inundated by a cacophony of words. How can we know when the word is from God?

Imperfect as it may be, our best recourse to "hearing the word" is our Christian community. Together, we have both the privilege and the responsibility to discern the Spirit and confirm the word and the will of God. Together, we are greater than the sum of our parts. Together, we can see that which remains hidden individually. In prayer, in study, in contemplative reflection, we come together to share our perceptions and faithfully to seek God's guidance and direction. Whenever we gather for worship, our collective invitation should be: "Speak, Lord, for your servants are listening." Thanks be to God that in the chaos of competing words and noise, we have one another with whom to sort it all out.

Elizabeth Quick
http://bethquick.com

1 Samuel 3

- Along with today's texts from Psalms/John, this text makes a great day for preaching about call and what we're meant to be doing.

- Samuel is confused about the voice he keeps hearing, thinking Eli is calling him. But his confusion doesn't keep Samuel from being willing, repeatedly, to respond.

- Eli plays such an important role, helping Samuel understand what's happening to him. It's an essential role in ministry to have supporters, encouragers, and guides for those trying to discern a call from God. To whom have you been an Eli?

Psalm 139

- It is both comforting *and challenging* to know that we can't go where God is not. We're reminded that God chases after us. We are "hemmed in" behind and before. God is strategically cornering us; a persistent God, who doesn't want to be ignored!

- This psalm affirms God and God's power *and our human* worth and goodness—a rare scriptural combination. You are fearfully, wonderfully made. Do you know it? How are we taught or discouraged from believing it?

John 1

- This is the second time in this chapter that Jesus tells someone to "Come and see." He's just said it to Andrew, when John the Baptist "introduced" Andrew to Jesus, and Andrew asked Jesus where he was staying. Now, he tells Nathanael. It's as if Jesus gives him a dare. "Do you want answers? I dare you to come and see for yourself."

- "Do you believe because of [this]?" Jesus doesn't want Nathanael to believe because of "magic tricks" but because of something deeper. Why do *you* believe in Jesus?

- "Follow me." Jesus doesn't give many details on which they can base their decision, does he? What's the most daring thing you've ever done? Have you ever trusted or acted based on so little?

Cameron Howard

Psalm 139

Thanks to social media, we all know a lot about one another these days. A quick scroll through my Facebook news feed tells me who is expecting a baby, who is having sushi for dinner, and who just bought a new novel for her e-reader. A web search for a new acquaintance tells me where he is from, what his job is, and how much money he gave to his favorite political candidates. But the searching and knowing of Psalm 139 are of a very different sort. The knowledge God has of us is not information about us, but rather the most intimate understanding of our inmost being. Such knowledge does not come from research; instead, God knows us deeply because God created us.

In verses 13-18, the psalmist imagines God's creative projects in terms of a handicraft, specifically knitting or weaving. Any crafter or artist understands the intimacy with which she comes to know her own work. "Your eyes beheld my unformed substance" (v. 16a NRSV): only the creator knows the details of the warp and the weft, the slub of the yarn, the sheen of the gesso on the blank canvas, or where the seams start, stop, and start again. Whereas we might more easily understand what it is like to be the *maker* of something, embracing our *made-ness* is less instinctive. Yet the psalmist emphasizes what is most important for us to understand about our status as ones created: "Wonderful are your works;

/ that I know very well" (v. 14b NRSV). We know that God's works are wonderful, and we are God's works; therefore, we are wonderful! In a world that judges us by our resumés, our places of origin, or our social media profiles, Psalm 139 is a welcome reminder that we are searched, known, and made wonderful simply by having been made by our creator.

Ann Scull
http://seedstuff.blogspot.com

Useful Images
See http://seedstuff.blogspot.com.au/2012/01/epiphany-2-b-january-15th-called-by.html (accessed April 15, 2013). One matches Psalm 139:17-18, and one is a reflection on ministry and calling.

Listening Song
Sons of Korah, "Psalm 139" on Rain (Sons of Korah, Australia, 2008) CD edition. This group simply sings the words of the psalm—beautifully.

Congregational Voice Drama
Tell or read the 1 Samuel story. Have the congregation respond to various words. For example, every time they hear the word Samuel have them shout "Yes, Lord!" Other responses might be: for *God* (Whoa!), for *run* (puff, puff, puff); for *sleep* get them to snore, and for *Eli* have them shout "I can't control my kids!" This is obviously for the children, but the adults have almost more fun participating in this than the kids (source unknown, but possibly me).

Film Clip
Simon Birch (1998). In this film, Simon struggles with his sense of call; he has issues with the difficulty of his call (he has a disability) and tries to determine exactly what God wants him to do and be. His minister is no help. There is a confronting scene in his minister's office that provides lots of opportunity for congregational discussion and reflection. This film is based on the book *A Prayer for Owen Meany* by John Irving.

Testimonies
Ask one or two people to share how they feel called to the particular ministry in which they are involved.

Response Activity
Ask, "What message about your faith might you like to pass on to the groups using our church building each week?" Have people submit their anonymous answers with their offerings. Afterward, collate all the messages on a handout and print enough to give out to all who come in contact with your church in the following week.

Julia Seymour
http://lutheranjulia.blogspot.com

1 Corinthians 6
Belonging to Christ does not allow rival claims. We are not washed onto the shores of grace so that our primary allegiance can be to our country of origin, our family of origin, or what we believe originates from within us. We are brought into a new kind of relationship, which alters the way we see the world.

What we do with our bodies, our time, and our possessions is no longer private when we are openly recognized as a member of the body of Christ. The church is not a private sin-analysis club, where we pick over one another's shortcomings. Nor is it a private-salvation society, where we rejoice in being chosen and pity the poor saps who are not as fortunate as we.

We are, instead, brought into a community in order to learn together how to live and die in Christ for the sake of the world. We are brought together to practice the radical life to which we are called in the safety of the community space. Then we plunge out into the world to carry out the mission of uncompromising grace.

If, like the Corinthians, we get caught up in what's okay and what's not—if we decide to skirt full body-mind-spirit morality and ethical living—then we undermine what it means to be included in God's radical work. Let us shudder at the thought of cheapening grace by conflating God's forgiveness with God's permission.

By being included in the body of Christ, we do not belong to ourselves. We do not live for ourselves or even for our children. We do not die for them. We live and die, body and mind and spirit, for the sake of Christ in the world.

Natalie Ann Sims
http://lectionarysong.blogspot.com

1 Corinthians 6 (Glorify God with Your Body)
- "Sacred the Body" (Ruth Duck)—This is one of very few good songs about the sacredness of the body. The tune is new, but it is both simple and beautiful, and should be learned very quickly by most congregations. "Sacred the body God has created, / temple of Spirit that dwells deep inside." Find the tune and lyrics at the Baylor University Christian Ethics Hymns Library (http://www.baylor.edu/christianethics/index.php?id=15937; an excellent resource!).
- "Come Build a Church" (Ken Medema)—Excellent words: "Come build a church of human frailty, / come build a church of flesh and blood." Not great for the congregation, but good for a choir or musicians (sound sample and sheet music: http://www.sheetmusicplus.com/title/Come-Build-A-Church/18402296)

John 1 (Jesus Calls Philip and Nathaniel)
- "I Have Called You by Your Name" (Dan Damon)—This is a great song for confirmation, ordination, and commissioning, but also ordinary Sundays. Easy, natural tune and good words about having courage to follow where God leads.
- "God Has Laid a Feasting Table / Invitation" (Shawn Whelan)—Feminine imagery of God gathering her guests together. Fun Cuban rhythm (lyrics, sound sample, songbook http://www.wholenote.com.au/songs/invitation.html).
- "Send Me Jesus" / "*Thuma mina*" (South African)—A very well-known short song that is particularly beautiful sung strongly with all four parts. The English translation also fits very well.
- "Jesus Calls Us Here to Meet Him" (John Bell)—Good words to a rollicking, or gentle, Scottish tune (depending on how you play it). The fourth verse, which is not in all sources, leads to Communion (tune PDF and Sound Samples: http://www.smallchurchmusic.com/index.php?KeyWordType=Title&KeyWordData=jesus+calls+us+here+to+meet).
- "Come with Me" / "Sing Hey for the Carpenter" (Iona)—I love this song; it's very joyous, especially the "Hey," reworded as "Yes" in some sources. The chorus is fun for kids too (lyrics: http://jmm.aaa.net.au/articles/18976.htm).

January 25, 2015

3rd Sunday after Epiphany

Jonah 3:1-5, 10; Psalm 62:5-12; 1 Corinthians 7:29-31; Mark 1:14-20

John Wesley

http://www.ccel.org/ccel/wesley/notes

Jonah 3:1

Exceeding great—The greatest city of the known world at that day, [Nineveh] was then in its flourishing state greater than Babylon, whose compass was three hundred eighty-five furlongs, but Nineveh was in compass, four hundred and eighty. It is said, her walls were an hundred foot in height, her walls broad enough for three coaches to meet, and safely pass by each other; that it had fifteen hundred towers on its walls, each two hundred foot high, and one million, four hundred thousand men employed for eight years to build it.

Mark 1

Repentance frequently means an inward change, a change of mind from sin to holiness. But we now speak of it in a quite different sense, as it is one kind of self-knowledge, the knowing ourselves sinners, yea, guilty, helpless sinners, even though we know we are children of God.

Sermon 14, The Repentance of Believers, Sermons of John Wesley http://www.umcmission.org/Find-Resources/Global-Praise—Worship-and-Spiritual-Growth/John-Wesley-Sermons/Sermon-14-The-Repentance-of-Believers

Liz Crumlish

http://somethingtostandon.blogspot.co.uk/

Jonah 3

It is said that it is a woman's prerogative to change her mind. Clearly this privilege belongs also to God—and the Ninevites. Hearing Jonah's message about their impending doom, they change their ways and turn aside God's wrath. Jonah must have been some preacher! It intrigues me that we don't celebrate his preaching prowess or even acknowledge the fact that his rhetoric convinced a whole city to repent and escape annihilation. Instead we make a parody of how he ran from God's call, stowed away on a ship, was tossed overboard and swallowed by a great fish. Nor do we pause to wonder that God gave Jonah the benefit of being commissioned a second time after refusing to accept the first challenge.

It sometimes appears that the mission of biblical interpreters is to cast a spotlight on how flawed many biblical characters were, even to point out the many failings of those now considered "giants of faith."

Is that to make today's disciples look better?

Is it so that our failings don't seem so terrible?

I'm advocating that, just for a moment, we celebrate Jonah's effective preaching and maybe even applaud the adventures he experienced in his circuitous journey to Nineveh. Let's give him cool points for striding into the middle of a city to proclaim God's word, a word that wasn't pleasant to hear if you were a Ninevite.

Jonah did all this even though, from the first time God called him, he was able to predict the outcome. Nevertheless, he put his heart and soul into it and turned around a nation. Isn't that worth celebrating?

Editor's Insights

Learning Honesty from Jonah (Jonah 3)

Sometimes I imagine Jonah telling this story about himself, with his closest friends, when he is honest about his life and what it really means to follow God. With his friends, he can be honest. He doesn't have to show his good side. He can show how very many times he didn't understand, how very many times he looked the other way, how very many times he argued with God and even tried to ignore God. I imagine him looking inside and having a bit of a laugh at himself and at the extent to which he tried not to follow.

Now and then, I like to have a bit of a laugh at myself and at all I do to try to get away from God's call. Most of the time, of course, I am faithful, and I am earnest, and I am, in my own mind, the very example of whoever does the "right thing" in a Scripture passage. I think the same of those who agree with me. But sometimes it really does a soul good to sit back and laugh with friends about our failures, and to think seriously about the grace of God in the midst of all of that. It's interesting to consider how that might look in various communities and relationships—sitting down, confessing not in hushed, fearful tones, but in laughter and in thankfulness for the grace of God who continues to call, continues to cajole, continues to teach, not just the Ninevites, but each of us as well.

Safiyah Fosua

Jonah 3

Just how big is a city that takes three days to cross by foot? Whether the description was a hyperbole or a metaphor, we cannot escape the fact that Nineveh was more like an urban city than a borough or a suburb. The traditional focus of Jonah 3 is upon the surprising receptivity of what we have come to think of as a wicked city, and the citywide conversion of the Ninevites. If we are honest about our stereotypes of large cities and city dwellers, we will have to admit that the appropriately ritual responses of the people of Nineveh surprise us, people we would have assumed to have very little knowledge of or interest in religious practices. Led by their king, they cover themselves in sackcloth, fast, and repent as a response to the word.

Though our eyes may have shifted from the reluctant prophet to the happy ending, the teller of the tale is not finished with his story of Jonah's conversion—for the book of Jonah is really two conversion stories in one. Jonah, who has learned his lesson, does not just complete the task from the edge of town; he embraces the city! Jonah, perhaps still reeking from the gastric juices of the large fish, took a one-day's walk into the city and began his preaching "in the thick of things," leaving us with questions about our own level of engagement with the cities around us. How deeply have *we* been converted? The overwhelmingly positive response of the Ninevites is a reminder that God loves the city as much as God loves the suburban or rural areas of our countries and that people in large cities are perhaps even *eager* to hear a word from God.

Todd Weir

http://bloomingcactus.typepad.com/

Jonah 3; Mark 1

Jonah is a patron saint of my cynical side. Sometimes it is impossible to imagine that those who disagree with me will ever change. The world beats me down, saying "you can't change the big picture; fall in line and don't worry about the world." My calling may say "head east to Nineveh," but I turn around and walk west and get on the boat with Jonah because it is too implausible to imagine an Assyrian repentance. Precious time is spent in the belly of the whale, out of touch with my calling. I am such a reluctant prophet when cynicism has a grip on me.

In Mark's gospel, Jesus calls Peter, Andrew, James, and John to be the first four disciples. While it takes three chapters for Jonah to get to Nineveh, in a remarkable four verses, these fishermen leave their nets, their security, and their families to follow Jesus. I know that I would want at least forty-eight hours to think through my decision, to weigh the consequences, to think about the family business and the implications of the career move. Of course, by the time I had done all that, Jesus would have moved on to the next town. The author tells us nothing of the disciples' inner deliberations, whether the fishing was good or bad, if they were religious people or not, if they got along with their parents or had a sense of wanderlust. Mark merely says, "And immediately... they followed him" (v. 18 NRSV; CEB has "Right away"). This connecting phrase, "and immediately," is the most common phrase in Mark's gospel, occurring thirty-three times in only sixteen chapters. (By the way, this phrase never occurs in Jonah!) Being able to hear and act on God's call in the moment is a precious gift of faith.

Linda Lee

Trust This Good News (Mark 1)

Jesus describes the coming of God's kingdom as a thing/place/experience of great value. In fact it is so great a treasure that those who discover it are willing to give up everything else they have valued in the past in order to hold on to it (see Matthew 13: 24-37).

In the Mark 1 passage, Jesus speaks of and embodies the hoped-for coming of the realm of God right now. Jesus has overcome the temptations of Satan in the desert and now reenters society to fulfill his Divine destiny. He has begun to call together those who will usher in this new realm of God after he is gone. Jesus assures them that God's realm is imminent, and that this is good news. "Now is the time! Here comes God's kingdom! Change your hearts and lives, and *trust this good news!*" (v. 15, emphasis added). Change and trust: two challenges for many human beings. Changing our hearts and lives means changing how we think, how we look at people and things, changing our self-perceptions, what we have believed, and what has been real for us. Changing our lives means giving up the lives we have now for something unknown. Jesus encourages his disciples then and now to trust that this unknown is good. As Christians, we spend much of our lives striving to be more like Christ, to follow him and to learn his ways. This is what Simon and Andrew did. Along with James and John, Mark says they made the life-changing decision to follow Jesus—immediately!

Following Jesus is the path to the kingdom of God.

For some of us it is an immediate life-forever-changed experience. For most, it is a lifelong journey. In whatever way it happens for us, God's kingdom come is the greatest treasure we will ever know.

John van de Laar

http://sacredise.com/

Mark 1

It's typical of Mark's gospel to throw us into the action with little preparation. After the briefest of introductions to John and his baptism of Jesus, Mark shifts directly to the content of Jesus' message. All the Gospels agree that the heart of Jesus' mission was the reign of God, but the second Gospel summarizes his message in a succinct pronouncement: "The time promised by God has come at last!... The Kingdom of God is near! Repent of your sins and believe the Good News!" (Mark 1:15 NLT). It's a proclamation that God's new order has arrived, and it requires a deep and significant change—a repentance—from those who would experience it. To describe what this means, the writer moves directly to the impact of Jesus' mission on the ones he called.

The first disciples are fishermen, and Jesus' call comes to them in continuity with who they are and what they do: They are to become fishers of people. It is comforting to know that God's call embraces our abilities and invites us to offer them for the sake of God's mission.

But this call also contains discontinuity. Jesus invites his followers into community. Ultimately this means that they must learn to love those who naturally would have been their enemies. Contrary to their natural inclinations, Jesus calls these first followers to become the manifestation of God's reign in their "unnatural" love for one another.

The time is still now. God's reign is still near, and we still are called to repent and believe it, which means to offer our gifts for God's purpose and to learn to participate in communities of "unnatural" love for one another. The question is whether we will be willing to attempt to live God's dream.

For more detail see: http://sacredise.com/blog/?p=1105

Martha Spong
http://marthaspong.com/

Mark 1

We expect it now, the leaving of the children. If they stay too close to home, we may wonder why. (Or we may wonder about other people's children. You know it's true.) We despair when the economy drives them home—this Boomerang Generation—and fall back into parental patterns we ought to have abandoned. We expect them to leave.

James and John, however, did not do something expected or what we might call "developmentally appropriate." In a culture where no one left home, they just took off. They left things behind: boats, nets, responsibilities, and dear old Dad. Immediately, they dropped it all to follow Jesus.

My children left home at the expected times. They reside at college and graduate school and in the adult world. In some ways, I am Zebedee. I stand in the boat, watching as they follow their hearts. But as the last one prepared to leave, I left too. I listened to a call from God to make a dramatic change in geography and personal circumstances. Like James and John, I got out of the boat and went.

I did not, however, leave immediately. I planned. I considered. I scheduled. I did not waffle about the outcome, but I made sure to take everything imaginable into consideration first. Which leaves me to wonder, did Zebedee do the same, eventually? If he did, I imagine he made careful arrangements for business and family, and issued judicious inquiries to discover where his sons had gone. I envision a deliberate journey to follow them.

I see myself, the last time we read this story in Mark's gospel, making my plans, my faithful and timely plans. It took us longer, but Zebedee and I are on the road with Jesus, too.

February 1, 2015

4th Sunday after Epiphany

Deuteronomy 18:15-20; Psalm 111; 1 Corinthians 8:1-13; Mark 1:21-28

Carolyn Winfrey Gillette

http://www.carolynshymns.com/

God, Send Your Prophets Here

LEONI 6.6.8.4 ("The God of Abraham Praise")

God, send your prophets here,
For all around we see
The sinful, broken values of humanity.
Accepting death and fear,
Our nations go to war
And so deny that peace is worth our struggling for.

Send stewards of the earth,
For it's becoming plain:
This world we haven't cared for cries aloud in pain.
Forgetting nature's worth,
Consuming for today,
We never realize what it is we throw away.

Send ones who love the poor,
For leaders arm the lands;
They buy their tanks and take the food from children's hands.
With greed, we long for more
While others cry for bread;
Remind us that we can't be full till all are fed.

Who are your prophets here?
We wonder, Lord, and search—
And then we realize you are calling us, your church.
Your kingdom, God, is near;
You show what life can be!
So by your Spirit may we answer, "Lord, send me!"

Biblical reference: Deuteronomy 18:15-20

Tune: Hebrew melody adaptation by Thomas Olivers and Meyer Lyon, 1770. Text: Copyright © 2011 by Carolyn Winfrey Gillette. All rights reserved. Email: bcgillette@comcast.net Web site: www.carolynshymns.com

John Wesley

http://www.ccel.org/ccel/wesley/notes

1 Corinthians 8:10

Now if Christ be in you—Where the Spirit of Christ is, there is Christ.

Mark 1:26

A loud noise—For he was forbidden to speak. Christ would neither suffer those evil spirits to speak in opposition, nor yet in favour of him. He needed not their testimony, nor would encourage it, lest any should infer that he acted in concert with them.

David Lose

1 Corinthians 8; Mark 1

In stories, "firsts" matters: first lines, first characters introduced, first plot moves. They set the tone and often preview what is to come. In Mark's gospel, it's significant that Jesus' first activity is to cast out a demon. This first reveals the heart of Jesus' ministry: he has come to oppose any and all things that stand between the children of God and life abundant.

Technically, the casting out is the second thing that happens. The first is that he teaches with authority. But we're mistaken to divide these two. Jesus comes to teach about the coming kingdom of God and to offer people a new way to understand and relate to God. But that kingdom and the new relationship it creates is rooted in God's implacable opposition to evil in every form. Thus, Jesus isn't a teacher *and* a miracle worker. He is a teacher who's message is embodied and made real in and through his miracles, all of which—feeding, healing, casting out demons, and raising to life—stand against all that robs God's children of life.

This has implications beyond understanding Jesus, however. It also shapes our life in community. When Paul mediates a dispute in the Corinthian congregation about food that had been offered to idols in religious ceremonies before being sold at market, he does so stressing not arcane theological teaching or complex moral precepts but instead asks, "What is the most loving thing to do?" If in some situations that means abstaining from meat, abstain cheerfully; and if in other circumstances it means eating, then eat freely.

Paul offers us another way to name Jesus' vision of the kingdom. Out of love, God comes to stand against all that robs us of life…and invites us to do the same.

Julie Craig

http://winsomelearnsome.com

Mark 1

You couldn't pay me to be the pastor of a megachurch these days. No, really. If you've read many headlines lately, you know that some high profile megachurch pastors are having a rough time of it. You could say that some of them have brought it on themselves with extravagant lifestyles that appear to be so far out of touch with the lives of their congregations, or by preaching one word and living by quite another altogether, but, really, isn't that what we all do now and again?

But the high-profile, big-name, well-paid, easily recognized Prophets For Our Time must do this in public, with the scrutiny of the whole world (or at least their sizable corner of it) shining on them like a megawatt beacon. Well, no thank you to that. You know what they say; the faster the climb, the harder the fall. Prophets have been falling off the pedestal about as long as God has been calling them.

Truly prophetic ministry, which stands in the gap between the Divine and the creature, and mediates on behalf of both, is unsettling and disturbing. It unravels our tightly woven tapestries of What We Think We Understand About God. Rather than predicting the future, prophecy is more concerned with describing the present and recalling the past. Prophets don't break open fortune cookies; they lug around mirrors into which they must peer constantly and hold up in front of the people to whom they are called to bring Truth. Prophecy is dangerous. Looking into that mirror is dangerous; holding it up for other people to look into can be treacherous.

Have you thanked your prophet today?

D. Mark Davis

http://leftbehindandlovingit.blogspot.com/

Mark 1

This story is told as a *chiasm,* a literary form based on the letter X (chi). I will lift out the common elements of the verses from my translation to show how the chiasm is formed.

21. And he was coming into Capernaum...on the Sabbath having come into the
    synagogue....
    22. And they were amazed...he was teaching them as having authority....
        23....a man in an unclean spirit, and he cried aloud.
            24. Saying, "What to us and to you, Jesus Nazarean? Have you
                come to destroy us?
                I know who you are, the holy of the God.
            25. And Jesus censured him saying,
                "Be silent and come out of him."
        26....and crying out a great voice the unclean spirit exited....
    27. And all were amazed..."What is this? This teaching with authority?
28. And the report of him came out immediately...into the whole region of Galilee.

The outer layers (vv. 21, 28) are related to space, time, and setting. The next layers (vv. 22, 27) indicate amazement at Jesus' authority, first his teaching then his exorcism. The next layers (vv. 23, 26) are the utterances of the man/unclean spirit. At the heart of the story is the dialogue between Jesus and the man/unclean spirit (vv. 24, 25).

The chiasm shoves us toward the curious wordplay regarding the man and the unclean spirit. When the spirit speaks, he says "us," conflating the man's identity with the spirit's. In contrast, Jesus says "him." Jesus' first step in exorcising this spirit is to see and address the man and the spirit as separate entities, thus keeping the man's personal integrity intact.

The amazing authority of Jesus begins with seeing a tormented man and not conflating him with his tormenting spirit.

Karoline Lewis

Mark 1

The exorcism of the man with the unclean spirit is Jesus' first public act in the gospel of Mark. A comparison of the inaugural events of Jesus' ministry in each of the four Gospels indicates what's at stake for the evangelist's portrait of Jesus. For Mark, Jesus is the boundary crosser, made clear by his immediate confrontation with the demonic. From the beginning of Mark's gospel, we have a God who regularly transgresses boundaries and is not where any God should be. Framed by the tearing of the heavens at Jesus' baptism and the tearing of the temple curtain at Jesus' crucifixion, Mark's story insists that because of Jesus, we cannot keep God behind the walls of our making. God will not be kept at bay; nor will God be located in the safe and clean spaces we think God should be. Yet, that is our propensity as humans, isn't it? We keep God at a distance, place God inside our boxes of secure theological expectations of how God should be and act. But in Jesus, God bursts through any borders we erect, and permanently. There is no going back for God. When something is torn apart, you can't put it back together like it was before. You can mend the tear, but you will always know that everything has changed. And in Jesus, everything has.

Julia Seymour
http://lutheranjulia.blogspot.com

Mark 1

In the centuries since the man with an unclean spirit was healed, our understanding of our bodies has increased in leaps and bounds. We know even more now about the miracles of our brains, our nervous system, our circulatory system, our skeletal system. We have come to understand even more that we are fearfully and wonderfully made. And we have come to know, as well, the depth of mystery that remains within us about how some things happen and some things work.

As we have become more sophisticated in our knowledge, the forces that oppose God and try to tempt us from faith have to increase their efforts as well. In our day and time, it is not demons that cause illnesses, but demons that accompany illnesses.

At the edge of our diagnoses are despair, loneliness, fear, doubt, guilt, grief, and a host of other pulls that steal our joy in life, our hope in Christ, and our faith in the truth of the Word of God.

These are precisely the demons that we are called to exorcise. You are. I am. We exorcise them by saying their names and banishing them. Despair is sent to hell through encouragement; loneliness, through companionship; fear, through prayer and information. And so it goes. By fervently exercising our faith through caring for our neighbors, we can exorcise their demons and ours.

Christ's love for the man in the crowd compelled the unclean spirit to flee his presence. Christ's love for us compels our demons to leave us. However, Christ's love for us also compels us to help the people around us deal with the negativity, the pain, and the unclean spirits that torment them.

February 8, 2015

5th Sunday after Epiphany

Isaiah 40:21-31; Psalm 147:1-11, 20c; 1 Corinthians 9:16-23; Mark 1:29-39

John Wesley

http://www.ccel.org/ccel/wesley/notes

Isaiah 40:24

Sown—They shall take no root, for planting and sowing are in order to taking root. They shall not continue and flourish, as they have vainly imagined, but shall be rooted up and perish.

1 Corinthians 9:17

Willingly—He seems to mean, without receiving anything. St. Paul here speaks in a manner peculiar to himself. Another might have preached willingly, and yet have received a maintenance from the Corinthians. But if he had received anything from them, he would have termed it preaching unwillingly. And so, in the next verse, another might have used that power without abusing it. But his own using it at all, he would have termed abusing it.

Liz Crumlish

http://somethingtostandon.blogspot.co.uk/

Isaiah 40; Mark 1

In the gospel of Mark, we often see Jesus enabling people to blend into their communities. Jesus acknowledges folk ostracized because of perceived shortcomings, be they physical, moral, or spiritual, and brings them back into community. For Jesus that was a costly exercise. It cost him energy and street cred. Often Jesus, in their place, took on their marginalization so that his physical, moral, and spiritual well-being was called into question. And there were few opportunities for him to recharge.

When Jesus healed Simon's mother-in-law, word soon got around and, it seems, by suppertime, the backyard was full of those seeking healing.

Jesus was simply unable to move around without attracting much unwanted attention.

The "Everlasting God" of Isaiah specializes in bringing the powerless to the fore and in giving courage to those who are afraid. Those who weary are called by name and given strength. Their eyes are opened to the reserves that reside within.

Perhaps effective discipleship today consists of blending well with our communities and bearing witness to Jesus who stands out from the crowd, offering wholeness and acceptance to all. Discipleship then becomes an enabling ministry in which people are alerted to their own strengths and encouraged to experience the wholeness that is God's will for all people.

Teri Peterson
http://clevertitlehere.blogspot.com

Mark 1

Someone had to stay behind.

So often when Jesus heals, the people ask to come along or begin to follow. This woman, apparently, stays behind when Jesus goes.

Sure, it wasn't as dramatic as raising the dead, but in some way it feels almost like more work to raise the living into fullness of life. So often, we experience transformation and then want to move on.

Yet Peter's mother-in-law doesn't immediately look for greener pastures; she keeps her deacon self here, right here where she's planted. Presumably, once Jesus changes her life, she shares that transformative power with others. After all, someone needs to live the good news right there in Capernaum. Jesus never intends to stay in each place forever, or even until everyone gets it. He teaches and heals, changing people from the inside out, breathing new life into bodies and communities, and when they're equipped then he gets back on the road.

In other words, Jesus models one of the pastoral roles: To equip the saints for ministry.

He certainly equipped Peter's mother-in-law to be a bearer of good news and a servant of her community. And so she becomes a model of another pastoral role: To stay behind and let grace grow in and through us right where we are.

Jesus needs this woman to answer her call to ministry right here, to carry on the mission right here, to embody the kingdom of God right here. She must have been faithful in her service, or she wouldn't be in the story. So we give thanks for her witness to the transformed life made possible when Jesus lifts us up.

Peter Woods

Mark 1

Superficially, this gospel passage has nuances of subterfuge and secrecy. As we examine it, though, it is actually a study in normalcy and simplicity.

It begins with a simple familial and pastoral visit by Jesus to Simon's mother-in-law. The absence of incantation, invocation, or any kind of prayer is interesting. Jesus simply takes the woman by the hand and lifts her up, realizing her inherent healing and prompting her desire for service. It is as if Jesus treats the woman as already whole, and so she is. He doesn't leverage healing; he recognizes it.

Perhaps the entire world would be whole if we could see in our daily reality, not our neurotic dis-ease with everything, but rather the inherent wholeness of the Divine Domain that is creatively God infused from the beginning?

The result is a spread of news and a gathering of need as the sun sets. The encroaching dark, so threatening to the sick and superstitious, is of no consequence to Jesus, the light of the world.

There is also a refreshing absence of ego in this Nazarene rabbi. He won't allow the oppositional energies at work in the shadow lands of the sick to name and proclaim him. Woody Allen's movie *To Rome with Love* parodies the fickleness of the paparazzi who proclaim grey Leopoldo "famous" only to exploit and abandon him on a whim. Is this part of why Jesus embargoes the proclamation of the demons?

The passage ends as it began. Jesus came from the synagogue to the ministry of healing and restoration. Now he returns to prayer, oblivious to the flurry of popularity in town and impervious to the seduction of celebrity. The church, at all levels, would do well to imitate the master in this.

Martha Spong
http://marthaspong.com/

Mark 1

My mother sat weakly in a comfortable chair, watching her grandsons play. Seven and two, they did not know the reason for our visit: Their grandmother was dying of cancer. The melanoma that began years before as a changed mole on her back was now in her liver. She grew frailer and fainter each day.

Although my father usually pressed money into my hand on the way out the door, Mother couldn't bear to think we might waste it on expensive food in the airport on our way home. While I made sandwiches, my mother mustered the strength to sit in a straight chair at the kitchen table.

She asked for a cutting board and two apples. She peeled and cored the apples, cutting them into neat slices, then putting them back together. She wrapped them in waxed paper, with a twist at the top that looked like a stem. It was the last time my mother would do something for another person.

When we opened the apples to eat on the plane, my eyes filled with tears. I will always remember the sacrament of apples, an outward and visible sign of an inward and spiritual grace. The apples carried her love; they healed the disappointments of an imperfect relationship.

The apples healed my mother, too. It's inconceivable, until the day we feel it. It's hard to grasp, until Jesus takes us by the hand and lifts us up off whatever sort of sickbed we inhabit. It's incomprehensible, until we feel the way love renews our strength, and the next thing we know, we're lifted up to serve. The next thing we know, we're slicing apples and wrapping them in waxed paper, with love.

John van de Laar
http://www.sacredise.com/

Mark 1

The start of Mark's gospel offers us not just a sound bite of Jesus' message, but a glimpse at how it operates in practice. It starts with Jesus healing Simon's sick mother-in-law. The description of Jesus' ministry to her is surprising in its detail, in spite of Mark's characteristic brevity, and there is a touching particularity to it. Then, once her fever has left her, Simon's mother-in-law serves Jesus and his disciples a meal. She has been served; and she immediately responds in kind.

Following this moment of individual attention, Mark shows Jesus ministering to a whole community, revealing how God's reign comes to both the individual and the world as a whole. The scene makes it clear that the new community of Jesus is getting to work. Among the crowds are those who have helped their sick friends get to Jesus. Hospitality would be offered. Organization would be necessary, and maybe even some crowd control. Jesus may do the healing, but the ministry is a community affair.

Finally, Mark gives a third glimpse into how this reign of God operates. Early the next morning, Jesus makes space to care for himself, going off alone to pray. He can do this because he knows that he now had a community that will keep things going while he is away.

If Mark wanted to give a three-dimensional picture of God's reign at work, he couldn't have done better. His description of these first couple of days of Jesus' ministry reveals, in remarkably few words, a community that provides individual care, community care, and space for self-care. All that's left for us is to emulate what we've seen so that others, in their turn, may learn from us.

For more detail see: http://sacredise.com/blog/?p=1112

February 15, 2015

Transfiguration Sunday

2 Kings 2:1-12; Psalm 50:1-6; 2 Corinthians 4:3-6; Mark 9:2-9

Amy Persons Parkes

2 Kings 2

"Hey, kids, we're going to go visit crazy ol' Uncle Elijah today. Remember, don't talk too loud or make any quick moves. And absolutely, do not open any door, drawer, or closet without permission!"

He prayed down fire to consume bull flesh, wood, stone, dust, and water; and he annihilated the priests of Baal who challenged him to the divine duel. He conversed with angels and hid in caves; he confronted people in power, denouncing their selfish ways and pronouncing their certain and grotesque deaths; and he killed the messengers—ignorant and innocent. Perhaps, even more inexplicable is the fact that Elijah has a friend.

Elisha's commitment to his "master" (v. 3) confounds me. I want to see Elijah and Elisha as the male version of Naomi and Ruth. Instead of Ruth's vow, "wherever you go, I will go" (Ruth 1:16a), I hear Elisha pledge, "I won't leave you" (v. 4b). But Elijah is no Naomi. Elijah seems to be the Mad-Eye Moody of Yahweh's prophets. We know that, deep down, he has a good heart; but other than the widow of Zarephath and her son, Elisha must be the only other person who sees it.

Yahweh's Mad-Eye Moody or not, Elijah has a friend who will not leave him, who is not ready to accept the coming transformation, who is more than happy to tell the know-it-alls not to talk about what's coming next. Elijah has a friend who desires to carry a part of his spirit into a world in which Elijah's body will not be present. Elijah has a friend who, grief-stricken, will wait and watch until the last vestige of his presence retreats into the Living Presence of the Almighty.

Some of us get Naomi; and then, there are those of us who get Elijah.

Ann Scull

http://seedstuff.blogspot.com

Listening Song

Kathy Troccoli, "Go Light Your Candle" on *Greatest Hits* (Franklin, Tennessee, Reunion, USA, 2003) CD Edition: This song fits well with the following story: "A Candle in the Darkness." You can help people to listen by projecting images that match with the words of the song.

Story

"A Candle in the Darkness" in Wayne Rice, *More Hot Illustrations for Youth Talks* (Grand Rapids: Zondervan, 1995, 17–18): This story connects particularly well with the 2 Corinthians reading but also with the other readings.

Prop: Use a self-igniting candle and explain: Daniel's light shone very brightly (light candle). Sometime ours does too, and at other times it is just a tiny glow. But, no matter what happens, once we have met God, there is no reason why our light should ever go out (*blow out self-lighting candle and then pause while candle reignites*). The trick is to stay close to God.

24

Response Activity: Ask the children to hand out a small candle to each person. Encourage everybody to light their candle each dinnertime during the week to remind them of the light of God.

Film Clip

Harry Potter and the Prisoner of Azkaban (2004): Show Dumbledore, in his welcome address, talking about turning on the light.

Sermon Introduction

Ask a few people to play a short game of the theater sport Space Jump (Google will help if you don't know how to play). Connect the game to our lives and to the gospel story: We are often so busy going from thing to thing that life often feels like a game of Space Jump. The disciples must have felt very much like they were playing a game of Space Jump with Jesus on the day of the transfiguration.

John Wesley

http://www.ccel.org/ccel/wesley/notes

2 Corinthians 4:4

The God of this world—What a sublime and horrible description of Satan! He is indeed the God of all that believe not, and works in them with inconceivable energy.

Mark 9:2

By themselves—That is, separate from the multitude: Apart—From the other apostles: and was transfigured—The Greek word seems to refer to the form of God, and the form of a servant, {mentioned by St. Paul, Phil. ii, 6, 7} and may intimate, that the Divine rays, which the indwelling God let out on this occasion, made the glorious change from one of these forms into the other. Matt. xvii, 1; Luke ix, 28.

Lowell E. Grisham

http://lowellsblog.blogspot.com/

Prayers of the People

Presider: God of eternal light and everlasting glory, send the Spirit of your Son Jesus Christ upon us, that we may be transfigured by the dazzling vision of his goodness, as we bring our prayers to you, saying: Give us the light of the knowledge of the glory of God in the face of Jesus Christ.

Litanist; You have caused your church to see the light of the gospel of the glory of Christ: Inspire our witness to him that all the earth may be raised to a new vision of your abiding presence and love. Give us the light of the knowledge of the glory of God

in the face of Jesus Christ.

Before you, O God, there is a consuming flame and round about you a raging storm: Humble our leaders and all who exercise authority among the nations of the world, that they may keep before them the vision of your peace. Give us the light of the knowledge of the glory of God

in the face of Jesus Christ.

Let your light shine in the hearts of this community and overshadow us with the cloud of your presence, that this place may be a place of transfiguring grace. Give us the light of the knowledge of the glory of God

in the face of Jesus Christ.

You see the suffering of people throughout the world who struggle in the face of poverty, violence, injustice, and illness; you know those desperate ones who have no hope or vision for themselves or their loved ones: Let your transfiguring grace bring light and hope to all who yearn for something new, O God. Give us the light of the knowledge of the glory of God

in the face of Jesus Christ.

Hear our prayers for all who need your light, especially ___.
We give you thanks for the light of your blessing, especially for ___.
Hear our prayers for those who have ascended with Elijah and Jesus into your eternal light, especially ___.
Give us the light of the knowledge of the glory of God
in the face of Jesus Christ.

Presider: Holy and ever-living God, grant us grace to ascend your holy mountain and to see the dazzling vision of your transfigured reality in our worship and prayer this day; and then strengthen us to listen to your voice and to follow you in faithful service, even when you are hidden from us, until at last we see you face-to-face in your eternal and everlasting glory, in the power of the Holy Spirit, through Jesus Christ our Savior. Amen.

Suzanne Guthrie

http://www.edgeofenclosure.org

Mark 9

Eternity breaks into this moment, Uncreated Light showing forth through the Incarnate Christ come into the world. The church completes the season of Epiphany with another theophany, another voice from heaven, echoing the baptism of Jesus. Theophany to theophany: parenthesis around this season of light and love.

A high mountain. The cloud of Presence. The voice of the Most High. The disciples fall into ecstasy. They see time disassemble. They see Jesus, Moses, and Elijah outside of time talking about something that will happen in time, Jesus' "exodus."

And the light! The Orthodox call it "Tabor Light." This light transfigured Moses, so that he had to wear a veil. This light blinded Paul on his way to Damascus. It is the light at the boundary of the soul, alluring us through meditation to continue deepening and remaining faithful when prayer is dark.

One thing I have learned about Tabor Light: you appropriate this light in prayer. You take in the light, and you become light, like a white blossom absorbing sunlight all day. And like the glow of that white blossom after dusk, you know you carry that light only when it is dark.

I love Epiphany, the season of befriending the Light. I love the liminal days between the Transfiguration and Ash Wednesday. I can linger on the mountain as the light fades. Soon, too soon, I must descent the side of the mountain facing Jerusalem.

Rick Morley

Mark 9

I never read the accounts of the transfiguration without feeling a strong sense of solidarity with Peter, who blurts out a bunch of nonsense because he didn't know what to say. I've been there. Haven't we all? Like Baby in *Dirty Dancing* awkwardly exclaiming that she "carried a watermelon," Peter felt he needed to say something because all of a sudden he felt so very small and insignificant. With all heaven breaking loose, and the holy heroes of ancient Israel showing up, he was, all of a sudden, hopelessly out of place and scared to death.

26

He wanted so desperately to say something, but apparently he also felt a desire to do something as well, as if this august occasion needed to be marked. Tabernacles needed to be erected to prolong this enlightening encounter, and designate the spot as holy. Doing something, anything, would give Peter an immediate sense of purpose, and assuage his self-doubt and need for affirmation.

But, as Peter learns, sometimes there's nothing to say and nothing to do. Sometimes all there is to do is stand there and soak in the holiness of the moment.

It takes a certain spiritual courage to speak up and act when the time calls for it. And, it also takes a certain spiritual courage to quiet the soul and be present to what God is doing here and now. How to know the difference between those two? Well, that takes a spiritual maturity that Peter doesn't yet have. But, he'll get there soon enough.

If we have the brave honesty to see ourselves in Peter here on the mountaintop, then perhaps we can also discern the moments of life and ministry in which what God wants from us is mindfulness and attention to the wondrous things he does.

Editor's Insights

Focus on the Sacred (Mark 9)

I do not understand transfiguration. I don't understand what it means or why this story is in our gospels. I've read a lot about it, and I've tried to consider it from many angles, but I don't understand it beyond the level of story and metaphor. I can't bring it into my own experience and my own life outside the walls of the church, which makes it difficult to live in my own life of faith or to consider as I seek to live in community with others. I can see lessons, I suppose, and I can see metaphors and things that are happening, but it's difficult to bring it home.

I do know a lot about one thing looking like another. I know a lot about things looking like glory and then fading. I know a lot about wanting to camp out and stay within the glow. I know a lot, also, about the hard work of following Jesus when it's not so pretty.

I'm still trying to figure out if these guys were seeing something positive or negative, if this story is the set up to the fall. Exactly who *are* Elijah and Moses here? But I do know about appearances, and about things meaning one thing and then meaning another. I know about things that have seemed essential in my life and faith becoming "images" as I walk on beside Jesus to live a more difficult chapter, one that calls into question the meaning of what I've held closest, dearest, and most sacred. I know about that in my real life, and I think others do as well.

The sacred comes into focus, and changes, and moves on. And it's easy. And it's hard. And we follow, no matter what it means we need to leave behind. And the sacred goes out of focus once again. We are called.

Thom M. Shuman

http://lectionaryliturgies.blogspot.com/

until

until
we see the faces
of those tossed onto
the world's garbage dumps,
    dazzling bright with
    hope and wholeness;

until
we respect the prophets
we have been yearning for
in the hip-hopped, do-ragged
        teenagers strutting
        through the malls;

until
we hear God's sweet
songs of peace and reconciliation
in the mother tongues
        of all we turn
        a deaf ear to;

until
we catch a glimpse
of you (out of the corner
of our shut-tight eyes)
        coming down off
        the shelf where we store you
        to enter our frayed lives;

maybe
we should have nothing to say...

        until

February 18, 2015

Ash Wednesday

Joel 2:1-2, 12-17 or Isaiah 58:1-12; Psalm 51:1-17; 2 Corinthians 5:20b–6:10; Matthew 6:1-6, 16-21

Natalie Ann Sims

http://lectionarysong.blogspot.com

Psalm 51 (A Prayer for Forgiveness and a New Heart)

• You might like to sing a favorite Kyrie.

• "Create in Me a Clean Heart, O God" (Digby Hannah)—This is a beautiful meditative song.

• "Create in Me a Pure Heart, O God" (Bruce Harding)—A nice round, with an optional descant part. Good for kids (available at https://www.melodicarts.com; free to join).

• "Have Mercy on Us, Lord" / "Khudaya, rahem kar" (Pakistan)—A nice Kyrie that can be used as a psalm refrain. It would be nice to get your congregation to sing something from South Asia. Also works well in English (sound sample at http://www.mennolink.org/cgi-bin/search.cgi?bk.sts.03.txt&track=17).

• "Lord Jesus Christ Son of the Living God" (Carol Browning)—A simple chant based on "The Jesus Prayer" with a beautiful (and optional) cantor, which is really worth using. Nice chords! (Sound sample: http://c1824532.cdn.cloudfiles.rackspacecloud.com/GC2_409-1.mp3; Lead sheet: http://c1824532.cdn.cloud-files.rackspacecloud.com/GC2_409-1.jpg)

• "O Tender God, Have Mercy" (Richard Bruxvoort-Colligan)—A gentle, modern version of the Kyrie (sound sample and lyrics: http://www.worldmaking.net/o-tender-god.php).

• "Jesus Christ, Son of God Have Mercy upon Us" (Iona Community)—A very simple call and response chant.

• "*Senzenina?*" / "What Have We Done?" (South African)—This beautiful chant asks the question that we often ask when things go wrong beyond belief. It's important to know what the song means when singing it. If you have some part-singers in your congregation, this would be particularly good. It is also on the soundtrack for *The Power of One*, so you could also play the recorded music (https://www.youtube.com/watch?v=MztK1bXbhIA). This could also work as a psalm response. (Free sheet music: http://humph.org/lw/concerts/13shakin/music/Senzenina.pdf)

• "On the Poor, on the Poor" / "*Kyrie Guarany*" (Pablo Sosa)—A simple Kyrie from Paraguay. The English translation varies widely. Good for kids. (Sound sample: http://www.giamusic.com/search_details.cfm?title_id=8096)

• "*Kyrie Eleison*" (Ghana / Reindorf)—Another common favorite. Easy to teach men the bass drone in the piano part (Sample: http://www.worshipworkshop.org.uk/songs-and-hymns/hymns/kyrie-eleison/)

John Wesley

http://www.ccel.org/ccel/wesley/notes

Joel 2:1

As the morning—As the morning spreads itself over all the hemisphere and first upon the high mountains, so shall the approaching calamities overspread this people.

Matthew 6:1

In the foregoing chapter, our Lord particularly described the nature of inward holiness. In this, he describes that purity of intention without which none of our outward actions are holy. This chapter contains four parts,

1. The right intention and manner of giving alms, ver. 1-4

2. The right intention, manner, form, and prerequisites of prayer, ver. 5-15

3. The right intention, and manner of fasting, ver. 16-18

4. The necessity of a pure intention in all things, unmixed either with the desire of riches, or worldly care, and fear of want, ver. 19-34

This verse is a general caution against vainglory, in any of our good works: All these are here summed up together, in the comprehensive word *righteousness*.

Todd Weir

http://bloomingcactus.typepad.com/

2 Corinthians 5–6

"Look, now is the right time! Look, now is the day of salvation!" (6:2b). These words bring me to a radical Lenten proposal. Perhaps the Christian focus on getting to heaven has become a selfish obsession that obscures the meaning of the gospel and our purpose as a church. Faith becomes avoiding the big sins and staying pure enough so we don't lose our heavenly prize. When we confess our sins, we are more likely to confess the sins of commission, of things we know we did wrong, but we are less likely to focus on the sins of omission, the good we did not do. Jesus did not model the spirituality of playing it safe. His great love for marginalized people in society raised the hackles of the Pharisees, who were playing it ultrasafe, who were secure in their sense of self-righteousness. They were far from God because they stood far off from those who suffered. We may want salvation because we want safety, but Jesus offers salvation because he wants us to be fully alive, embodying God's love and justice. Christians and churches who play it safe may wake up one morning to find that the world has so changed around them that they are swallowed up, like Jonah in the belly of the whale.

As Lent begins, let us hear Paul's exhortation with new ears. Today is the day of your salvation! And tomorrow! Don't forget Friday and Saturday, Sunday and Monday! In fact, work out your salvation daily, as Paul says in Philippians. Walk with God. Take courage as you face the trials of life: afflictions, hardships, calamities, sleepless nights, and hungers. God's salvation is near, with the power to see it through.

Mary J. Scifres

Treasures (Matthew 6)

Since reading Jesus' words of wisdom quoted in a Harry Potter novel several years ago, I have been haunted by the deep truth that treasures of our heart often go unnoticed and unattended. Matthew 6:21: "Where your treasure is, there your heart will be also" (NRSV) is etched upon the gravestone of Professor Dumbledore's mother and sister, whom he loved dearly but betrayed with foolish decisions and actions in his young adult years. In the book *Harry Potter and the Deathly Hallows*, Harry struggles to reconcile the wise, compassionate mentor he has known for the last six years with the stories he discovers of the power-hungry, self-absorbed young wizard Dumbledore had once been. The story haunts me when I realize how often each of us struggles to truly focus our time, attention, gifts, and priorities on the things we value most. In losing our focus, we may lose the treasure we value most. We so often store up treasures of productivity, wealth, vacuous fun, and manic schedules, neglecting the true treasures of love, people, faith, and discipleship. Even in discipleship, we often say yes to every church invitation and forget to say yes to Christ's deepest call in our lives. Churches and institutions face this temptation when we increase endowment funds and decrease ministry offerings or fill up rental calendars and slow down our schedule of outreach programs.

As we reflect and repent this Ash Wednesday, perhaps we should turn back (repent from) those things that fill our time but not our hearts. Reflecting on what we value most and what God calls each of us to do and be can help us return and refocus on what matters most: Christ's call; our life purpose; the love of God, neighbor, family, friends, and self that fills our souls and makes us whole.

D. Mark Davis

http://leftbehindandlovingit.blogspot.com/

Matthew 6

Matthew's text almost seems ironical when it is the reading for Ash Wednesday, especially if the occasion includes the imposition of ashes on one's forehead. Among the warnings against public acts of righteousness is the teaching in v. 16 not to disfigure one's face as a sign of fasting. To read this text while imposing ashes raises a tension between a meaningful, well-intended act that is part of the church's tradition and a plainspoken teaching from the Gospels. The paradox is that the very church tradition that has handed over the practice of imposing ashes on Ash Wednesday is the same church tradition that has identified Matthew 6 as the appropriate reading for this occasion.

Of course, Jesus' teachings (part of the "Sermon on the Mount" in Matthew 5–7) are not addressing Ash Wednesday per se. They aim at the public performance of piety, when acts of righteousness are intended for show. In contrast, Jesus encourages acts of mercy that are performed "in secret" for the God who sees and who rewards in secret.

It would be a stretch to say that Jesus is teaching against the imposition of ashes itself, any more than he is teaching against alms, prayer, or fasting in this chapter. Nor is Jesus against the public nature of faith; his encouragement to "let your light shine before people, so they can see the good things you do and praise your Father who is in heaven" (5:16) is in this same sermon. His warning is that any act of piety can become corrupted when recognition itself becomes the goal. This warning is a continual challenge to the church, that intends faith to be a public witness but whose acts of mercy and practices of piety are best performed under a cloak of anonymity.

Matthew L. Skinner

Matthew 6

Devotional practices, like the imposition of ashes, help us commune with God. If we use them to draw attention to ourselves, we misuse them.

Jesus' words in verses 1-6 and 16-18 about giving, praying, and fasting affirm those who perform such acts. His concern, one shared by other Jewish teachers of his time, is the motivation behind the devotion. People who act piously to promote themselves amount to "hypocrites," a Greek term for stage actors who wore masks. If we engage in religious behavior to congratulate ourselves, we put forward a false identity and essentially attempt to hide our true selves from

God and others. By contrast, genuine piety yields rewards from God—not in earthly health and wealth, but in participating with God in the ultimate realization of God's kingdom.

Jesus uses humor in these verses. References to blowing a trumpet, keeping one hand shielded from the other, praying on street corners and in closets, and purposely distorting one's face—the images should make us giggle. The humor exposes the ridiculousness of misused devotion: something meant to express our dependence upon God ends up praising ourselves and asserting our self-sufficiency.

The truly amazing thing about this passage resides in Jesus' insistence that God sees and blesses our worship and service, no matter how understated they are. Serve God however you can, but go about it as if no one notices. God sees.

The conversation heads in a new direction in verses 19-21, as Jesus contrasts treasures "on earth" with those "in heaven." The stuff we accumulate is temporary. Instead, Jesus encourages us to live in expectation of God's coming judgment. The treasure we seek is right standing before God. This right standing, Jesus declares, is always God's gift, an aspect of "the kingdom of heaven" (see Matthew 5:3-12).

February 22, 2015

1st Sunday in Lent

Genesis 9:8-17; Psalm 25:1-10; 1 Peter 3:18-22; Mark 1:9-15

Julia Seymour

http://lutheranjulia.blogspot.com

Genesis 9

The flood decision is made because of the corruption of the world. How can you tell when a world is this corrupt: When things begin to be worse for coming generations instead of better? The center of a rotten thing cannot hold, and the space created will consume the children of future generations.

Scripture says Noah did not have children until he was five hundred years old. He waited, possibly, because he did not think the world was a good place into which to bring children. Everyone did what they wanted, focused on themselves and their needs first, and failed to consider God's preference, desires, and commands toward relationship and fruitfulness—which means bearing, supporting, and being a part of a society that values children.

Valuing children does not mean becoming child-centric. Not everyone can or should have children. However, we all live in a world in which all kinds of decisions—economic, political, spiritual, educational, and environmental—affect children. If our thoughts are not on the impact of what we choose and how we choose it, then we have stopped considering the future generations. We have stopped valuing children.

This is a story that is not for children; it is about children. It reveals God as resolute. The price of destruction is too great for a creator to pay. The pain of the loss is not worth the break in relationship. So God makes plans, plans for generations, plans for hope and a future. There will still be judgment, but there will also be mercy. There will not be massive destruction that comes from the hand of God as a judgment. God takes the long view and the long view includes many, many, many children.

Elizabeth Quick

http://bethquick.com

Genesis 9

- One of the first covenants established with God's people. What does God commit to here, and why?

- Have you ever made a personal covenant with God? Have you kept your part of the promise? Has God?

- The rainbow is a symbol of a promise. Symbols are important reminders of promise; we use rings, for example, as symbols of promises made in marriage. What symbols are important reminders in your own life?

- Have you seen many rainbows? When I see them, I am always filled with joy, such beauty after dark and gloomy skies. How do they make you feel? Do you remember God's promise when you see them?

Mark 1

- Our text starts with the baptism of Jesus. Short and sweet, like everything in Mark. He barely mentions the actual event, and says nothing about what brings Jesus to John. Make sure you compare Mark's recording with the accounts in the other Gospels. In Mark, God speaks directly to Jesus. Other accounts have God's voice speaking *about* Jesus to the crowds. Which do you prefer?

- Where the temptation lasts several verses with many details in Luke and Matthew, with a conversation between Jesus and Satan, Mark sees no need for such an account, simply recording that Jesus was tempted for forty days, driven into the wilderness by the Spirit. What do you make Mark's account? What does his brief style say about what is most important to him about Jesus' temptation?

- Mark again emphasizes that, for Jesus, the good news is the coming near of the kingdom of God, which calls us to repentance. Do you see this as good news? Why was it so important for Jesus to tell this? Is this what most people mean when they talk about the good news of Jesus today?

Mark Stamm

Genesis 9; 1 Peter 3; Mark 1

In its origins, Lent was a time to prepare for baptism. It served that purpose even before it took its current position on the calendar as the forty-day period leading to Easter (Paul F. Bradshaw and Maxwell E. Johnson, *The Origins of Feasts, Fasts, and Seasons in Early Christianity* [Collegeville, Minnesota: The Liturgical Press, 2011], 93–98). Given those origins, we do well to read these texts through a baptismal lens. What do they say to those beginning their Christian journey as well as to those baptized years ago?

For Jesus, baptism led directly to his wilderness mission, even to conflict with malevolent powers and untamed beasts (Mark 1:12-13). Authentic Christian ministry and witness will share in these dynamics, yet God provides sustenance. Jesus' call to repent and believe is a call to turn from sin, yet it pushes deeper. Jesus also bids us turn toward God and God's reign. Even in the midst of difficulty, can we imagine that God is about to do something wonderful, even liberating? Such dreaming is part of our Christian vocation, and can be the first step toward deeper justice.

Consider Noah's ark, but only after tuning out the literalists and then using your imagination. Finding the boat doesn't matter, but taking the ride does. The ark stands (floats?) as a sign of God's care, even in the midst of judgment. Through our baptism, we have a place on the ark with Noah and his family and with all those in relationship with God. In that same baptism, we also are judged, drowned if you will. Notice that God's covenant of "never again" is made not only with human beings but also "all the earth's creatures" (Gen 9:15-17). Here is warrant to care for all of creation, for such caring is part of our baptismal vocation.

Martha Spong

http://marthaspong.com/

Psalm 25; Mark 1

Matthew and Luke tell involved stories about Jesus' temptation in the wilderness. Mark is, by contrast, economical. One verse: "He was in the wilderness forty days, tempted by Satan; and he was with the wild beasts; and the angels waited on him" (Mark 1:13 NRSV).

That's it. We have to imagine Jesus hungry and thirsty, hot all day and too cold at night. We have to remind ourselves that the wilderness was a desert full of scorpions and snakes and scrubby, prickly shrubs, where the little wadis dried up depending on the time of year. We have to imagine what it was like for Jesus, not on day one or two, but on day twenty-three or thirty-one or forty. How wretched did he feel? How did he keep his wits about him?

I know how my mind works when I am away from home and disconnected:

• I wonder what they're doing right now.

• I wonder what the weather is like.

• I wonder what they're having for dinner. (Maybe this one especially.)

The questions get more serious when we use the time away is to contemplate the future, as Jesus must have done on his rather extreme retreat. Driven into the wilderness by the Spirit, Jesus stayed until the time was right to come out and begin declaring the kingdom of God to be at hand. To get from baptism to revolution—what desert path did he walk?

Hungry, thirsty, thrown back on whatever he could remember, perhaps he whispered this week's psalm:

> Make me to know your ways, O Lord;
> > teach me your paths.
> Lead me in your truth, and teach me,
> > for you are the God of my salvation;
> > for you I wait all day long. (25:4-5 NRSV)

Walkabout ended; he emerged, declaring God's kingdom at hand.

John Wesley
http://www.ccel.org/ccel/wesley/notes

1 Peter 3

The just for the unjust—The word signifies, not only them who have wronged their neighbours, but those who have transgressed any of the commands of God; as the preceding word, just, denotes a person who has fulfilled, not barely social duties, but all kind of righteousness.

Mark 1:12

And immediately the Spirit thrusteth him out into the wilderness—So in all the children of God, extraordinary manifestations of his favour are wont to be followed by extraordinary temptations.

Kwasi Kena

1 Peter 3; Mark 1

Life, liberty, and the pursuit of happiness—words deeply embedded into our North American ethos. We hold doggedly to the notion that we have certain inalienable rights endowed by God, including freedom and the opportunity to pursue prosperity. Some believe these ideals have been adopted as Christian values. If so, then today's passages may threaten our culture-laden view of Christianity.

In Mark 1, Jesus submits to baptism by John the Baptizer. This was a baptism of repentance. Jesus, being sinless, had no need to repent, but he submitted as an act of obedience that demonstrated the path humanity should take.

After Jesus came up from the water, the same Spirit that descended upon him drove Jesus into the wilderness to be tested. What? God's Spirit sent Jesus to be tested by Satan? That seems so unfair. Does the fact that God set up this severe time of testing stand at odds with our pursuit of happiness? If, in the quest for success, God's Spirit sent you into a difficult place that prevented you from obtaining "achievable prosperity," would you resist the Spirit's leading? Ancient Jewish belief held that a righteous person prospered and a sinful person suffered—it was simple cause-and-effect thinking. Do we presume the same?

In 1 Peter, Christ volunteers to suffer unjustly for sinful humanity. Again, this seems contrary to the agenda of Western ideals. Which of us, in pursuing happiness, would voluntarily abandon that quest to endure suffering to benefit others, who may despise us? How many would question God for expecting selflessness?

The message of the two passages disturbs the peace: God's Spirit may drive us into difficult situations to test our character, and imitating Jesus may require voluntary suffering. What holds more sway over your life, the quest for personal achievement or imitation of Christ?

Editor's Insights

Holy Spirit Power (Mark 1)

The Spirit throws him out in the wilderness to be tested. The Spirit does the same to us. How many times have I used "Holy Spirit" as shorthand for "what I think," so that it cannot be countered by others? It's the "Spirit." It's "my Jesus." It's "our God." But it seems that these stories about the Spirit are not so easily domesticated. It's not "my spirit." It's God's Spirit. It's the Holy (separated, other) Spirit. It's not only the "feeling" of everyone worshiping and feeling good about the worship. Maybe it's not primarily that. It's a Wild Wind. This Wind thrusts us, violently, into wilderness after wilderness in our lives, where we see who we really are.

I can tell the stories in such a way that I end up following the Spirit and making the right choices and my life is blessed. I can do that every time. I also can tell the stories in such a way that I missed the mark. I can do both of these things at the same time. I think of this at this time of year when I think about the Spirit throwing Jesus around in the wilderness. He gets the "right answer" and that is the "wrong answer" and that is the "right answer." The world changes, the Spirit comes again, throws us out in the wilderness, me and Jesus, and we struggle to find God again. Where is God in these questions? Where is the Spirit? And how does Satan enter in? We live. We choose. Our choices are right; our choices are wrong. The Spirit continues to call and thrust us into uncomfortable places where we learn who we are, where we learn to be of some earthly good.

Thom M. Shuman

http://lectionaryliturgies.blogspot.com/

Gggrrrooowwwlll (Mark 1)

my kitten, Apathy,
       settles down in my lap
             as if it were a nest,
                    contentedly purring so long
                          that i become
       convinced
there is nothing
i can
       (or need) to do
     for the brokenness of the
       world;

putting the leash on
                              Envy,
          he drags me through the
                    day,
                    stopping to sniff
                    every place the rich
                              leave their mark,
                    sitting at the end of the
                              driveway, looking
                    up at the mcmansion,
                    turning to stare at me,
                    with a look on his face,
          "wouldn't you like to live there?"

Lust, Temptation, Greed
chase each other
                    around and around
                    the fish tank (like the
                              3 Stooges at work),
          pausing every five minutes
          or so,
                    to swim to the top, imploring
                              "feed us, feed us!"

oh my!
if only it were
          lions and tigers and bears
                    i have to contend with,
                    but in my wilderness
          they are so domesticated,
                    so everyday,
                    so comfortable,
          that i never notice
                              my
          wild beasts.

March 1, 2015

2nd Sunday in Lent

Genesis 17:1-7, 15-16; Psalm 22:23-31; Romans 4:13-25; Mark 8:31-38

Teri Peterson

http://clevertitlehere.blogspot.com

Genesis 17; Mark 8

"Walk with me and be trustworthy," God says to Abram (Genesis 17:1b). "You are not thinking God's thoughts, but human thoughts," Jesus says to Peter (Mark 8:33b).

In other words, the covenant is about relationship. God is not interested in a checklist of rules but in a relationship that evolves and grows and deepens through time, a relationship built on back-and-forth and on trust.

Abram and Sarai have been following the call to "go" for several years, without much to show for it, but still they persevere. Peter has just named Jesus as Christ a few moments before this exchange. Abram and Peter know what it is to walk with God. They've been building a relationship for some time, which must have made it hard for them to hear these things from the mouths of those they considered friends. And yet they could be said only by a friend—a true friend, someone whose words we trust, someone who can challenge us and hold us accountable to being who we are called to be, someone who knows the relationship we have is not threatened by Truth.

That kind of covenant relationship often comes with a name change—whether it's a baptismal name, a new name taken along with holy orders, or a name change after a wedding. So, too, our name, *Christian*, is a sign of our part in God's covenant story, a symbol of walking with the One who says, "Take up your cross and follow me." The moniker is a symbol of our new life—may we bear it well.

Chuck Aaron

Genesis 17; Mark 8

The Genesis reading and the Mark reading both represent significant transitions. Within the Genesis narrative, God changes Abram's name to Abraham, marking the new relationship. God takes the initiative to establish covenant with Abram/Abraham. In Mark, the narrative has emphasized Jesus' healing ministry, with the opposition to Jesus building. Peter has recognized Jesus' identity in healings and exorcisms. Now Jesus clearly teaches about the suffering and crucifixion that await him. The contrast startles Peter. The contemporary reader might also ask how the one who heals and restores, who gives life, also becomes the one who suffers and dies. How can Jesus offer healing and life, and then ask his followers to give up that life by assuming the cross?

The Mark passage provides a transition between Jesus' healing ministry and the journey to Jerusalem where death awaits. Although the healings seem incongruous with the call to take up the cross, in reality the two represent the same ministry. The confrontation with the unclean spirit in chapter 1 defines Jesus' ministry for Mark. The healings speak to Jesus' power over demonic forces. Jesus calls his disciples to take up the cross because confrontation with demonic forces places the church in danger. Demonic forces oppose Jesus' ministry. Disciples who push back against them should expect danger and threat.

The Genesis passage and the Mark passage also teach about faith. Although Abram falls on his face in worship, he falls on his face in laughter in verse 17. Peter exhibits faith in Jesus as the Messiah, but displays a lack of faith in Jesus' teaching about crucifixion. These two passages indicate that faith can exist side by side with unfaith. Abraham shows unfaith in God's promises; Peter shows unfaith in the call to risk.

Paul Bellan-Boyer

The Heart of Praise (Psalm 22)

Psalm 22 gets a lot of attention for the way Jesus spoke its words from the cross: "My God, why have you forsaken me?" (v. 1 NRSV). For thousands of years people have turned to this psalm for the way it speaks to their experiences of suffering and abandonment.

Its pain and sense of abandonment speak straight to Good Friday. Yet the psalmist continues his prayer past this point of desolation, just as the life of Jesus continued past his cross and death.

Think of Lent not only as a season of penitence but also of praise. When the brokenness of this world (and our lives) touches us, then we have the greatest opportunity to recognize God's magnificent mercy.

Sometimes the best commentary we can make on scripture is to let it speak for itself: "All the ends of the earth shall remember / and turn to the Lord." "The poor shall eat and be satisfied." And, most personally, the Lord "did not hide his face from me, / but heard when I cried to him" (vv. 27, 26, 24 NRSV).

Salvation *is* personal. We pray for and confess the redemption of the whole world, but we need salvation and know it right where we live.

The psalm, like the lives of believers, like the life of God's self, refuses to deny the real experience of sin, suffering, destruction, and simultaneously refuses to affirm their primacy, their victory, their claim to truth. Still more, we refuse to assent to their claim upon humanity: "For dominion belongs to the Lord" (v. 28 NRSV).

The cross stands at the heart of darkness. God's will for wholeness, for *shalom*, places the empty tomb at the heart of life. Praise the Lord! Stand in awe before God! May your hearts live forever.

Liz Crumlish

http://somethingtostandon.blogspot.co.uk/

Psalm 22; Mark 8

Making journeys is not so unusual these days. People move to find work. People move to study. Young folk think nothing of travelling for gap years. We're a very mobile society.

Not so in Abraham's day. What a statement of faith that he should pack up his whole life and, with his family, go where God calls.

So I have great sympathy with Abraham when it seems that God calls for one more incredible stretch, makes one more demand—to believe that he could start, not just a family, but a whole nation. It's clear that Abraham seldom had much clue about what God was up to.

Although we read of Abraham spending time in discernment and building altars in testimony, there are occasions when he tries to second-guess God and short-circuit the process.

And yet, Abraham has become one of the exemplars of faith, maybe precisely because of his cluelessness. Although he didn't know why, he did as God asked.

Sometimes those asks were huge: asked to pack up his whole life and travel, asked to believe that he could father a nation, asked to sacrifice his one and only heir with no idea that God would provide an alternative.

Abraham might well have been clueless about God's plans, but he certainly wasn't found wanting in his faith.

In Romans 4:18, we see Abraham held up as an exemplar of "hoping against hope" (NRSV). God's people are called to practice such unlikely faith today so that God's improbable will can come to pass.

John Wesley

http://www.ccel.org/ccel/wesley/notes

Romans 4:17

Who against hope—Against all probability, believed and hoped in the promise. The same thing is apprehended both by faith and hope; by faith, as a thing which God has spoken; by hope, as a good thing which God has promised to us. So shall thy seed be—Both natural and spiritual, as the stars of heaven for multitude.

Mark 8:34

And when he called the people—To hear a truth of the last importance, and one that equally concerned them all. Let him deny himself—His own will, in all things small and great, however pleasing, and that continually: And take up his cross—Embrace the will of God, however painful, daily, hourly, continually. Thus only can he follow me in holiness to glory.

D. Mark Davis

http://leftbehindandlovingit.blogspot.com/

Mark 8

On this second Sunday of Lent, Mark's reading provides some firsts: the first mention of a cross and the first of three times that Jesus discloses his forthcoming death to his disciples. In each case the disciples will respond inappropriately, after which Jesus will issue a call.

Verse 31 states the disclosure itself rather simply, "It is necessary for the son of man to suffer greatly and to be rejected by the elders, the chief priests, and the scribes, and to be killed, and after three days to rise" (my translation). The strength of the verb *dei* ("It is necessary that") is lost when translated simply as "must" (ESV). It is Mark's way of signifying that the events that follow are not simply tragic, but divinely purposive.

Peter's response is outrageous to those of us who live on this side of two thousand years of theologies of the cross. But in the moment, it was a genuine response to the real prospect of Jesus' death. Peter "rebuked" Jesus (see Mark 1:25, 9:25 and especially 8:30; CEB has "spoke harshly" and "ordered"). This is the language of real opposition. Peter represents a genuine religious attempt to bring in the reign of God without a cross. Jesus, in turn, rebukes Peter with those stunning words, "Get behind me, Satan!" The crossless path on which Peter insists is the real temptation that faces Jesus in his work. But, for Jesus, it is necessary to take the journey toward death.

Then Jesus issues a call, saying that if any would be his disciple they too must take up their crosses and follow. The reign of God comes only by way of the death of the son of man, and one follows the son of man only by embracing that way of death as one's own.

Suzanne Guthrie

http://www.edgeofenclosure.org

Mark 8

Life is difficult. But awakening to personal complicity with evil in the world cruelly adds to the difficulty. Aligning with God against injustice, oppression, exploitation, and violence propels us toward the cross. In Lent, giving up illusion is the primary sacrifice: illusions about God, the world, safety, self-satisfaction; or, even clinging to the easier, friendlier Jesus of Galilee and Epiphany rather than traveling with the suffering Jesus of Jerusalem and Holy Week.

Peter tries to cling to an illusion. "God forbid you should die!" Jesus' harsh rebuke is devastating: "Get behind me, Satan." Perhaps Jesus' harshness reflects a continuing struggle—an echo of the illusions tempting him during his own desert fast before beginning his ministry. Certainly, Jesus does not want to die a criminal's death by torture. Why wouldn't he lash out as Peter witlessly touches this raw nerve?

From time to time, it is necessary to abandon the illusion of what we previously called *faith*. Faith draws us to a dark realm behind reason. Reason is merely a placeholder of discernment; the content of the pages can shock with their unreasonable wonder, complexity, beauty, horror, emptiness.

But dark faith is not the same thing as blind faith. Blind faith draws on ignorance and illusion, while dark faith draws us toward the crucible of liberation from fantasy, compulsion, and self-justification. To go forward in dark faith sometimes means risking faith itself to face truth. Difficult truths, perhaps like that personal complicity with evil mentioned earlier. In any case, dark faith leads to the cross. There's no way around the darkness.

March 8, 2015

3rd Sunday in Lent

Exodus 20:1-17; Psalm 19; 1 Corinthians 1:18-25; John 2:13-22

Two Bubbas and a Bible

http://lectionarylab.com

Exodus 20

Here's my personal Ten Commandments inventory:

No other Gods? No Baal or Fertility Cult worship.

No graven image? No bowing to idols.

Lord's Name in Vain?—No.

Remember Sabbath Day? Always in church.

Honor parents? Cards, phone calls, gifts. Done.

Not kill? Not even a fight since seventh grade.

Not steal? Does sneaking fries count?

False witness? Daddy said, "Always tell the truth. Don't have to remember what you said."

Covet neighbor's house, wife, slaves, ox, or his ass? No.

Based on this record, I didn't need Jesus to die for me. I've got the being-good thing covered. If "other gods" and "graven images" are earthly things to which I have devoted a great deal more time and energy to than I have to "THE God," however, then I'm guilty.

Suppose taking the Lord's name in vain means using religion for less than holy reasons—oops!

And the Sabbath could be about creating enough silence and space in my life to allow God to seep in and nurture and lead and refresh me. Oh my!

Honoring father and mother may have something to say about how I deal with those who have taken on the responsibility for leadership in my life; have I been responsive and cooperative? Dang!

Well, I really haven't killed anyone; but I haven't prevented or protested a lot of the violence that goes on in my name, funded by my dollars.

Adultery? Well there is that Lust in the Heart thing.

You shall not steal? What was it Augustine said, anything you have more than you need is stolen from the poor? Ouch!

False Witness? I do not lie, but I can "spin" like a whirling dervish.

Okay, I still haven't coveted anybody's donkey and nobody can say that I did!

John Wesley

http://www.ccel.org/ccel/wesley/notes

Exodus 20:1

God has many ways of speaking to the children of men by his spirit, conscience, providences; his voice in all which we ought carefully to attend to: but he never spake at any time upon any occasion so as he spake the ten commandments, which therefore we ought to hear with the more earnest heed. This law God had given to man before, it was written in his heart by nature; but sin had so defaced that writing, that it was necessary to revive the knowledge of it.

John 2:14

And the changers of money—Those who changed foreign money for that which was current at Jerusalem, for the convenience of them that came from distant countries. (John 2:14)

Carolyn Winfrey Gillette

http://www.carolynshymns.com/

"I Have Brought You Out of Egypt" (Exodus 20)

NETTLETON 8.7.8.7 D ("Come, Thou Fount of Every Blessing")

"I have brought you out of Egypt," Moses heard the Lord God say.
"I have saved you! I have freed you! People, listen and obey.
Have no other gods before me; don't make idols for yourselves.
I will judge those who reject me; worship me and no one else."

"Do not use the Lord's name wrongly; use God's name for what is good.
Keep the Sabbath; keep it holy; rest and worship as you should.
Honor father, honor mother; do not murder! Honor life!
Do not wander to another from your husband or your wife."

God continued these commandments: "Do not steal another's things;
And you shall not bear false witness—see the anguish that it brings.
Do not seek with bitter longing what you see across the street.
Keep these laws and find within them where my love and justice meet."

God of grace, we see your promise in the covenant you give.
For your law is wise and wondrous as it shows us how to live.
Loving God and loving neighbor, may we follow where you call.
Saved by grace, may we together seek to live your gracious law.

Biblical reference: Exodus 20:1-17

Tune: Wyeth's *Repository of Sacred Music*, 1813. Alternate Tune: BEACH SPRING 8.7.8.7 D *The Sacred Harp*, 1844. Harm. James H. Wood, 1958. Text: Copyright © 2012 by Carolyn Winfrey Gillette. All rights reserved. Email: bcgillette@comcast.net New Hymns: www.carolynshymns.com

Eric D. Barreto

1 Corinthians 1

The cross, says Paul, is foolish in the eyes of the world. The cross, however, has become such a distinctive symbol of the church that its offense has largely been lost. In antiquity, the cross was not a natural symbol around which a community might gather. The cross was an unalloyed symbol of shame, death, and chaos.

How would Jesus have died had he arrived in our midst recently? Imagine if his demise occurred not on a cross but in an electric chair as the victim of an unjust criminal process (see Luke 23:47), on a noose as the victim of a lynching, or in a gas chamber as the victim of genocide. Imagine then that his followers would have eventually worn these deadly implements around their necks as a symbol of their faith. In this way, we only approximate the foolishness about which Paul writes. Jesus died without any sense of nobility in the eyes of the world, a criminal accused and clearly guilty. Yet we draw our eyes to this symbol of shame and see in it not the fear the Romans hoped to inspire or the death it hoped to inflict on yet another victim of imperial cruelty. Instead, a symbol of cruelty becomes an instantiation of the defeat of death and injustice. A cross that stripped someone of life and humanity becomes the turning point around which all hope turns. A cross, meant to disempower its many victims, morphs into God's ultimate victory. This is foolishness in the eyes of the world but not for the faithful. God reigns through what appears to be weakness. True power is in the cross and not in the accumulation of wealth or the deployment of mighty armies. True power is lovely and beautiful, especially on a cross.

Sharron Blezard

1 Corinthians 1; John 2

Hindsight is 20/20, and we humans understand much of life only in reverse and after the fact. Jesus' disciples were no exception. This week's gospel lesson from the fourth evangelist recounts Jesus' dramatic cleansing of the temple in Jerusalem. There is a lot going on here, and you may want to look at some historical source material to set the stage fully for preaching on this text. Oppression under the heel of empire, the commoditization of religion, and economic abuse of the marginalized fuel Jesus' anger, and he makes mighty quick work of cleaning things up.

What a sight that must have been! Think of how things generally go today when someone challenges established practices and authority. It is usually not too pretty. Jesus had some explaining to do, and the religious folk ask him for a sign (in other words, "Who made you the big cheese, you marginal rabbi hick from Galilee?"). Of course, in typical Jesus fashion, he gives them a sign that on the surface makes no sense at all.

John is big on signs, so fortunately for us, we get an explanation.

Folks still have a tough time getting what Jesus is all about, and Christians have not done the best job of sharing the good news and living out faith in love. Not everyone will understand or be open to the amazing grace and mercy that is so freely given. Paul makes that clear in the epistle lesson this week. People still want signs, seek wisdom, crave power, and ignore truth by looking for it in all the wrong places. Yet Christians celebrate what the world derides as foolishness, believing instead that nothing is impossible with God—not even redeeming this beautiful, broken creation with a crazy, amazing, incarnate love.

Julie Craig

http://winsomelearnsome.com

John 2

The picture of Jesus that hung in my grandmother's house, right above her electric organ—and also in the house in which I lived when I was a child—was a rather famous rendition of him, a copy of the painting by Walter Sallman. I'll bet you've seen it too. In the portrait, which is comprised of umber, gold and bronze tones, Jesus sits in three-quarters profile, looking serenely into the distance, his light brown hair gleaming and brushed back from his face, highlighting his high cheekbones; his beard neatly trimmed and his light-colored eyes softly yet intently focused on some point of reference off to his slight left field of vision.

This was the Jesus I saw in my dreams—the dreams in which he spoke with me outside, near my parents' tomato patch. The eyes in the Sallman portrait were the ones that spookily followed me when I walked down the hallway in my childhood home. The two things I remembered thinking about that portrait of Jesus way back then were that I wondered how that picture of Jesus had survived all those "hundreds" of years, and I marveled at how much Jesus looked like my older brother. I honestly thought that someone had painted Jesus when he was alive, and that a copy of it had survived to the 1960s, when it was copied for the rest of us. Why else would everyone I loved and trusted have the same picture of Jesus hanging on their wall?

Sometimes the picture of Jesus we hold in our minds and in our hearts is really hard to shake, isn't it? But the Jesus in this story is so very different from that one.

Todd Weir

http://bloomingcactus.typepad.com/

John 2

Jesus welcomed the beggars and hugged the lepers, while driving out the sellers of doves and moneychangers from the temple. I state what should be obvious, but we seem to get it backwards today. We shun the downtrodden, the sick, and the poor and welcome the wealthy and the commercial interests.

Anne Murray reached the twenty-first spot on the Billboard 100 in the 1970s singing "Put Your Hand in the Hand":

> For the buyers and the sellers were no different fellas than what I profess to be,
> And it causes me shame to know I'm not the gal that I should be.

The lyrics merge the temple buyers and sellers together as one. It is not just wealthy corporations or the rich who come into conflict with Jesus. Sellers do not exist without buyers, and most of us are buyers. If I am honest with myself, even though my politics and values are progressive in nature, I tremble when I look at my spending. Consumerism is in the air we breathe. It is easier to let Jesus into our hearts than into our wallets. Bringing our bank accounts, church budgets, and credit cards in line with the gospel and following the commandment, "Thou shalt not covet," is the toughest challenge of the North American church.

March 15, 2015

4th Sunday in Lent

Numbers 21:4-9; Psalm 107:1-3, 17-22; Ephesians 2:1-10; John 3:14-21

Linda Lee

More Than Enough (Numbers 21)

That which causes suffering can also be the vehicle for healing, both internal and external. The snakes came upon the Hebrews in the wilderness as consequence of their turning away from God. The people suffered from them. Yet God used this same source of suffering to heal them. Every time they looked at the instrument of their suffering, they remembered the cause of their suffering. Their memories caused them to turn back to God. And because they turned back to God, they were healed.

There are times on our Christian journey when we become aware of the ways we have sinned against God. We find ourselves suffering as we experience the normal consequences of self-absorbed choices.

At these times, it seems that our disobedience, that is to say, the ways we have turned away from or ignored God, are ever before us. Overcome by these imperfections, we often become ready to call out to God. God knows our tragic human flaws and loves us anyway.

Thanks be to God that the very mistakes we've made, harm we have caused, and the harm done to us can become symbols of our healing. Every time we look at them, we remember the suffering resulting from our choices or of those we love; and we remember we can make a different choice this time and be healed. God's nature, which is love, cannot resist expressing itself; God pours out abounding mercy and grace on us.

During this season of introspection and reflection, it is good to both confess the ways in which we have turned away from God and to let go. In this way, we can receive the lavish grace and love of God revealed to us in Jesus Christ, and we make choices that make us and others whole.

Lowell E. Grisham

http://lowellsblog.blogspot.com/

Prayers of the People

Presider: Gracious God, you loved the world so much that you sent your only Son, not to condemn the world, but in order that the world might be saved through him; let your light renew all things as we pray: We give you thanks, O God, for you are good; your mercy endures forever.

Litanist: Loving God, you have shown your church the immeasurable riches of your grace and kindness toward us in Christ Jesus and raised us with him to be seated in the heavenly places: Let your light shine through our deeds, that Christ's love may be known throughout the world. We give you thanks, O God, for you are good;

your mercy endures forever.

Mighty God, you resist fools who take to rebellious ways, and you deliver those who cry to you in their trouble: Turn the hearts of all who govern or hold authority in the world, that they may love the light rather than darkness and do all such good works as you have prepared for them. We give you thanks, O God, for you are good;

your mercy endures forever.

Saving God, you give us the true bread that gives life to the world, and you raise up signs of hope in our suffering: Send your word into our community that we may be healed and tell of your acts with shouts of joy. We give you thanks, O God, for you are good;

your mercy endures forever.

Compassionate and healing God, you are light for those who live in darkness, and your saving love extends through all the earth: Be with everyone who suffers throughout the world that they may be delivered from their distress. We give you thanks, O God, for you are good;

your mercy endures forever.

Let your gift of eternal life be manifest in all who turn
    to you for help, especially those for whom we pray: ___.
Let all give thanks to you for your mercy and the wonders you do for your children. Hear us as we offer our sacrifice
    of thanksgiving, especially for ___.
You have lifted up the Son so that all may have eternal life. Let your light shine upon those who have died to save
    them from the grave, especially ___.
We give you thanks, O God, for you are good;

your mercy endures forever.

Presider: Almighty God, you are rich in mercy; out of your great love you loved us even when we were dead in our trespasses, and you have made us alive together with Christ: Let your gift of grace shine through our faith, that we may bear your light of eternal life throughout the world, in the power of your Holy Spirit, through Jesus Christ our Savior. Amen.

Cameron Howard

Numbers 21; John 3

John 3:16, arguably the most well-known Bible verse of them all, is juxtaposed this week with one of the most enigmatic passages from the little-read book of Numbers. The story of the serpent on the pole in Numbers 21 describes a worldview that is no longer directly accessible to us. Something about looking at that specially-fastened bronze serpent was thought to have healing powers; in similar fashion, Jacob set peeled rods in front of Laban's sheep so they would breed striped, speckled, and spotted lambs when they bred in front of the rods (Genesis 30:37-43). Can what we look at actually change the course of our lives? Can images be life giving?

While we might dismiss these stories from Numbers and Genesis as prescientific strategies for manipulating natural phenomena, they do inspire reflection on the Christian worshiper's everyday spirituality. The Israelites wandering in the wilderness invited the poisonous serpents with their complaints, and the uplifted pole reoriented them to repentance and gratitude. With what images are we surrounded? What commands our attention? Are we surrounding ourselves and our families with images that are life giving or death dealing?

When the gospel of John refers to this bronze-serpent incident, the lifting up of the serpent on the rod becomes the most important element, mirroring the lifting up of Christ on the cross. That lifting up is no magic trick or prescientific experiment, but rather reorients one's life to salvation in Jesus Christ. In most Christian sanctuaries today, no matter the denomination, somewhere hangs either a crucifix or an empty cross. Often the cross is lifted up in a way that focuses the worshiper's gaze upon it. Beyond being a requisite symbol of the identity of the congregation, the cross can direct the worshiper away from the concerns of the world and toward the encounter with God.

John Wesley

http://www.ccel.org/ccel/wesley/notes

Numbers 21:8

A fiery serpent—That is, the figure of a serpent in brass, which is of a fiery colour. This would require some time: God would not speedily take off the judgment, because he saw they were not thoroughly humbled. Upon a pole—That the people might see it from all parts of the camp, and therefore the pole must be high, and the serpent large. When he looketh—This method of cure was prescribed, that it might appear to be God's own work, and not the effect of nature or art: and that it might be an eminent type of our salvation by Christ. The serpent signified Christ, who was in the likeness of sinful flesh, though without sin, as this brazen serpent had the outward shape, but not the inward poison, of the other serpents: the pole resembled the cross upon which Christ was lifted up for our salvation: and looking up to it designed our believing in Christ.

John 3:16

Whosoever believeth on him—With that faith which worketh by love, and hold fast the beginning of his confidence steadfast to the end. God so loved the world—That is, all men under heaven; even those that despise his love, and will for that cause finally perish. Otherwise, not to believe would be no sin to them. For what should they believe? Ought they to believe that Christ was given for them? Then he was given for them. He gave his only Son—Truly and seriously. And the Son of God gave himself, Gal. iv, 4, truly and seriously.

Marci Auld Glass

http://www.marciglass.com

Numbers 21; John 3

This story should be scary. It is not a coincidence that God uses the animal that scares us most to scare us straight. And it seems to work for the Hebrew people. They repent and beg Moses, asking him to intercede on their behalf to their God, against whom they had sinned.

So, the killer serpents, or "snakes on a plain," as it were, lead the people to repentance.

But God does not just get rid of the snakes. The dangers of the world are still there with them. God takes a symbol of fear and death and turns it into a symbol of life. Once the people have repented of their sin and turned again to trust in God, the thing that had been killing them becomes the thing that saves them.

And it works very well, by all accounts, for years and years. Because centuries later, when King Hezekiah is leading reforms and cleaning out the temple, around 700 BCE, listen to what he does, as recorded in 2 Kings 18:4. "He crushed the bronze snake that Moses made, because up to that point the Israelites had been burning incense to it. (The snake was named Nehushtan.)"

The chronicler of Hezekiah makes this report to let us know about what a good King Hezekiah was, but I find it interesting because it shows that Moses not only made this serpent but also that *it worked*, because people were still praying to it centuries later. If the people believed that the bronze serpent, and not God, was the agent of their healing, then Hezekiah was right to destroy it. Whenever we mistake the signs and symbols for God, and we begin to worship the signs and symbols instead of God, then we have made idols that need to be crushed.

(Excerpt from http://marciglass.com/2009/03/22/snakes-on-a-plain/)

Liz Crumlish

http://somethingtostandon.blogspot.co.uk/

Psalm 107; Ephesians 2; John 3

I have a T-shirt that proclaims, "You can take the girl out of Scotland, but you cannot take Scotland out of the girl!" It seems that the Israelites could have worn similar T-shirts about Egypt. They grumbled their way through the wilderness, constantly wanting to be back in Egypt.

We see the story of Moses the leader and the people grumbling against him repeated in so many guises in Scripture. No matter how much God is revealed, memories are always short. And it seems that a leader is only as good as the last miracle.

It's a story that we see repeated today in business, in education, in politics—and in the church. Leaders are expected to continuously improve on their previous performance—no matter how wonderful that performance—and folk are not satisfied but are always upping the stakes.

Still eyes rise heavenward as leaders ask, God, what am I to do with these people? It's called scapegoating. As long as folks have someone to blame for all that is wrong, they are absolved of responsibility. If we can place all that seems wrong on the shoulders of leaders, then we ourselves don't have to do anything to change.

It's much easier just to stay in the wilderness and grumble than step up to the mark and try to make things different. Stepping up might mean putting ourselves in the firing line. The plight, or blight, of the Israelites is our plight too. We cannot let go of the past and look forward to the future that God has planned for us. God calls us out of Egypt, out of our standing on the sidelines, out of our propensity to grumble, and leads us into a brave new world.

Thom M. Shuman
http://lectionaryliturgies.blogspot.com/

Call to Worship

We come, to offer all we have to God:
our minds, our bodies, our hearts, our hopes.
We come, to offer all we are to God:
our relationships with families and friends,
our longing to draw closer to other pilgrims.
We come, to offer all we would be to God:
our faith, our discipleship, our yearning to follow Jesus.
We come, to offer ourselves to God:
who offers life, joy, and peace in Jesus Christ.

Prayer of the Day

When once we let sin
coil itself around our hearts,
you wrap us in the
comforting shawl of grace.

When once
we obsessed over us,
you freed us to give
ourselves away to the world.

Ceaseless Creator,
your love overwhelms us
each and every day.

Where once
we sat by the edge of the way,

with sin and death on either side,
now we can pull up a chair
next to you, to rest our lives on you.

Where once
we hungered for love
and thirsted for compassion,
now we are filled at your Table.

Healing Hope,
your grace flows through us
each and every day.
When we are tempted
to submit our resumes
to the Evil One,
you put us to work,
caring for the outsiders.

When we are tempted
to mutter our way
through each moment,
you teach us songs of grace.
Faithful Spirit,
your peace surrounds us
each and every day.

You are with us each and every day,
God in Community, Holy in One,
even as we pray as we have been taught,
Our Father...

March 22, 2015

5th Sunday in Lent

Jeremiah 31:31-34; Psalm 51:1-12 or Psalm 119:9-16; Hebrews 5:5-10; John 12:20-33

Dan R. Dick

Jeremiah 31

What is written in your heart? Matthew reminds us that, "where your treasure is, there your heart will be also" (6:21). God speaks an amazing word of intimacy and new relationship through the prophet Jeremiah. No longer is the covenant between God and God's people one of mere Law—rules and regulations grounded in fear and intimidation. The relationship is no longer carved in stone, written on parchment, hidden in the Holy of Holies—the new covenant is organic, dynamic, and living.

The story related throughout Hebrew Scripture is one of covenants made and broken. Repeatedly, God reaches out offering to "be their God, and they shall be my people." God makes it; humans break it—again and again and again. Since the beginning of the Christian era, the covenant rests in Jesus, but the question rises—are we any different? Even with the grace and reconciliation of the Christ, human beings are still human beings: testing limits, crossing boundaries, taking for granted, and, ultimately, failing to keep covenant. How often do we forget the basics? How regularly are we less than loving, less than kind, less than respectful, and less than generous? How often do we ignore compassion, mercy, sacrifice, and justice in favor of personal comfort, security, enjoyment, and entitlement? Our written gospel resides most commonly in books—print or digital—not in the muscle of the human heart. Our "good news" is too often external. God's challenge to us is not that we believe in a book or that we follow a set of teachings. God's challenge is that we become the very body of Christ—the living embodiment of God's grace and love. While the heart resides at the core, what is written there is evident for the whole world to see. What is written in your heart?

John Wesley

http://www.ccel.org/ccel/wesley/notes

Jeremiah 31:33

And write it—The prophet's design is here to express the difference betwixt the law and the gospel. The first shews duty, the latter brings the grace of regeneration, by which the heart is changed, and enabled for duty. All under the time of the law that came to salvation, were saved by this new covenant; but this was not evidently exhibited; neither was the regenerating grace of God so common under the time of the law, as it hath been under the gospel.

Psalm 51:4

Thee only—Which is not to be, understood absolutely, because he had sinned against Bathsheba and Uriah, and many others; but comparatively. So the sense is, though I have sinned against my own conscience, and against others; yet nothing is more grievous to me, than that I have sinned against thee.

Safiyah Fosua

Jeremiah 31; Psalm 119; Hebrews 5; John 12

This excerpt from what interpretation calls Jeremiah's "Little Book of Consolation" points to the classic tension between head religion and heart religion, the tension between what we *know* about our faith and how we *live* faith from the heart. Jeremiah wrote to people who knew God's word but were on the verge of being consumed by their sins and their enemies for failing to live what they knew. The revival of religion they had experienced years before, under King Josiah, had waned and there they were, in the sin-rut again, with the prophet's feet nailed to his soapbox while he screamed judgment and warning against the people and their leaders because of their sin. After such railing, the consolation offered in verses 31-34 is almost too good to be true. The tension between head knowledge and righteous living is resolved by changing *where* the Law is written—from stone tablets to the human heart.

Our culture often envisions covenant relationships in terms of loyalty or commitment. This may have been true in part for adherents to the old covenant, but God has given us a new covenant. This new covenant brings God into such intimacy with humankind that it minimizes or even eliminates our human propensity for breaking God's heart. But how? We find clues in the remaining readings for this week: reconciliation with God through Christ and a diligent aspiration to become the people of God through Christian practices such as study and prayer. The passages from Hebrews and John remind us that the mission of God in Christ was to reconcile the world to God, and Psalm 119 reminds us to become familiar with God's nature, with God's ways, and with God's will; thus writing the word (Word) on our hearts.

Ann Scull

http://seedstuff.blogspot.com

Useful Image

Church and Manse: See http://seedstuff.blogspot.com.au/2012_03_01_archive.html (accessed April 22, 2013). This image reminds me that God calls us not only to all kinds of exciting places but also that being like Jesus doesn't mean we have to be flashy and showy.

Listening Song

Plus One, "Written on My Heart" on *The Promise* (New York, Atlantic, U.S.A., 2000) CD edition. This song is based on the Jeremiah reading.

Prayer of Confession

Bits of Psalm 51 make a great prayer of confession—use a modern translation or paraphrase. Print or project the words along with some relevant images.

Jeremiah Reading

Have enough snazzy envelopes for one per person. The matching paper sealed within should have the Bible reading printed on it, or print the reading onto A4 parchment and roll up and tie with a colored ribbon—one per each person. Give these out as people arrive, and then ask people to open them/unroll them as the Bible reader comes forward to read.

Kid's Story

Angela Elwell Hunt, *The Tale of Three Trees* (Oxford, England: Lion Publishing, 1989). Use this beautiful children's story at Christmas, Easter, or at any time for that matter. I like using it particularly with this gospel reading because Jesus predicts his own death.

Discussion

What if "some Greeks" (based on the John reading) turned up at your faith community this week and said "We want to see Jesus"?

1. Who would they be?
2. What would you do?
3. What would you say?
4. Would they see Jesus?

Discuss these questions in groups of three.

Response Activity

Requires small pieces of paper, pencils. Ask people to include with their offering how they intend to specifically follow and serve Jesus this week. Reassure everyone that this is between them and God and not to be shared with others.

Two Bubbas and a Bible

http://lectionarylab.com

John 12

The appearance of the Greeks who sought after Jesus has always been something of a reminder to me that we never know who is going to be intrigued with our message about the Christ. These guys seem to come from left field, so to speak, and Philip seems a little puzzled as to what to do with them.

Ever have someone like that come to your church? We all say we want to reach new people—but then you get somebody who is really from beyond the edge of your normal constituency, and you find yourself asking the internal question, "How in the Sam Hill did they get here?"

To Jesus, it seemed to represent an important development; it is almost as if he says, "Okay, boys; if the Greeks are showing up, then it's just about time to kick this thing into high gear."

Does Jesus know that means the stuff is about to hit the fan? He seems to intimate such knowledge with his prayer about being troubled and asking God to save him from the hour.

Certainly, the humanity of Jesus is a significant aspect of our shared faith. We can't always make Jesus into Superman when he must surmount a difficult obstacle, calling on some sort of magical power not available to the rest of us.

What God had him do was hard and he must have found himself somewhat reluctant, at times, to carry it forward.

And, yet, the Savior is willing to play the part of the kernel of wheat falling to the ground—there is new life yet to come even in the midst of an impending burial.

Natalie Ann Sims

http://lectionarysong.blogspot.com

John 12

• "Our God Who Weeps" (Kate Scull)—Very simple folklike tune and challenging and hopeful lyrics. A beautiful song and easy to sing. (Lyrics sample: http://www.wholenote.com.au/songs/ourgodwhoweeps.html)

- "Praise the One Who Breaks the Darkness" (Rusty Edwards)—Good words of Christ's ministry to all. Can be sung to the familiar tune NETTLETON, or the less familiar and very lovely tune JOEL. (Lyrics: http://www.oremus.org/hymnal/p/p090.html)
- "He Comes to Us as One Unknown" (Timothy Dudley-Smith)—Great words to a very standard-sounding hymn tune. (Lyrics and tune: http://www.oremus.org/hymnal/h/h114.html)
- "Tree of Life" (Marty Haugen)—Great, very positive words about the suffering of Christ: "Tree of life and awesome mystery, in your death we are reborn; / though you die in all of history, still you rise with every morn." (Lyrics: http://www.mljmusic.com/Portals/0/Lyrics/CMP5lyrics.pdf, scroll down)
- "What Wondrous Love Is This?" (US Folk tune)—I just really like this old hymn. Versions vary widely in their inclusiveness; if you want inclusive language, use the *New Century Hymnal*. Here's an awesome bluegrass version: https://www.youtube.com/watch?v=Nu9KjxaVEC4&feature=PlayList&p=2B9206D30F66333C&playnext=1&playnext_from=PL&index=18.
- "When Christ Was Lifted from the Earth" (Brian Wren)—Powerful words of Christ's sacrifice and acceptance of all people, without the cultural imperialism of some similar hymns. The new hymn tune (WINCHCOMBE) is not too hard, but could be replaced with many others if required. I think WILTSHIRE would work.
- "The Word of God Is Source and Seed" (Dolores Dufner)—"The Word of God is source and seed; It comes to die and sprout and grow. / So make your dark earth welcome warm; Root deep the grain God bent to sow."
- "When a Grain of Wheat" / "*Hitotsubu No*" (Toyohiko Kagawa)—Not easy for a congregation, but this Japanese song would be good for musicians to sing for the congregation. (Sheet music: http://new.gbgm-umc.org/media/worship/110509dljapanworshipgrainwheat.pdf)

John van de Laar

http://www.sacredise.com/

John 12

The cross of Christ is both judgment and liberation.

Jesus calls his death the moment when the world will be judged and Satan cast out. It's a judgment no one can avoid—the whole world is drawn to Jesus as he is lifted up—because we are all masters at projecting our darkness on to others and crucifying them for it. The cross reveals all of this destructiveness for what it truly is.

But, having seen the truth about ourselves, we face a choice—to ignore this truth and continue living in darkness or to allow the Satan in us to be cast out. When we accept that the cross has judged us, Jesus' words become a difficult challenge. If we seek to save our lives, we will lose them to the darkness we mistakenly think we can hide or avoid. But, if we can find it in ourselves to accept the judgment and allow our destructiveness to be crucified, only then can we find life—free from what destroys us.

This process is both painful and glorious. In a Gethsemane-like moment, Jesus considers asking for release from his sacrifice (v. 27). But, then in a moment reminiscent of the Transfiguration, a heavenly voice, responding to Jesus' prayer, proclaims that God has been glorified and will be again (v. 28). Jesus' death—and our willingness to follow him to the cross—is glorious because it is the necessary surgery that heals our brokenness. In this sense, also, Jesus draws all people to himself. He reveals to us that there is an alternative way to live. We can leave behind our denial and darkness, and we can embrace the death that leads us to authentic, abundant life.

For more detail see: http://sacredise.com/blog/?p=1137

March 29, 2015
Palm/Passion Sunday

Palm Texts: Psalm 118:1-2, 19-29; Mark 11:1-11 or John 12:12-16
Passion Texts: Isaiah 50:4-9a; Psalm 31:9-16; Philippians 2:5-11; Mark 14:1–15:47 or Mark 15:1-39, (40-47)

Carolyn Winfrey Gillette

http://www.carolynshymns.com/

Lord, What a Parade!

LYONS 10.10.11.11 ("O Worship the King, All Glorious Above")
Lord, what a parade! The crowd quickly grew;
What noise they all made in welcoming you.
"Hosanna!" they shouted. "It's David's own son!
Hosanna! Come save us! God's reign has begun!"

They welcomed you in, a conquering king,
Yet what kind of reign would you really bring?
It wasn't a warhorse you rode on that day;
A creature of peace carried you on your way.

Did those in that crowd expect something more
Than one who reached out in love to the poor?
Did they think a savior with armies was best,
Or did they remember: the peaceful are blessed?

Lord Jesus, it's true—we give you glad praise,
Yet living for you will challenge our ways.
So may we be open and welcome your reign.
Hosanna! Come save us! Renew us again!

Biblical reference: Matthew 21:1-11

Tune: attr. Johann Michael Haydn, (1737-1806). Text: Copyright © 2011 Carolyn Winfrey Gillette. All rights reserved. Email: bcgillette@comcast.net Web site: www.carolynshymns.com/

Teri Peterson

http://clevertitlehere.blogspot.com

Mark 11

"Hosanna!" the crowd cries. "Save us from Rome!"
And Jesus goes into the temple alone, looks around, and quietly leaves the way he came.

This anticlimax begins to turn the tide from "Hosanna! Blessed is the One who comes in the name of the Lord!" to whispers of "Crucify! Crucify this one who did not meet our expectations! Crucify this one we have so misunderstood. We thought he was the one to rescue us."

"Hosanna! Save us!" the people shout. And Jesus, in his parody parade, does exactly that, but not the way we expect. He comes—into the city, into the houses, into the crowd. He shares our life—joys and sorrows, pain and death. God comes in the flesh to be with us, to give us courage and strength, to walk the journey. God comes, not with political power and military might, not with coercion and crushing, not with violence that only begets more violence, but with compassion, with care, with love. "Hosanna!" we shout. "Save us! Come again into our lives, our world, our community. Walk with us the road of this world's suffering and this world's joy. Redeem us, make us whole again; reconcile us to one another."

"Hosanna! Blessed is the One who comes in the name of the Lord!"

In some traditions, these words are part of the Communion prayer—evidence that God's story doesn't always go the way we expect. We say these words with palm branches waving, then pray them on the way to a table where we remember again that we, together, are the body of Christ, the ones who come in the name of the Lord, the hands and feet of the one who saves us by coming into the world to share a common life. May it be so.

Julia Seymour

http://lutheranjulia.blogspot.com

Mark 11

Jesus rides on a colt that has never had a rider. He's coming into a kingship that has no predecessor. By riding a colt with no previous rider, Jesus is revealing, perhaps too subtly, that what he brings is very different from what previous rulers have offered.

Yet the crowds miss that. Most of the disciples don't understand it. They're too busy calling for salvation, and they know exactly what they want that to look like.

This is one of the challenges of Holy Week—letting go of what we want salvation to be and allowing ourselves to be open to what it is. Easter helps us not to fear death; however, most of us are still afraid of dying. Holy Week has a lot of dying.

The recollections of betrayal and false accusation and crucifixion cause us to tremble, but the dying begins here, with branches in our hands. Dying well takes honesty. How honest are we ready to be?

Are we honest about our discomfort at being touched? Our uncertainty at the story of the crucifixion? Our sense of being overwhelmed or underwhelmed by a story that's been told many times? Are we willing to be honest that Jesus isn't the king we are expecting?

Are we prepared to die to the notion that goodness, our right behavior, can make us right with God? Are we prepared to be honest that we don't always look for Jesus in others, and we do not always let people see Jesus in us? In this Holy Week, are we prepared to die, within ourselves and in our actions, to our prejudices, fears, and insecurities? Are we prepared to crucify injustice, anger, judgment, and mistrust? Will we cry, "Hosanna to the King of Kings," and mean, "Save us, Jesus, save us"?

David Lose

Philippians 2; Mark 11:14–15

Each year pastors are asked to choose between emphasizing either Palm Sunday or Passion Sunday. They have distinct emphases, it is argued, and doing both is too much, too confusing.

Perhaps. But I think a few notes of frenzy and confusion are in order to capture the mood and events of the week we call "holy." It is a week of great swings in emotions, fortunes, and more. The key to navigating it all is locating a particular element that ties the various passages and emphases together. The element I choose to reflect on is courage.

Notice, for instance, that in the accounts of both the Triumphal Entry and the Last Supper, Jesus makes preparations. He identifies ahead of time someone with a colt and makes arrangements to use it on that day. Similarly, he contracts with someone earlier for a room in which to share the Passover meal with his disciples.

Jesus *chooses* his actions. His fate is not some tragic accident or unexpected twist of fate. Rather, he looks his destiny in the eye and chooses to embrace it, even when it includes, as Paul notes, death on the cross.

This is the very definition of courage, as courage is not having no fear, but rather acting faithfully *in spite of fear*.

For this reason, Paul sings, Jesus is praised—not because of his divine nature or status of equality with God, but rather because out of love he gave all those things up, taking on our lot and our life in order to be joined to us in every possible way. The result is that wherever we may go and whatever we may experience, we know that Jesus has already been there. And where Jesus now is, we are promised we shall someday be.

Elizabeth Quick

http://bethquick.com

Mark 11

- This is a passage that aches to be visually depicted. That's why, I think, we wave the palms or have processions on Palm Sunday. We need to see it, experience it, be part of it. How do you proclaim this text using all our senses?

- "Go into the village ahead of you, and as you enter it you will find tied there..." (v. 2 NRSV) I read this not as Jesus prophesying what will happen, but simply as Jesus telling the disciples the plans he has made. We never seem satisfied with things just happening in the realm of the natural. We seem to need to add a supernatural element to scripture, as if it is not powerful enough otherwise.

Philippians 2

- "Did not regard equality with God / as something to be exploited" (v. 6 NRSV). Such a compelling statement. Imagine if Christ had used his equality to exploit. What would that look like? Perhaps this is what the devil tempted Christ to do in the wilderness—to exploit his equality with God.

- How would you empty yourself? What practices or disciplines help you empty yourself so God can use you?

- When we read of every knee bending and every tongue confessing that Jesus is Lord, do you see this as something that people are compelled by force to do, against their will? Or do you think this is a vision of everyone being transformed by the persuasive witness of Jesus' life, death, and resurrection?

John Wesley

http://www.ccel.org/ccel/wesley/notes

Mark 11:1

To Bethphage and Bethany, at the Mount of Olives—The limits of Bethany reached to the Mount of Olives, and joined to those of Bethphage. Bethphage was part of the suburbs of Jerusalem, and reached from the Mount of Olives to the walls of the city. Our Lord was now come to the place where the boundaries of Bethany and Bethphage met.

Mark 15

The unanimous outrageous clamours of the people have Christ put to death, and particularly to have him crucified. It was a great surprise to Pilate, when he found the people so much under the influence of the priests that they all agreed to desire that Barabbas might be released, v. 11. Pilate opposed it all he could; What will ye that I shall do to him whom ye call the King of the Jews? Would not ye then have him released too? (v. 12.) No, say they, Crucify him. The priests having put that in their mouths, they insist upon it; when Pilate objected, Why, what evil has he done? (a very material question in such a case), they did not pretend to answer it, but cried out more exceedingly, as they were more and more instigated and irritated by the priests, Crucify him, crucify him. Now the priests, who were very busy dispersing themselves and their creatures among the mob, to keep up the cry, promised themselves that it would influence Pilate two ways to condemn him.

http://www.ccel.org/ccel/henry/mhc5.Mark.xvi.html

Editor's Insights

Seeing Me at the Crucifixion (Mark 14–15)

We have liturgical permission, it seems, to put very little emphasis on the crucifixion of Jesus. Yet, somehow, we must think through (feel through) what it means in our lives and in our faith. We are called here, to look at the world from here, to respond from here. This is where it all starts.

I don't know much about substitutionary atonement. I do understand about crosses. I understand about crucifixions in many, many ways. I see them daily in my own life. I see them on my way into the town, warning me not to say or do anything that is against whomever I'm getting my power and my patronage from. I see myself on crosses, sometimes willingly, sometimes not, sometimes honestly, sometimes with not quite so much honesty, sometimes playacting that my petty inconveniences are sufferings in the name of Christ. Sometimes I actually put my life on the line—in terms of power, community, wealth—for others, for everyone. Sometimes all of those things.

And sometimes I see myself in the crucifiers, whether they are "the Jews," "the "Judeans," "the Romans," or whoever. I, too, construct crosses for others. I, too, laugh at folks on their way to do what they think is being done in the name of the Lord. I, too, construct realities that keep me safe and powerful, while others—yes, because of my constructed realities—are on their way to torture, or maybe not quite torture, but a whole lot of pain.

Where am I at the crucifixion? All around. On all sides. Inside and outside. Victim and torturer. Not literally, but I'm there. Just on this one day, I want to say, I'm there.

April 2, 2015

Holy Thursday

Exodus 12:1-4, (5-10), 11-14; Psalm 116:1-2, 12-19; 1 Corinthians 11:23-26; John 13:1-7, 31b-35

John Wesley

http://www.ccel.org/ccel/wesley/notes

Exodus 12

This was to be annually observed as a feast of the Lord in their generations, to which the feast of unleavened bread was annexed, during which, for seven days, they were to eat no bread but what was unleavened, in remembrance of their being confined to such bread, of necessity, for many days after they came out of Egypt, v. 14-20. The appointment is inculcated for their better direction, and that they might not mistake concerning it, and to awaken those who perhaps in Egypt had grown generally very stupid and careless in the matters of religion to a diligent observance of the institution.

John 13:8

If I wash thee not—If thou dost not submit to my will, thou hast no part with me—Thou art not my disciple. In a more general sense it may mean, If I do not wash thee in my blood, and purify thee by my Spirit, thou canst have no communion with me, nor any share in the blessings of my kingdom.

John Petty

http://progressiveinvolvement.com

1 Corinthians 11

In Genesis 2:7, we are told, "The Lord God formed the human from the topsoil of the fertile land [NRSV has dust of the ground]." We read in Genesis that out of the ground the Lord God formed every animal of the field and every bird of the air. Out of the ground, the Lord God made the trees, and the grass, and the animals, and us too.

God apparently thought this was a pretty good idea. Six times, the Lord God said that what he made was "good." Finally, when God looked over everything God had made, it was not just good, but "supremely good" (1:31).

The sacraments reaffirm that the world is good, that the earth and its inhabitants are the objects of God's love, and that this created world—this ground—is the place where God meets us.

This is the world to which Jesus came; born in the sticks, to a couple of hick Jews, from a podunk town. Jesus, born into the thick fabric of everyday human life that all of us share.

One of my seminary professors used to talk about what he called "a sacramental view of life." What he meant was that if Christ can come to us as a baby from the sticks, if Christ can come among us even in a little piece of bread and sip of cheap wine, then Christ can come to us any way and every way through the people and places and events of our everyday world.

Philip Melanchthon (1497–1560), one of the early Protestant reformers, is believed to have said that when you look at it a certain way, there are "thousands of sacraments" because Christ can and does come to us in a thousand

59

different ways. Or, as the poet Gerard Manley Hopkins once put it in a sonnet, "Christ plays in ten thousand places" (*The Poems of Gerard Manley Hopkins*, ed. W. H. Gardner and N. H. Mackenzie [London: Oxford University Press, 1967], 90).

Julie Craig

http://winsomelearnsome.com

John 13

I think of the feet. Every time I read this, always the feet. The feet connect us to the ground—if we're lucky. They trip us up sometimes; when your feet hurt, your whole body knows it. Feet are soft and vulnerable after being closed up tight in socks and boots for the winter. In the northern climate where I live, Maundy Thursday is often one of those days when boots and socks are a necessity.

My father's feet have been his point of vulnerability his whole life. Suffering from hyperhidrosis, he needs ventilated shoes. Unfortunately, he also needed steel-toed shoes to work on the plant floor as a machinist. After much searching, he eventually found a company that sells ventilated, steel-toed shoes and bought one very expensive pair to wear to work. When that pair wore out, he'd buy another. They were, as I remember, his only splurge during his working years.

I'm told that on the day my parents went to court to adopt me, my father wore shoes into which he had cut holes himself. He was nervous standing before the judge on that summer day; he was afraid the judge might find him unfit because of the holes in his shoes. He needn't have worried. The adoption was finalized that day. But the vulnerability he showed reminds me of grace, and redemption, and love.

Many congregations have moved away from foot washing it seems, preferring the less intimate act of hand washing or no washing at all. I'm sure there are many good reasons given, but I will always think of the feet, and the feet will always be love to me.

Liz Crumlish

http://somethingtostandon.blogspot.co.uk/

John 13

To begin the service:
It was on the Thursday...
Back to the city:
sharing Passover with his friends,
showing them how to serve,
washing their feet,
serving at table,
being God incarnate,
layering everything with new meaning,
the depth of which they could only grasp
after his death.
After instituting a memorial,
he went out into the garden
to await his betrayer's kiss.
Knowing agony
but remaining resolute
to do God's will.

Then on he goes to arrest and trial
witnessing all his friends,
fleeing and failing,
yet still looking on them
with eyes full of love,
and a heart full of forgiveness,
and a mind resolved
to save the world.
Hallelujah, what a Saviour.
To end the service:
Not over
We know it's not over
But for now we go and wait
on the authorities
doing their worst
Offloading the responsibility
and blame
as they achieve
their inevitable outcomes
All the while knowing
We would have done the same. . . .

Karoline Lewis

John 13

"Do you know what I've done for you?" is the key question for preaching the foot washing. Unique to John's gospel, the foot washing has the potential both to be misinterpreted and drastically reduced to a replicated act only for the sake of ritual. While there's nothing wrong with foot washings, we must understand this act of Jesus in the larger context of what it means to be a disciple of Jesus. The foot washing is only the beginning of the Farewell Discourse, the chapters in which Jesus speaks of his imminent departure and what life will look like when he ascends. He will talk about laying down one's life for one's friends, the disciples thrown out of their synagogues *and* doing greater works than his. Before we sentimentalize foot washing, we would do well to remember that very soon, Jesus will no longer call the disciples servants but friends. To be Jesus' friend is to be Jesus' disciple, "This is my commandment: love each other just as I have loved you. No one has greater love than give up one's life for one's friends" (John 15:12-13). To love as Jesus loves is not a feeling or foot washing, but to be the very presence of God's love and grace in the world. When Jesus asks Peter, "Do you love me?" it is not simply an affirmation of affection but an invitation to discipleship that demands risk, that calls for extravagance, and that is nothing short of abundance, grace upon grace.

Rick Morley

John 13

This is the night before Jesus dies on the cross, as the creeds say, "for us and for our salvation." This night sees the commencement of the events that hold for Christians the greatest soteriological significance.

On this night, we find Jesus in a remarkably penultimate matter, setting the boundaries for the community of those who will live in his name after his death and resurrection. Two things will define this new community, Jesus says: service and love.

Jesus washes Peter's feet and the feet of the other disciples after some almost comical protest. And then Jesus gives the reason for the foot washing: He washes their feet as an example, an example that his disciples are to follow. It's a model of service, for sure, but it's a particular kind of service that Jesus is going for: It's hands-on. It's messy. It's intimate. And it's a reminder that, in Christian community, hierarchy and privilege don't rule the day. All of us are to get down on our knees and wash one another's feet.

And then comes the moment that makes this Thursday "Maundy." From the Latin word mandatum, meaning "commandment," Jesus gives his disciples a "new commandment." One might even say a *final* commandment. "Love each other."

The word that always sticks out to me here is "new." What's new about this? Hasn't love been the foundation of Jesus' teaching all along? Well, what's new here is the addendum. We are to love one another "as I have loved you," as Jesus has loved us. That this conversation happens on the eve of Jesus' sacrificial death makes this commandment particularly poignant. And, like the foot washing before, this new kind of love is just as messy, hands-on, and intimate.

Martha Spong

http://marthaspong.com/

John 13

For my second Maundy Thursday with my last congregation, I got the notion we should try foot washing. When I floated it to the deacons months ahead, they assured me it had been done before. I let the idea go, thinking I would come back to the logistics later. Just before Lent, I discovered it had been done only once before, urged on by someone now gone. Worse, at the time it felt odd to people. It would have been helpful to know this sooner.

Raised a rather urban Southern Baptist, I suffered from the assumptions of my schoolmates—"Are you a foot-washin' Baptist?" I didn't know what they meant. I had to look it up. Now I did the same thing, checking every resource I could find about how to carry off a foot washing. Episcopal friends told me their altar guilds supplied plentiful clean water throughout the ritual. Meanwhile, my deacons worried about coming dressed the right way for baring their feet in the still-cold Maine weather. They worried about putting pressure on the congregation. I worried the service would be a failure.

Overwhelmed, I felt my resemblance to Peter, who managed to misunderstand both by resisting and by overcommitting. No one wants to get an important thing wrong, to blurt out an inelegant answer or splash water all over the carpet, or ask God to wash the wrong parts of us.

Finally, I said, "What about hand washing instead?" Marvelously—really, it was a marvel—it all came together then. We no longer drowned in the logistics. One deacon brought a rustic white basin and pitcher; another shopped for two dozen white hand towels. Perceived obstacles fell away, graciously and gracefully.

By candlelight, warm water poured over each hand with blessing. We used every towel and needed no more.

April 3, 2015

Good Friday

Isaiah 52:13–53:12; Psalm 22; Hebrews 10:16-25 or Hebrews 4:14-16; 5:7-9; John 18:1–19:42

Mary J. Scifres

Forsaken?! (Psalm 22)

Although this "fourth word" of the traditional Seven Last Words of Christ does not occur in John's gospel (see Mark 15), today's psalm brings the quote to mind. Surely, Jesus was remembering a song of sorrow or a word of scripture from his youth as he faced his imminent death on the cross. How sorrowful to feel so forsaken! How deeply wounded and broken to face the cross alone!

How sorrowful we all feel when we are forsaken by people we love, when we feel forsaken even by God! How deeply wounded and broken we are when we face the death of dreams and hopes, plans and ideals! Good Friday is a time to face our brokenness, and realize that Jesus has walked this lonesome valley and knows this brokenness in intimate, personal ways. Still, death comes; shrouds cover our hope; and life's cruelties break our spirits. Even Jesus ultimately "bowed his head and gave up his spirit" (John 19:30 NRSV). Jesus knows this lonesome valley. Jesus knows the deep grief of feeling forsaken, even by God, even by parents and loved ones, and even by church family and friends. Still, we never are forsaken, even as we sense being forsaken. For Christ is with us, Immanuel, always, forever. And God's Spirit never gives up on us, even if we give up on God. For within each of us, the Spirit dwells, the light shines, and the darkness will not overcome it.

John Wesley

http://www.ccel.org/ccel/wesley/notes

Hebrews 5:7

And being heard in that which he particularly feared—When the cup was offered him first, there was set before him that horrible image of a painful, shameful, accursed death, which moved him to pray conditionally against it: for, if he had desired it, his heavenly Father would have sent him more than twelve legions of angels to have delivered him. But what he most exceedingly feared was the weight of infinite justice; the being "bruised" and "put to grief" by the hand of God himself. Compared with this, everything else was a mere nothing; and yet, so greatly did he ever thirst to be obedient to the righteous will of his Father, and to "lay down" even "his life for the sheep," that he vehemently longed to be baptized with this baptism.

John 18

A garden—Probably belonging to one of his friends. He might retire to this private place, not only for the advantage of secret devotion, but also that the people might not be alarmed at his apprehension, nor attempt, in the first sallies of their zeal, to rescue him in a tumultuous manner. Kedron was (as the name signifies) a dark shady valley, on the east side of Jerusalem, between the city and the Mount of Olives, through which a little brook ran, which took its name from it. It was this brook, which David, a type of Christ, went over with the people, weeping in his flight from Absalom.

D. Mark Davis

http://leftbehindandlovingit.blogspot.com/

John 18–19

The events that unfold at the arrest, trial, torture, and death of Jesus are horrific on many levels. The gospels tell them in a way that invites not only horror at the depth of human cruelty, but also the real brokenness that comes with hearing this story in God's world. God's role in this story may be the most difficult of all. First, the human roles:

Annas and his son Caiaphas hand Jesus over to Pilate. John puts this responsibility squarely on the shoulders of the Jewish religious leaders, reflecting the experience of John's community, who felt betrayed by their leadership. The chief priests' villainy reaches its highest point when they say, "We have no king except the emperor" (19:15).

Peter's act of denying Jesus is parallel to Jesus' act of claiming his identity. Twice Peter says, and once more it is implied, "I am not" when asked if he is a disciple of Jesus (18:17, 25, 27). Twice Jesus said and once more implies "I am he" at his arrest (vv. 5, 6, 8).

Pilate acts reluctantly but cowardly in this story. Dismissing the matter of truth (v. 38), Pilate capitulates to the voices that posit Jesus against Caesar.

Ultimately, however, this is a story of Jesus' encounter with God. God has given Pilate his authority over Jesus. A challenge facing the interpreter of this text is whether the second half of John 19:11 refers to God or Judas. The first half of that verse would imply that it is God. If so, we have a story of the culpability of God in handing Jesus over—a mind-boggling thought. It makes this story more than a tragedy of bad human choices and a story of brokenness at the very core of life.

Lowell E. Grisham

http://lowellsblog.blogspot.com/

The Prayers of the People

Presider: Gracious and loving God, in Jesus you have poured out your divine life in sacrificial love, bearing our sins and brokenness unto death: Hear us when we cry to you and deliver us from evil, as we pray: Those who seek you shall praise you: "May your heart live forever."

Litanist: Eternal God, in Christ's passion you have borne our infirmities and carried our diseases; out of Christ's anguish you have brought light to the world: Empower our witness through the church that all people may know the wonder of your love. Those who see you shall praise you:

"May your heart live forever."

Almighty God, startle the nations into silence before you and deliver all who suffer from perversions of justice, violence, and abuse, that all who rule or hold authority may exercise their powers wisely in the service of truth and for the benefit of the needy and poor. Those who see you shall praise you:

"May your heart live forever."

Gracious God, do not hide your face from this community, but deliver those who trust in you, for you are our strength; hasten to help us. Those who see you shall praise you:

"May your heart live forever."

Benevolent God, out of Christ's anguish you have brought life: Shed abroad the power of your compassionate heart, and be with all who cry in the daytime and hear no answer, who cry at night and find no rest. Those who see you shall praise you:

"May your heart live forever."

Suffering God, visit with your love all prisoners and criminals, the violent and their victims, the broken and those who mourn, that none may be forsaken in their suffering: We pray especially for ___.

Hear our grateful thanks for your sacrificial love and for all of the goodness and grace we experience in our lives, as we offer our prayers of thanksgiving, especially for ___.

All who go down to the dust fall before you for through Christ you have opened to us the new and living way: Hear our prayers for those who have died, especially ___. To you alone all who sleep in the earth bow down in worship.

Those who see you shall praise you:

"May your heart live forever."

Presider: Through the cross of Christ you have saved the world from its darkness, O God, and brought light and life to our violence and death: Be with us as we walk the way of the cross, and finish the work of your Spirit, that all people may put their trust in you and be delivered, through Jesus Christ, who died for us, and lives forever in glory everlasting. Amen.

Suzanne Guthrie

http://www.edgeofenclosure.org

John 18–19

Here in my soul, I see the bureaucrats sitting in uninformed judgment. They don't have all the facts. They don't have all the information they need. They don't see the big picture. Annas, Pilate, Caiaphas, the Sanhedrin: my Committee of the Interior.

They like to hear themselves hold forth with loud opinions, no matter the long-term consequences. They appeal to the day's shouting rabble, the crowd at hand, the crowd addicted to drama, to adrenalin, to the quick-moving surface of passing events.

Shallow bureaucrats impressing one another with their cleverness will crucify my true life. One rises and clears his throat. "It is expedient for you that one man should die for the people." The others nod, pretending they understand. So, too, in the world.

Woe to the ones who stop to think before they speak. Woe to the ones lingering in the library. Woe to the fact checkers. Woe to those who contemplate the darkness, who face and embrace unpleasant truths. Woe to those who tell the story from the beginning and hold out for a graceful ending. Woe to those holding ambiguity in their weakening grasp. Woe to the weary reconcilers.

I know the arrogant class. They look just like my Committee. I hear myself speak; therefore, I must be right! Don't you worry your pretty head, little lady, I'm in charge.

You may be in charge, but you're destroying the already diminishing life in me. You will kill me out of your empty ignorance. And just for the slightest, most temporary, greedy thrill.

And so, when I contemplate the Passion, and hear the self-satisfying pundits condemning Christ to death before going out for lunch, I can't exactly hold them up as the enemy. I know these men. I know them all. They live in me.

And I am crucifying You in me. Forgive us. We do not know what we are doing.

Amy Persons Parkes

John 18–19

One dying man went into a coma only hours after his son replaced the broken spark plug on his lawnmower. Crossing off the final item on his "to-do" list, he let go of consciousness. Stories of this sort are endless. The close relative arrives to say good-bye. A long-anticipated phone call is made. One last gift is acquired for an occasion yet to occur. The dying have a sense of timing, and the living are often puzzled by it.

Jesus has his own sense of timing. In the throes of his suffering, Jesus recognizes his mother and the disciple whom he loves gathered at the foot of the cross among some of his inner circle. Seeing them, Jesus initiates an exchange; he negotiates his own replacement. For all the years he has been son to her, perhaps Jesus is saying to his mother, "Here, let this one whom I love take my place. Let him be me." For the all the years he has been teacher, friend, mentor, perhaps Jesus is saying to the disciple, "Here, take my mother; she taught me. Let her be me." Jesus gives them to one another and in so doing, gives them himself. Echoes of John 17 ring in our ears, where Jesus said, "All mine are yours, and yours are mine" (v. 10a NRSV). Jesus prayed, "that they all may be one. As you, Father, are in me and I am in you, may they also be in us" (v. 21ab NRSV), and "so that they may be one, as we are one, I in them and you in me, that they may be completely one" (vv. 22-23a NRSV).

Did Jesus take our place? Or do we take the place of Jesus? The latter idea inverts a theory of substitutionary atonement.

Thom M. Shuman
http://lectionaryliturgies.blogspot.com/

Call to Worship
Here, in the midst of these people, we come to worship you.
We come with the groans of our lives and the whispers of hope in our hearts.
Here, in the midst of these people, we come to remember you.
We come, trusting you have not forgotten us; that here, promises will be fulfilled.
Here, in the midst of these people, we come to have our hearts touched.
We come, knowing you hear our souls; we come, to praise you for your steadfast love.

Prayer of the Day
On this day, God of all tears,
you call us in the midst
of our busy lives
to look at the suffering and death
of the One who came to carry
the pain of the world into your heart.
Give us eyes to see your love
this day.

On this day
you would gather everyone
to your side,
Grace of Calvary,
but we leave you
to carry the cross alone.
You came simply as love incarnate,
but hate and bitterness
were the gifts we offered to you.
You poured out your love
so our emptiness might be filled.

Give us ears to hear your pain
this day.

On this day,
you would pray for us,
for we cannot find the words
on our own,
Shattered Spirit.
Hear the cries of those in need.
Listen to the lament of the lonely.
Cradle the whispered hopes of children.
Set free the dreams of prisoners and captives.
Give us hearts to pray with you
this day.

God in Community, Holy in One,
we lift our prayers to you in the name of the One
who suffered and died for us
this day
and who teaches us to pray, saying,
Our Father . . .

April 5, 2015

Easter Sunday

Acts 10:34-43 or Isaiah 25:6-9; Psalm 118:1-2, 14-24; 1 Corinthians 15:1-11; John 20:1-18 or Mark 16:1-8

Mark Stamm

Isaiah 25; 1 Corinthians 15; John 20

The writer of John doesn't tell us why Mary Magdalene went to the tomb early that morning, simply that she went. After telling Peter and "the other disciple" what she had seen, Mary wept. Grief was deepening. Even when she encountered the Risen Jesus, she didn't recognize him. One finds such inability to recognize Jesus, even bewilderment, throughout the Resurrection appearances (compare Luke 24:13-35 and Mark 16:8). We also experience such confusion, even as persons of faith. Be clear—encountering the Risen Christ does not lead to a simple "happily ever after" place. The Boston Marathon bombing and the explosion of a fertilizer plant in West, Texas, both happened during Eastertide. Who knows what will happen by the time you read this?

While Mary doesn't say that all is resolved, she does proclaim, "I've seen the Lord" (John 20:18). How can we invite persons to join her in a similar witness?

Turning to 1 Corinthians 15, notice that Paul doesn't try to prove the veracity of the Resurrection. Rather, he recounts testimony about Christ's appearances, including his own testimony (v. 8). We can neither prove nor fully describe Resurrection. It remains "a mystery" (v. 51 NRSV). But we can learn to name the Lord's appearing in our midst—in grief that yields to hope, in recovery from addiction, in deliverance from abuse, in the rebuilding of devastated communities, in churches that find new purpose. Where have you seen glimpses of Resurrection?

The Isaiah 25 text provides a vision of a great feast on God's mountain, with the promise that God will swallow up death forever. Feast nurtures such visions. We may experience a glimpse of that future at the Lord's Table and in other places of hospitality. Therefore, don't neglect Eucharist on Easter Sunday.

Kwasi Kena

Acts 10

"Now do you understand?" How often do parents say that after explaining the same concept for the umpteenth time to a child? Repetition, exact or with slight variation, is a communication device used frequently in oral cultures. Repetition indicates importance. The people living during ancient biblical times primarily communicated orally, transmitting values and spiritual truths through stories filled with key repetitions. Today's passages are a sample of the oft-repeated retelling of Christ's resurrection.

In the Acts passage, Peter highlights Jesus' earthly ministry: his preaching, healing, death, and resurrection. In 1 Corinthians, Paul summarizes the good news: Christ died for our sins, was buried and resurrected in accordance with scripture. Both John and Mark attest to Christ's resurrection through their empty-tomb accounts.

This repetition of Christ's resurrection is understandable. His resurrection was different. Sure, people had been raised from the dead before—remember the son of the woman at Zarephath's(1 Kgs 17:17-23), Jairus's daughter (Mark 5:35-41), the widow of Nain's son (Luke 7:11-17), and Lazarus (John 11:41-44)? In those cases human agency played a role. But Jesus was buried, alone, in a sealed tomb, with Roman guards posted. Without any human intervention, God resurrected Jesus from the dead. This was news. This was monumental. No one had ever been raised from the dead by God alone.

Christ's resurrection marked the beginning of a new understanding of God's power. Now people understood that God could conquer death, hell, and the grave without any human help. God was and is omnipotent. Belief in the resurrected Jesus makes us part of the body of Christ and a participant in God's resurrection power. On Easter, Resurrection Sunday, there is no need to be creative. Just repeat the story. Rehearse the resurrection. Review how God raised Jesus from the dead until people believe.

John Wesley

Acts 10:34

I perceive of a truth—More clearly than ever, from such a concurrence of circumstances. That God is not a respecter of persons—Is not partial in his love. The words mean, in a particular sense, that he does not confine his love to one nation; in a general, that he is loving to every man, and willeth all men should be saved.

Mark 16:3

Who shall roll us away the stone—This seems to have been the only difficulty they apprehended. So they knew nothing of Pilate's having sealed the stone, and placed a guard of soldiers there.

Marci Auld Glass

http://www.marciglass.com

Mark 16

"Overcome with terror and dread, they fled from the tomb. They said nothing to anyone, because they were afraid."

And here Mark ends his gospel. In the Greek, it even ends on a preposition, causing Mark's eighth-grade grammar teacher to hang her head and weep!

Your Bibles have some other verses after this ending—both a shorter and a longer ending. But scholars agree editors trying to help Mark out added these. "Surely he couldn't have meant to end there?"

It appears he did.

And before you flee in terror and amazement, headed for a church that is reading one of the other resurrection stories, let me invite you to spend some time with your discomfort over this ending.

Because, no matter what happens next for the fleeing women and the disciples, there is a real ending taking place in this story. Jesus is dead. They headed to the tomb to anoint his dead body with spices, after all, not to take him a sandwich and a change of clothes. He had died a horrific death on a cross, and they were witnesses to his death. He was dead, dead, dead.

They were never going to go out for lunch with him again. They were not ever going to pick up their phones and hear his voice at the other end of the line.

And as you know from dealing with death in your own lives, to pretend that the death hasn't happened is not helpful. To move on from death to happy ending too quickly is also not helpful.

I appreciate Mark's willingness to remind us to pause—even if it involves terror and amazement—before we move on to the good news of the resurrection.

(Excerpt from http://marciglass.com/2012/04/08/after-the-ending/)

Teri Peterson

http://clevertitlehere.blogspot.com

Mark 16

I don't know what the women were thinking that morning when they ran away in fear. I don't know what most of us are thinking when we run away from good news either. I do know what I would be thinking if I were those women, though:

What if it's true?

What if the grave wasn't robbed, and God has truly broken the bonds of death?

What if it's true that Jesus, who was dead, is now alive, having burst out of the tomb, and is now cavorting around in Galilee?

What if it's true, what we've been saying all these weeks together—that God is doing a *new thing*—even now it springs forth…can't we see it?

If all those things are true, then the things Jesus said and did must be true too, and the things he asked us to do, the calling he gave us, the standards he set, the love he poured on us and commanded us to share—those must also be true.

And now I'm just as scared as those women must have been!

Fear seems an odd place to end this story. It feels as if there ought to be more. (And, of course, through the centuries, people who felt the same way tried to add more, but they never quite captured Mark's style or message.) And yet fear is common in our culture, so perhaps it's the best place to end: with our common experience.

Or maybe Mark doesn't give us an ending because, as he said in his first sentence sixteen chapters ago, he's only telling the beginning of the good news of Jesus Christ, the Son of God. Fear, death, and loss are not the last words. The good news—love, grace, and hope—keeps going. Christ is risen indeed!

Ann Scull

http://seedstuff.blogspot.com

Dawn Service

Have a short reflective service near a lake or beach if possible—if you live inland, then choose a high point—if you live inland on a plain then find a nice river—if you live inland on a plain in a desert (like many Australians) then you will have plenty of beautiful places to choose from. Have a campfire or a fire pot instead of an Easter candle. As part of the service, cook enough fish and damper (Australian soda bread) or Middle Eastern flat bread over your open fire for everyone.

Call to Worship

Project a series of pictures about Good Friday while playing Moby, "Grace" on *Songs* (New York: Elektra, USA, 2000) CD edition. Move straight into the drama: "The Three Women" from *Wild Goose Worship Group, Stages on the Way* (Glasgow: Wild Goose Publications, 1998, 192–94). As the three women say their final lines together, "He is risen," project their words. Woman 1 then removes the black cloths that have been covering everything around the church, Woman 2 lights the candle, and Woman 3 gives out the musical instruments and announces the first song. Then make enthusiastic music!

Listening Song

U2, "Beautiful Day" on *All That You Can't Leave Behind* (Dublin and France: Island Records, UK, Interscope Records, USA, 2000). This is a great song for Easter day.

Children's Talk

"Cut the Tie," found at http//talks2children.wordpress.com/2010/09/06/cut-the-tie/ (accessed April 29, 2013). I used this one three years ago and people still talk about it. They were astounded, and the elderly gentleman who had his tie cut was just wonderful!

Dramas

"The Message" in Verena Johnson, *Let's Make Another Scene* [Adelaide, Open Book, 1995] 66. This drama is based on the gospels.

"Easter Eggcitement" in Verena Johnson ed., Mega Drama 1 (Adelaide: Open Book Publishing, 2001, 94). This drama is based on the John reading.

Julia Seymour

http://lutheranjulia.blogspot.com

Mark 16

Easter's changing date means it is a moveable feast. It sounds like a picnic on the go, something that comes with us, that we carry, that carries us. A moveable feast is a banquet, a glorious table spread with all kinds of amazing foods. Or when you are hungry or exhausted, a moveable feast is a shared crust of bread and the slug of liquid that helps you keep going. Easter is both of these.

The women probably ate little the day before, since it was the Sabbath and because they were still stunned from the crucifixion. At some point, each of them set aside ointments, cloths, and spices to tend Jesus' body, to mend it, to commend it to God through washing and prayer. Grieving, these women were not ready for a feast of any kind.

Ready or not, they arrived to hear of resurrection. They are stunned and afraid. Minutes before, they had a momentous task, honoring the body of Jesus. Now they have a different, monumental task, becoming the body of Christ. Carrying words as a balm, hope as the fragrance, faith as a spice. They nibble at the edges of this feast, easing the hunger of their grief.

Why does the angel tell them to go the disciples and Peter? The messenger is clarifying for the women that there are no side tables at God's feast, no people wait for scraps in the kitchen, and no one is turned away from the banquet of resurrection. Even Peter, who denied, has a place at the Easter feast.

A moveable feast comes whether we're ready or not. It offers us hope until we taste joy. It offers expectation until we drink from faith. A moveable feast fills us with courage until we are stuffed from encounter.

April 12, 2015

2nd Sunday of Easter

Acts 4:32-35; Psalm 133; 1 John 1:1–2:2; John 20:19-31

John Wesley

http://www.ccel.org/ccel/wesley/notes

Acts 4:32

And the multitude of them that believed—Every individual person were of one heart and one soul—Their love, their hopes, their passions joined: and not so much as one—In so great a multitude: this was a necessary consequence of that union of heart; said that aught of the things which he had was his own—It is impossible any one should, while all were of one soul. So long as that truly Christian love continued, they could not but have all things common.

John 20:21

Peace be unto you—This is the foundation of the mission of a true Gospel minister, peace in his own soul, 2 Cor. iv, 1.

Matthew L. Skinner

Acts 4; John 20

The summary in Acts 4 recalls 2:43-47, the creation of a growing community characterized by worship and mutuality. Now, the great generosity of some members results in "no needy persons" (v. 34) among the fellowship. This description echoes a promise God made to the ancient Hebrews before they entered the promised land (Deuteronomy 15:4).

A caring community that is "one in heart and mind" (v. 32): What causes this? Acts does not credit it to the right social organization, human determination, or ethical fortitude. God makes it happen. God assembles the community of believers at Pentecost, by the Holy Spirit (Acts 2; see also John 20:22, where Jesus literally breathes the Spirit *into* his followers). Through the Spirit's power, this collection of people becomes a place where the full transformative power of God's salvation can be experienced and expressed.

People in Acts 4 do not give up private possessions for the sake of one another because ownership is necessarily inconsistent with discipleship. Their actions indicate they have been called to participate in the salvation God makes possible. They understand what this salvation is about, for they demonstrate it, surrendering their advantages to enter into true solidarity with others. The risen Lord Jesus, who sends the Holy Spirit, empowers the community of disciples to manifest the kind of discipleship he envisions and models in Luke's gospel (Luke 6:35; 12:33-34; 14:33; 18:22).

The discipleship described in Luke, embodied here in Acts, challenges our tamer expressions of church and communal support. We might begin with the passage's ability to illustrate the unity that God desires and makes possible. Any unity built on seeking to live with a single "heart and mind" must express it somehow. Self-sacrificial sharing offers but one way of exemplifying the new realities made possible through Jesus' resurrection. Help your listeners imagine additional ways.

Peter Woods

Acts 4; John 20

There can be no doubt that materialism is the dominant zeitgeist of our age. Probably because we are so afraid of penury and privation, we have come to believe that the hoarding of material wealth will be a fortress against that which we fear the most. Don't we speak about "hedge" funds?

The post-Resurrection, pre-Pentecostal disciples were afraid too. Living as they did, not in a materialistic culture, but in the physical power culture of Rome, they also hedged themselves in. They were locked up—physically, emotionally, and spiritually—not for fear of poverty, but as John records, for "fear of the Jews." (Whenever I preach on texts where John speaks of "the Jews" I take a moment to disentangle this phrase from its resultant anti-Semitism and the embarrassment the church must forever bear.)

John never meant to be anti-Semitic. He is referring to "those in power" or those "who threaten us." Would "for fear of the gangsters, the criminals, or the banks" be a modern-day equivalent?

Fear closes us in. It shuts us down.

Two encounters with the risen Christ follow. In both meetings, Jesus leads with a blessing of peace, Shalom, and displays his wounds. Vulnerability and not defense is the counterintuitive key to the prison of fear.

How different is the courage of the post-Pentecostal church we meet in Acts 4:32-35. No more fear and defense, but rather a communalism that doesn't hoard but helps the other in need.

Meeting the resurrected and wounded one, who overcame the worst of human aggression through the power of forgiveness and love, can unlock the most fearful of us today.

Martha Spong

http://marthaspong.com/

John 20

To avoid risk, they locked the doors.

We've locked the doors and sat around our own tables, fearful, haven't we? Will our neighborhood ever be the same again? Will the storm knock out the power? Will the police find the terrorist?

Average daily anxiety gets us worked up enough; when there's a good reason to be afraid, for real, our brain chemistry can rearrange our judgment.

It had to be that way in the house where the disciples locked the doors. According to John's gospel, Jesus drew attention and trouble from the beginning of his ministry. Their Jesus waltzed into the temple in chapter 2 and laid it down. When he returned later, he vanished his way to safety, inspiring murderous rage in the religious leaders.

The disciples knew the rage. They felt fear and despair. Jesus was dead. What good could come of it? They expected more violence, reprisals, perhaps their own deaths.

They locked the doors, quite reasonably.

But someone went out to get news and supplies. Someone had to do it, like my wife making the last trip to the supermarket before a snowstorm. Someone had to take the risk. Since someone particular missed the visit from Reappearing Jesus, no more restrained by locked doors than by death, we may deduce the one who went out for whatever they needed was Thomas.

He did more than doubt. He risked. Risking his life, Thomas offered himself up to die with Jesus (John 11:16). Risking laughter, Thomas asked the direct, even obvious, question (14:5). Risking arrest or worse, Thomas left the safe house (20:24).

And when he returned, he took the risk again and expressed his doubts. Would we take the same risks?

Editor's Insights

Doubting with Thomas (John 20)

I am Thomas. I am the one who wasn't there. I am the one who refuses to pretend that I get it (even when others pretend that they get it in order to go along with the group). I'm the one who asks about the emperor's clothes. I am the one who is disappointed when I do, and the one who turns up my cynicism another notch. But this time, this time it's real. I'm the one who struggles with how to respond when I finally find something that is actually, truly, real. How does one respond to a miracle that's not a mir-"I"-cle? How does one respond to the real thing when the response means giving my life to something I, finally, know is real, but do not at all understand?

John van de Laar

http://www.sacredise.com/

John 20

"Doubter" is an unfair title for Thomas. He was one of Jesus' most courageous disciples, but he refused a second-hand faith. There is raw honesty here, and it moves the message of John's gospel—the call to a deeper seeing—to a climax. Thomas is shown, at first, as the epitome of faith that is not really faith. He wanted a miracle that would enable him to believe. John's gospel constantly contrasts this kind of faith with true belief. The other disciples were no better, though. None of them had really *seen* yet.

A week later, Jesus appears in the upper room again. This time Thomas is there, and Jesus immediately offers the proof he seeks. Thomas responds as none of the others had: "My Lord and my God!" (v. 28). Jesus' famous reply—"Do you believe because you see me? Happy are those who don't see and yet believe" (v. 29)—is the climactic challenge of John's gospel. We can either see—believe shallowly in miracles—or we can truly *see*.

Where before Thomas had been looking for proof that Jesus was risen, he now sees Jesus in a whole new way. He believes, not just in a resurrected teacher, but in an incarnate deity. And his faith is more than an idea—it is a transforming encounter. This is the faith that Jesus calls for, and that John seeks to generate in his readers.

This leaves us with a searching question. Do we get hung up on the proof of the resurrection or are we ready to lay aside the miracles and enter the mystery? The resurrection is not really about a scientific fact. It's about an eternal truth. And until we have really seen this, we haven't encountered resurrection at all.

For more detail see: http://sacredise.com/blog/?p=943

Natalie Ann Sims

http://lectionarysong.blogspot.com

John 20

- "Peace I Leave with You My Friends" (Ray Repp)—Slow, simple and excellent words. A congregation will pick this up the first time through, I think.

- "Faith Will Not Grow from Words Alone" (Elizabeth Smith)—Excellent strong words of a questioning faith to a familiar hymn tune (DUNEDIN).

- "Jesus Is Risen from the Grave" (Iona Community)—Good, simple rhythm and tune. You can even make up some verses if you like. Good for KIDS. If you missed the Thomas verse at Easter (or missed singing this song), you could sing it this week instead.

- "God Give Us Peace That Lasts" (John Bell)—Lovely prayer for peace, hope, and love to a simple hymn tune. This can also be sung to LOVE UNKNOWN. "God give us peace that lasts, not through the fear of might, / but through the force of love, and love of life and right."

- "Peace before Us Peace behind Us" (David Haas)—I just love this one. Reflective. Careful not to get too schmaltzy because it's long. Less is more. Good for kids.

- "Let It Breathe on Me" (Magnolia Lewis-Butts—A lovely old gospel tune welcoming the Spirit, especially nice with harmonies; I like to sing just the first verse.

- "Sent by the Lord Am I" / "*Enviado soy de Dios*" (traditional Cuban)—Great rhythm, good words, and not too hard to sing (provided you sing it a little slowly the first time!). I prefer the translation "Sent out in Jesus' Name."

- Recorded music: "Doubting Thomas" (Nickel Creek)—One of the most powerful songs I know about being a postmodern doubting, but faithful, Christian. (Lyrics: http://www.cowboylyrics.com/lyrics/creek-nickel/doubting-thomas-16069.html)

April 19, 2015

3rd Sunday of Easter

Acts 3:12-19; Psalm 4; 1 John 3:1-7; Luke 24:36b-48

Thom M. Shuman

http://lectionaryliturgies.blogspot.com/

Call to Worship

We are witnesses,
to the love God has poured into us.
We are witnesses of God's love,
sharing it with each person we meet.
We are witnesses to everyone we encounter,
little children like us, sisters and brothers in God's family.

Call to Reconciliation

We know how easy it is to trick ourselves into believing that every thought is pure, every act is just, every choice is correct. But if we want to be God's children, to grow in hope, to walk in the Light, we must admit our mistakes, so we may open ourselves to the healing mercy of God's love. Join me, please, as we pray together, saying,

Unison Prayer of Confession

Emptier of tombs, we find ourselves running down the street after lies, rather than walking with you. We find it easy to love other people, as long as they don't annoy or bother us. We hunger for love and search for affirmation, yet find it difficult to let others love us for who we are.
Forgive us, Compassionate Heart. You listen to the whispers of our hearts, and then sing of the promises of hope. You grace us with peace, so our hearts can rest in you. You continue to transform us into Easter people, brothers and sisters of our Lord and Savior, Jesus Christ.

Silence is kept

Assurance of Pardon

Not everything has been revealed to us, but this we do know: as God's children, we are blessed, we are loved, we are forgiven.
Our lives have been transformed by the abundant mercy given to us in Christ Jesus our Lord. Thanks be to God! Amen.

John Wesley

http://www.ccel.org/ccel/wesley/notes

Acts 3:19

Be converted—Be turned from sin and Satan unto God. See chap. xxvi, 20. But this term, so common in modern writings, very rarely occurs in Scripture: perhaps not once in the sense we now use it, for an entire change from vice to holiness.

Luke 24:45

Then opened he their understanding, to understand the Scriptures—He had explained them before to the two as they went to Emmaus. But still they understood them not, till he took off the veil from their hearts, by the illumination of his Spirit.

David Lose

Acts 3; 1 John 3; Luke 24

Most of us know what a paradox is. It is the ability to hold two seemingly contradictory impulses together. The Christian faith and life is full of paradoxes. Jesus is, we confess in the Nicene Creed, both fully human *and* fully divine. How can he be two different things fully? It is a paradox—we don't understand how, quite frankly, but we know both statements are true.

Today's readings are animated by a similar paradox. Peter describes his Jewish audience as those who "handed over" and "rejected" Jesus (Acts 3:13b, 14), in language that makes us uncomfortable given the long history of prejudice Christians have shown Jews. At the same time, the one offering this sermon and indictment himself denied and deserted Jesus. How is it that the one who deserted his Lord now accuses others of handing him over?

Similarly, John says that no one who abides in Jesus sins, and that those who sin do not know Jesus. Yet all of us sin, including the one who wrote this letter.

At Emmaus, the disciples are at one and the same time frightened by Jesus' sudden appearance, overjoyed to see him, and filled with wonder and disbelief. How does all that happen at once?

Across these readings we are invited to behold a paradox. God is holy, righteous, and pure and cannot tolerate those who are sinful. Yet although we manifestly are *not* holy, righteous, or pure—including Jesus' own disciples—we are nevertheless called children of God and used by God to share the news of God's love with all people.

How can this be? We do not know. It is a paradox. We may not understand it, but we know both statements are true.

Elizabeth Quick

http://bethquick.com

Acts 3

- Sometimes Peter sounds so accusatory, especially in his early preaching, as if still fresh from losing Jesus as a daily physical presence, he's looking for someone to blame.

- Peter's words are also interesting considering his own role in Jesus' passion. Do you think he's speaking to himself as much as to the crowd?

- This scene takes place just after Peter heals a "crippled man." How do Peter and Jesus differ in their styles of healing?

1 John 3

- We are God's children. More than creator and created, more than master and servant. We're parent and child, a relationship that communicates God's overflowing, unconditional love for us.

- Verses 2 and 3 are traditionally used in funeral liturgies. What we will be has not yet been revealed. So much potential that is inside of us. What's the best you can imagine yourself being? What is God revealing you to be?

- "No one who abides in him sins; no one who sins has either seen him or known him" (v. 6 NRSV). What do you think the author means? Obviously, Christians continue to sin. Do we still abide in God? Sin can put distance between us and God, but does it keep us from knowing God? Maybe our blindness, our unknowing, lasts only as long as we remain separate from God.

Luke 24

- Instead of just a doubting Thomas, Luke recounts a whole group of frightened and terrified disciples, which seems a likely scenario. What would it take to convince you that someone had risen from the dead?

- "Then he opened their minds to understand the scriptures" (v. 45 NRSV). I love this verse, but I'm jealous: what did Jesus say to them? I've always been a questioning, looking-for-answers sort of believer. I'd like a Q&A session with Jesus too!

Chuck Aaron

1 John 3; Luke 24

The combination of the Acts reading, the reading from 1 John, and the reading from Luke gives a comprehensive interpretation of healing.

In the Acts passage, Peter and John continue the healing ministry begun by Jesus when they heal the lame man at the gate of the temple. The reading for today gives Peter's sermon following the healing. At least one message of Peter's sermon is that in spite of the crucifixion, the name of Jesus brings healing. God redeems the betrayal and handing over. Healing arises out of rejection. Peter attributes the healing to "faith," but does not say how faith plays a role. In the healing story itself, the man does not display faith that the disciples will heal him; he wants only a handout. This aspect of the story suggests that healing and grace do not depend on our mustering enough faith to motivate God to act. God takes the initiative.

The Luke pericope presents a full picture of the soundness of Jesus' body after the resurrection. Jesus stands, speaks, eats, and points to his flesh and bones. Jesus has an intact, functioning resurrection body. Jesus then gives instruction to the church for its mission, including the necessity of waiting for the Holy Spirit, which comes at Pentecost.

First John 3 promises the full presence of Christ and our transformation to be like him. Part of this transformation involves purification. If Luke promises physical healing, 1 John promises moral and spiritual healing.

The church continues to offer healing in its ministry. Our resurrection will produce a full healing of our bodies and purity of spirit. These promises offer reassurance to those limited by physical problems and to those struggling with guilt and remorse.

Carolyn Winfrey Gillette

http://www.carolynshymns.com/

Children of God (1 John 3)

LYONS 10.10.11.11 ("O Worship the King, All Glorious Above!")
We're children of God; we're welcomed and claimed.
We're given new birth, renewed and renamed.

The world may not know yet to whom we belong,
But we are God's children and love is our song.

We're children of God, who takes away sin.
In Christ we abide; our life is in him.
We offer forgiveness, seek justice and peace,
And reach out to others, that love may increase.

We're children of God and so our delight
Is living the life that's good in God's sight.
One day we'll be like him, transformed from above
To sing for eternity God's song of love.

Biblical reference: 1 John 3:1-7

Tune: LYONS 10.10.11.11 ("O Worship the King, All Glorious Above!") attr. Johann Michael Haydn (1737–1806); arranged by William Gardiner, *Sacred Melodies* (London: 1815). Alternate Tune: HANOVER ("Ye Servants of God, Your Master Proclaim) attr. William Croft in *The Supplement to the New Version of Psalms,* by Nahum Tate and Nicholas Brady, 6th edition, 1708. Text: Copyright © 2013 by Carolyn Winfrey Gillette. All rights reserved. Email: bcgillette@comcast.net Website: www.carolynshymns.com

Two Bubbas and a Bible

http://lectionarylab.com

Luke 24

What happened to Jesus was not a random act of ugliness, not simply another in a long series of cruelties and indignities that powerful and corrupt people have foisted upon the weak, the innocent, and the good.

Jesus' life, suffering, death, and resurrection were a part of God's long-term effort to deal with the very human problems of sin, evil, hatred, discord, and death. The history of the world is one long litany of bad things people as individuals and as communities and as nations have done to one another.

The only way forward is the way of the Christ, the way of the cross. Jesus came and lived among us and showed us that the one who had the most right to revenge, the best claim to satisfaction, chose to go another way. God, in Christ, turned away from revenge and embraced justice; turned away from our death and through his own death gave us life.

"Repentance and forgiveness of sins is to be proclaimed in his name to all nations" (v. 47 NRSV).

This is the world's only hope, our only way out of the continual cycle of offense and revenge, of wrong piled upon wrong in a deadly game of king of the hill. The only way to bring an end is the gospel call for repentance and forgiveness—not simply in a private and individual way but also in a communal and corporate manner.

What if we heard it and witnessed to it in this way: "We—as a people—are called to turn together from ways that lead to death, and we—as a people—are called to turn together to follow ways that lead to newness of life."

April 26, 2015

4th Sunday of Easter

Acts 4:5-12; Psalm 23; 1 John 3:16-24; John 10:11-18

John Wesley

http://www.ccel.org/ccel/wesley/notes

Acts 4:8

Then Peter, filled with the Holy Ghost—That moment. God moves his instruments, not when they please, but just when he sees it needful.

John 10:12

The wolf—signifies any enemy who, by force or fraud, attacks the Christian's faith, liberty, or life. So the wolf seizeth and scattereth the flock—He seizeth some, and scattereth the rest; the two ways of hurting the flock of Christ.

Todd Weir

http://bloomingcactus.typepad.com/

Psalm 23

When it comes to the word *want*, we have to keep our wits about us. "I shall not want" (CEB has "I lack nothing") is not a promise of a consumer paradise or freedom from troubles. So what does Psalm 23 offer that the mall can't already give? Listen to the promises—tranquility, peace of mind, knowing the right path, overcoming fear, hospitality, blessings, goodness, and mercy. Reading the psalm this time, something struck me that never occurred in hundreds of previous readings. In the first three verses of the psalm, notice the tense for God. The psalmist refers to God in the third person five times as "he" or "him." In verses 4-5, the poet shifts to the intimate form "You," referencing God again five times.

This clarifies to me what it means to say "I shall not want." The spiritual life is a movement from looking to God from a distance, a third-person God who is far away from us, to beginning to experience God as "You." We all have to start somewhere with God. We have some idea or hint of a divine being as we rest in a green pasture, or as we look at the still waters. We have moments in worship, perhaps when we light candles on Christmas Eve, when our souls are restored. As we read Scripture and listen to sermons, we find wisdom to be on the right moral path. And then at some moment in our lives, we come face-to-face with the reality of death, evil, enemies that would hurt us. In these times, we need a God we can call "You." As we pass through these times, we come to know the true nature of the living God, a good shepherd, who will walk with us.

Dan R. Dick

1 John 3

Western culture tends to favor "either/or" thinking. In the West, we love to categorize and divide and compartmentalize. One of the most basic divisions in our culture is that between head and heart. Our cognitive, intellectual processes are viewed as disconnected and discrete from our affective and emotional orientations. Two natural extensions of such thinking result in a division between thought and action, as well as a separation of doing from being. We can satisfy ourselves that we are good people based on what we believe—completely separate from how we behave. This is not a unique or new phenomenon. The author of John's letter instructs his community to "love, not in word or speech, but in truth and action" (v. 18 NRSV). Talking about love, having loving thoughts, abstractly believing love is a good idea—these are not enough. Loving only those who are close to you, whom you like, or who are convenient doesn't qualify either. The kind of love John's author speaks of is active and engaged, not passive and abstract. Love is both who we are and what we do. Love is a verb.

The integration of doing and being, thinking and acting, believing and behaving should be full-time work for Christian disciples. As we learn to be more Christlike, we shift from learning to teaching, from following to leading, from thinking to doing. As our actions align more fully with our thinking, we are transformed. Through God's Holy Spirit, we become the incarnate body of Christ for the world. We become God's love in the world "for God is greater than our hearts" (v. 20 NRSV), and by God's grace, we become greater than our limitations. Love is no longer just a good idea. Love is the reality that defines who we are.

Natalie Ann Sims

http://lectionarysong.blogspot.com

1 John 3 (The Importance of Love and Generous Living)

- "God Is Love and Love Is Giving" (Ross Langmead)—A simple kids' song about God's love. A round; good for kids. (sound sample: http://rosslangmead.50webs.com/rl/Downloads/SongsMP3/GodIsLove.mp3)

- "Love Is the Touch of Intangible Joy" (Alison M Robertson)—words of different kinds of love—deep friendship, romantic love, and the love of God. Each verse ends with "God is where love is, for love is of God." Tune is simple enough for a congregation to sing first go, and it has gorgeous chords. (lyrics: http://knoxwaterloo.ca/home/?p=3785)

- "A New Commandment I Give unto You" (Unknown)—This is a classic chorus, and much loved. Note that more recent publications use "others" rather than "all men" to make it inclusive for all people.

- "God of Freedom God of Justice" (Shirley Murray)—Powerful lyrics. Can be sung to either TREDEGAR (new, but not too hard) or PICARDY (very familiar). (lyrics: http://www.oremus.org/hymnal/g/g203.html)

- "Holy Spirit Come to Us" / "*Veni sancte spiritus*" / "Tui amoris" (Jacques Berthier)—Good if you have a cantor, but works equally well if you don't. (midi: http://www.taize.fr/en_article10308.html?letter=V)

- "Love Knocks and Waits" (Daniel Charles Damon)—Lovely words and a simple lilting melody. Groovy bossa nova mp3 sample at http://www.damonstuneshop.com/AUDIO/Love%20Knocks%20and%20Waits....mp3. I reckon I would play it faster for our congregation. (lyrics and sample sheet music: http://www.hope-publishing.com/html/main.isx?sitesec=40.2.1.0&hymnID=2331)

- "When the Church of Jesus Shuts Its Outer Door" (Fred Pratt Green)—Sung to tune KING'S WESTON, this hymn has strong words of reproach and mission. Could work as a confession, sending out, or offering song. (Lyrics: http://www.hymnary.org/hymn/UMH/592)

John Petty

http://progressiveinvolvement.com

John 10

The "good shepherd" is one of the earliest and most popular images for Jesus. In fact, before the cross became a universal symbol of Christianity, the image of the good shepherd may well have been the most popular image of the early Christians. The cross does not appear in the catacombs below Rome, for example, but Jesus the Good Shepherd does.

In a Jungian archetypal sense, the "good shepherd" is a guide for a person's spirit. The good shepherd helps and leads a person toward ego maturity. Psychologically, "sheep" does not refer to persons *per se*, but rather to that part of the human psyche that listens for a True Voice.

Of course, many entities in life purport to do this. These competing voices—the market, this-or-that celebrity—all make their appeals. This is confusing. Which one, among all these contenders, is a true good shepherd? Which one has a "voice" the sheep can hear?

For the Fourth Gospel, that good shepherd—the one with the True Voice—is, of course, Jesus. The Fourth Gospel tells us that this "good shepherd" does not operate out of selfish motives, as "thieves" and "outlaws" do (10:1, 8). The good shepherd does not take anything away, but will, instead, give up all he has for the benefit of the sheep.

Moreover, this good shepherd *knows* his sheep. The word is *ginosko*, which refers to an intimate and personal knowledge. The good shepherd not only cares for the sheep with no ulterior motive of his own, but knows their deepest and most private yearnings.

This sense of intimacy between Jesus and his followers pervades the Fourth Gospel. The relationship between the two is like that between Jesus and his Father. The intimacy they enjoy is of the same kind as that between the "blessed community" and Jesus.

Karoline Lewis

John 10

Good Shepherd Sunday, the fourth Sunday of Easter, always has as the gospel reading from John 10. It is important to remember that this section of John is situated in the Shepherd Discourse, which is Jesus' interpretation of his healing of the man blind from birth (ch. 9). Jesus does not stop talking at the end of chapter 9, which our modern Bibles have led us to believe. The story of the shepherd and the sheep is a metaphorical rendering of what Jesus and the blind man have already acted out. The blind man was "expelled" (9:35) and then found by Jesus, a sheep not of this "sheep pen" (10:16). The blind man, marginalized from his family, community, religious life, and God, is brought into the fold of Jesus' disciples. The blind man is graced with abundant life, everything that he needs for sustenance and nourishment, a stark contrast to his former life, begging for a scrap of mercy. Fast forward to the arrest scene in John, where Jesus will again act out what it means to be the Good Shepherd. With the sheep (his disciples) safely in the fold (the garden, only in John), Jesus comes out of the garden to face Judas (the thief, 12:4), the soldiers, and police. There is no kiss from Judas, no handing Jesus over, no betrayal. Instead, Jesus willingly hands himself over, asking one of the most important question of John's gospel, "Who are you looking for?" (18:4). Jesus lays down his life for his sheep. He is simultaneously both shepherd and door. What happens if you bring the arrest of Jesus back into the preaching of the Good Shepherd passage? Perhaps a sermon on Jesus as shepherd will find a richer backdrop than simply shepherding practices in ancient Palestine.

May 3, 2015

5th Sunday of Easter

Acts 8:26-40; Psalm 22:25-31; 1 John 4:7-21; John 15:1-8

John Wesley

http://www.ccel.org/ccel/wesley/notes

Acts 8:27

An eunuch—Chief officers were anciently called eunuchs, though not always literally such; because such used to be chief ministers in the eastern courts. Candace, queen of the Ethiopians—So all the queens of Ethiopia were called.

John 15:5

I am the vine, ye are the branches—Our Lord in this whole passage speaks of no branches but such as are, or at least were once, united to him by living faith.

Marci Auld Glass

http://www.marciglass.com

Acts 8

Thankfully, the Ethiopian was willing to accept advice when offered, because he had uncovered a discrepancy in Scripture.

The book of Deuteronomy kept him from worshiping in the temple. Yet, the book of Isaiah promises *all* nations, all peoples, will worship God together. The Ethiopian is reading a prophecy of hope, of freedom, of inclusion, but is unable to square it with what his tradition tells him.

"How can I understand unless someone guides me?"

Luckily, the Spirit sends Philip. The Ethiopian doesn't just need someone who can quote Scripture; he needs someone who knows the God of Scripture. He needs someone who recognizes that God's movement is *always* toward greater inclusion. The family of God is an ever-expanding one.

So we need to be open to advice when offered. But we also need to be discerning in the advice we accept. Some people would have given a very different answer to our Ethiopian friend. There are people today who would say, "I'm sorry. You are a eunuch. This prophecy from Scripture doesn't apply to you. It says so, right here in Deuteronomy. I'd like to baptize you, but Scripture says no."

When we discern the advice out there, we have to ask ourselves, is this person speaking about a God I recognize? Do they know about the love of God? Have they experienced salvation in a way that makes them more compassionate?

Thankfully, the Ethiopian met Philip.

Whenever you start to doubt that your voice matters, remember this story. There are people traveling down all kinds of wilderness roads. And they need to hear about God's love. But if we aren't speaking it, they're going to be stuck listening to someone who wants to claim God is about hate, prejudice, or exclusion.

(Excerpt from http://marciglass.com/2012/05/06/on-the-wilderness-road/)

Amy Persons Parkes

Acts 8

Education is not wisdom, just as age is not maturity. Power and influence do not always equate with capability or competency; and intellectual ability is not the same as understanding. But we often forget all of these things.

I am refreshed when I read the story of the Ethiopian official. He is a man of means, a person of influence in the court of a queen, and he is perplexed in his attempt to grasp the deeper meaning of the sacred words he is reading; yet he willingly opens himself to learn something new from someone else. In fact, he seems to understand a basic principle of a life lived in humility. We need guides. We need mentors and conversation partners and covenant commitments in community. We need other voices who have heard other stories. We need other people willing to share their successes and their failures, their faults and their virtues.

None of us, no matter how educated or powerful or influential or smart, will be able to navigate a life of faith on our own. And for my part, I offer my thanks to the Ethiopian, who accepted the grace of God's intervention in his life without asking Philip, "Where did you earn your degree?" "What is your most recent successful project launch?" "How long have you been in ministry?" "Who do you know that I know?"

Perhaps, instead, he simply said, "Please share with me what you think. I want to know."

Suzanne Guthrie

http://www.edgeofenclosure.org

John 15

The deeply interior life touches the universal. The contemplative life, "with its long slow growth and costly training," as Evelyn Underhill puts it (*Mysticism* [New York: E.P Dutton, 2002], 413), prepares the human person for the life of compassion, union with the Holy and with people.

Life is grounded in community—a vineyard of neighbor planted with neighbor. Vines and root systems enmesh. We drink the same water and breathe the same air. Humans live in overlapping spheres of human interaction in one global community and an increasingly fragile ecosystem.

Jesus taught that you can't love God and not strive to love others. "What you have done to the least of these" links inextricably to God.

But growing in love is terribly difficult, stunted through false starts, twisted mistakes, well-meaning disasters. Factor in poverty, addictions, mental illness, disordered loves—willful, ignorant, and biological. Add the usual character flaws of greed and envy and fear. Note what happens to the human person during war, famine, displacement, stress of all kinds. Every stress affects every part of the vine.

You are not born mastering the impossible standard of loving neighbor as yourself, loving enemies, honoring the stranger in your midst, and laying down your life for your friends. Those lessons come at a cost, often through tragedy and pain, a tremendous suffering for such awakening—"Long, slow growth and costly training"—much pruning, practice, prayer.

Love's impossible enterprise finds nourishment deep in the darkness of Divine Love—the strength to bear blights; the too much rain and too little sun, or too much sun and not enough rain. Love demands deep roots for the length of days to withstand generations of love's disasters.

John van de Laar

http://www.sacredise.com/

John 15

John 15 is part of Jesus' final conversation with his disciples. It begins in John 13 with Jesus washing their feet and announcing the "new commandment"—to love one another as he loved them (13:34). This commandment is then repeated in 15:12 and explains what Jesus means when he calls his followers to "produce fruit" (v. 16).

Jesus' words indicate that fruitfulness is not so much something we do as something we are. A tree does not have to strive to be fruitful. If it is healthy and connected to a source of water and nutrients, it *will* bear fruit—it can do no other. In the same way, if we "remain in" Jesus, we will bear fruit. Our values, priorities, desires, and dreams will all line up with those of God's reign. We will automatically become lovers of God and of people. We will automatically become concerned for the well-being of others and of our planet. We will find compassion flowing freely because that is the heart of Christ.

Jesus describes different ways that the branches behave. Although we can think about these branches as different kinds of people, we all contain these traits within us. We have parts that have grown dead and need to be cut off and thrown away. These are the habits and attitudes that keep us from being true lovers of God and others. We need to be "pruned"—some of our capacities for love need to be disciplined and "shaped" to make us more effective lovers. And we all bear good fruit in the ways we already reveal God's love in our lives. "Remaining in" Jesus, then, is about daily deepening our communion with him so that his love manifests increasingly clearly in every facet of our lives.

May 10, 2015
6th Sunday of Easter

Acts 10:44-48; Psalm 98; 1 John 5:1-6; John 15:9-17

Natalie Ann Sims

http://lectionarysong.blogspot.com

Acts 10 (The Gentiles Receive the Spirit and Are Welcomed with Baptism)

- "Draw the Circle Wide" (Gordon Light)—A great song about welcoming all people. Chorus is "Draw the circle wide, draw it wider still. / Let this be our song." (in *Worship and Song* [Nashville: Abingdon Press, 2011], 3154)

- "Filled with the Spirit's Power" (J. R. Peacey)—A rollicking hymn; a classic and the lyrics are still good to sing today. I prefer the tune WOODLANDS for this hymn.

- "In My Father's House" (Paul Somerville)—Excellent words and an inspiring chorus of living together and learning from our differences within the church. (lyrics, sound sample, and source: http://www.songsthatunite.org.au/artists/product/179-in-my-father-s-house)

- "Holy Spirit Go before Us" (Elizabeth Smith)—Great words of evangelism and justice to a simple lilting melody. If you think your congregation can't cope with a new tune this week, it can be sung to AUSTRIA.

- "From the Waiting Comes the Sign" (Shirley Murray)—Lovely haunting song. Lines 1, 3, and 5 may be sung by a cantor, with the congregation responding on the other repetitive lines. Sung, this way, the repetition makes it quite good for kids.

- "Let Us Build a House" / "All Are Welcome" (Marty Haugen)—This song has wonderful lyrics of hope for what a Christian community can be like, and a chorus that joyfully says, "All are welcome, all are welcome, all are welcome in this place." (lyrics: http://www.mljmusic.com/Portals/0/Lyrics/All%20Are%20Welcome.pdf)

- "Where the Spirit Is There's Freedom" (Per Harling)—An excellent joyous upbeat song from the World Council of Churches. (lyrics: http://babasiga.blogspot.com/2007/05/where-spirit-is-theres-freedom.html)

Matthew L. Skinner

Acts 10

In Acts 10:44-48, preachers find a great opportunity to explore the question: What do the death and resurrection of Jesus Christ make possible? This passage gives one answer: The circle encompassing who can belong to the people of God expands in shocking, perhaps unexpected directions. A conventional dividing line evaporates.

These verses narrate the conclusion of Peter's divinely coordinated visit to Cornelius, a Gentile centurion in the Roman army. Peter has discovered that "God doesn't show partiality" to certain people (v. 34). He has told Cornelius the basics about Jesus. Then God breaks in.

The Holy Spirit interrupts Peter's sermon. Rather, the Spirit ends it. God acts. God comes to the Gentile audience. The key detail is Peter and his Jewish colleagues' certain, instant recognition that this is the same Spirit that previously came to them. There is no difference, and so the case is closed: These Gentiles now belong fully to the church of God, simply because God has made them equal members. Nothing prevents them from being baptized—now. No one expresses concern about established divisions and legal distinctions between Jews and Gentiles (although others will raise questions at the beginning of Acts 11). Peter and his company stay where they are, willing to receive hospitality in a Gentile's home (compare v. 28) because all of them now share complete unity in Christ.

Jesus' resurrection involves more than the raising of a dead man. It sets into motion, according to the New Testament, whole new ways of existing in the world. It destroys old systems; inclusion and exclusion, belonging and alienation, acceptable and unacceptable, life and death—many of these demarcations get obliterated or shaken up. Where have we replaced them with new ones of our own design, which God may yet knock down?

Todd Weir

http://bloomingcactus.typepad.com/

Acts 10

Acts makes it clear that the Holy Spirit is guiding all the action. It is not merely that the twelve apostles were brilliant, that they had a great business plan, or were willing to work hard. Their success is following the right consultant, the Holy Spirit. The created church moves throughout the Mediterranean world by people who have dreams, called during moments of prayer, or in the case of Paul, a dramatic vision of the risen Christ. Throughout the history of the church, things happen when the Spirit moves people. Read the journals of all the great spiritual leaders and hear their inner thoughts—Martin Luther, John Wesley, Martin Luther King, Jr.—to name a few—there was some moment in their lives when the Spirit moved them to step out in faith.

What does this mean for us? I think our biggest challenge is to believe that the Holy Spirit is still speaking today, and not only to great leaders and preachers and perhaps even presidents and politicians but also to all baptized believers. The Holy Spirit is a gift for all God's people. It is also present in every church. We affirm that each week when we say the creedal statement, "I believe in the Holy Spirit." To believe in the Holy Spirit is to believe that God still moves in the church. Perhaps the Spirit is already speaking to you, with a nagging thought urging you into a new direction in life, with hopes and dreams for the church and the world.

The biggest challenge of the spiritual life is to be open. It is much harder to listen for God than it is to preach. Amazing things happen when we begin to listen for the Holy Spirit. God is still speaking!

Peter Woods

Acts 10

Genetics is a fascinating phenomenon. I am sure we have all had the experience of phoning a friend's home and having one of the children answer. The voices, the tone, and intonation are so similar that we are fooled into thinking it is the parent and not the child speaking. It is uncanny how our children sound just like us.

The early followers of Jesus did not have telephones, but they realized that what they heard when Jesus spoke was the voice of a direct descendant of God. It was this lineage, this inheritance of love, grace, and wisdom, so clearly expressed in the words and actions of Jesus that made the penny (or drachma) drop. He is the son of God!

It is the same realization we have when we call our friend's house. Something in the voice of this kid on the phone comes directly from the parent. Jesus, in an age before genetics, was in the same genus as God. Jesus never called it genetics, he called it "abiding." It means remaining in the genus, staying true to type. The inheritance from God that came to Jesus was obedient love, most fully expressed in a sacrificial lifestyle.

But the lineage of resemblance did not end with Jesus. The fact that Jesus was celibate does not mean he had no offspring. Every time we connect with God. Every time we abide, obey, and sacrifice in love we become his voice and being in the world. Just like the child on the phone we say, "Please hold, I'll get my parent."

John Wesley
http://www.ccel.org/ccel/wesley/notes

Acts 10:47

Can any man forbid water, that these should not be baptized, who have received the Holy Ghost?—He does not say they have the baptism of the Spirit; therefore they do not need baptism with water. But just the contrary: if they have received the Spirit, then baptize them with water. How easily is this question decided, if we will take the word of God for our rule! Either men have received the Holy Ghost or not. If they have not, Repent, saith God, and be baptized, and ye shall receive the gift of the Holy Ghost. If they have, if they are already baptized with the Holy Ghost, then who can forbid water?

John 15:11

That my joy might remain in you—The same joy which I feel in loving the Father, and keeping his commandments.

Ann Scull
http://seedstuff.blogspot.com

Listening Song

Third Day, "I've Always Loved You" on *Time* (Franklin, Tennessee, Essential Records, USA, 1999) CD Edition.

Call to Worship

Show a series of images and quotes about friendship.

Prayer of Confession

"Who Am I?" by Dietrich Bonhoeffer, http://www.dbonhoeffer.org/who-was-db2.htm (accessed 22 April 2013)

Kid's Story

Sam McBratney and Anita Jeram, *Guess How Much I Love You* (London: Walker Books, 1994).

Film Clip

Crocodile Dundee (1986)—interview in which Mick compares himself to the apostles, claiming he and God would be "mates." Discuss what difference it makes if you and God are best mates.

Stories

"I Am the One Jesus Loves" and "He's Very Fond of Me" found in Philip Yancey, *What's So Amazing about Grace* (Grand Rapids, Mich.: Zondervan, 1997), 68–69. These stories go well with the Gospel reading.

Discussion

Linked to the Gospel and the stories above:
• What makes a good friend a best mate?

- How differently would we see ourselves if we viewed ourselves as "the one Jesus loves"?

- How would our lives change if we really believed the words of Jesus: "You are my friends.... You didn't choose me. I chose you."

- Give everyone a business card/postcard/bookmark with the words "I am the one Jesus loves" printed upon it. Find an example to use at http://seedstuff.blogspot.com.au/2012/05/easter-6-b-may-13.html (accessed 22 April 2013)

Useful Quote

"The feeling you have when you wake up in the morning and realize that it is the beginning of the holidays or the beginning of summer" (C.S. Lewis, *The Lion, the Witch and the Wardrobe* reprint edition [HarperCollins, 1994],43).

May 17, 2015
Ascension of the Lord

Acts 1:1-11; Psalm 47 or Psalm 93; Ephesians 1:15-23; Luke 24:44-53

Martha Spong

http://marthaspong.com/

Acts 1; Ephesians 1

We've all been there: the train leaves the station; the bus pulls away from the curb; the one we love starts the car, backs out of the driveway, and waves one last time. Times have changed, of course. When I was a little girl, we could walk to the edge of the tarmac with my father and watch him climb the stairs to a Piedmont jet, waving and blowing enthusiastic kisses, hoping he would turn around one last time.

When I deliver my older children to airports, or to bus and train stations, I bid them farewell expecting a return or a reunion. We do this so regularly, it feels normal. I remind the college students to text on arrival. We connect via Skype or Facetime to keep up with what's going on at home and in their other worlds. Wherever we are, we are part of one another.

For Jesus' friends, it was a different kind of farewell. Their loved one moved out of sight on the Great Cloud Elevator that some believe will return him to us. It was not normal, unusual even for Scripture, the first supernatural departure since the whirlwind lifted Elijah. If he waved, Scripture does not record it.

Thus began our long-distance relationship with God's right-hand man. We can't Facebook message him—although in various guises we can follow him on Twitter. We can't text him and expect a quick response. We must employ more "old-fashioned" forms of communication. We pray. We worship. Most important, we live in community together as his body, knowing him to be the head of that body. He is part of us; we are part of him. Without him, we have no guidance. Without us, he has no body.

John Wesley

http://www.ccel.org/ccel/wesley/notes

Acts 1:5

Ye shall be baptized with the Holy Ghost—And so are all true believers to the end of the world. But the extraordinary gifts of the Holy Ghost also are here promised.

Luke 24:45

Then opened he their understanding, to understand the Scriptures—He had explained them before to the two as they went to Emmaus. But still they understood them not, till he took off the veil from their hearts, by the illumination of his Spirit.

Eric D. Barreto

Acts 1; Luke 24

Luke is alone among the Gospel writers in narrating the ascension of Jesus. In Mark, we catch a glimpse of an empty tomb. In Matthew, Jesus gives the Great Commission. John concludes that much more could be said about Jesus' life. Yet only Luke details how and why God grants Jesus a place at God's right hand. For Luke, this is a crucial hinge between his two volumes; the story repeats at the close of the gospel *and* the beginning of Acts. The stories are not identical, however, for they serve distinct narrative functions. The former marks the conclusion of volume one, the latter the very start of a burgeoning group of believers who will embody Jesus' world-changing good news.

What do we make of Jesus now seated at the right hand of God? Does he remain with us, or is he established and isolated in a heavenly throne room? Too often, interpreters of Luke's writings have posited that Acts is marked by Jesus' absence. They assume that the activity of the apostles fills the theological vacuum Jesus leaves in his wake. This is an incomplete understanding of Lukan theology. Jesus remains a powerful presence in Acts. Jesus appears to Saul on the road to Damascus and to Stephen as he breathes his last. Jesus' name is invoked in healings. Jesus remains the originating force of these communities of faith. Certainly, Jesus has ascended, but he remains ever in our midst.

Why do you stand gazing into the heavens? This could be a question posed to many Christians. Jesus' ascension does not liberate us from following God's call. Jesus empowers us from the right hand of God to be bold and faithful, especially in light of his promise to return once again.

Marci Auld Glass

http://www.marciglass.com

Acts 1; Luke 24

Both stories describe the same event, but in the gospel, it is conclusion. In the book of Acts, it marks the beginning.

And we understand that. There are things that seem like endings. Clearly, nothing could ever happen after a death, or loss, or tragedy, or after watching Jesus ascend into the clouds. That's all she wrote. End scene.

But the story goes on.

Luke says they returned to Jerusalem and worshiped with great joy . . . which is great and all . . . but I think they also returned to Jerusalem wondering what just happened.

Forty days of Jesus' resurrected presence must have upset their equilibrium. At first, you wonder, "What in the heck is going on?" but then, after a while, you get used to resurrected Jesus just showing up at your gatherings, eating fish with you, teaching you, and disappearing again.

But now he has instructed them to be witnesses, he has blessed them, and he has ascended. This feels final.

As they return to Jerusalem, where they worship in the temple with great joy, I wonder if some of the joy is *because it is over*. As much as they loved Jesus and wanted him to stay, perhaps there is also relief. He has gone back to the Father where he belongs. They are left where they belong, with his recent teaching and instruction, ready to be the witnesses he's called them to be. Ready to move on.

Endings are like that. We don't want them to come. We would rather stay in our places and situations, and perhaps have been for a long while. But change happens. Loved ones die. Jobs and relationships end. Jesus ascends. In the midst of the sadness of endings, we also find joy, when we gather, worshiping in the temple.

Excerpted from http://marciglass.com/2012/05/22/letting-go/

Cameron Howard

Psalms 47; 93

The two psalms appointed for Ascension Sunday are enthronement psalms, which celebrate the kingship of God. Psalm 47 emphasizes God's dominion over all nations (vv. 3, 8) and peoples (vv. 1, 3, 9); God is king of kings indeed. God exercises that dominion particularly through God's chosen people Israel, in whom God's glory is revealed (v. 3). In Psalm 93, the scope of God's reign is depicted even more cosmically: God established the world (v. 1a). God is ancient and eternal (v. 2). God is praised by the floods (v. 3). God's majesty is greater than any element of creation (v. 4).

Both psalms are noisy. In Psalm 47, God is praised with clapping (v. 1), shouting (vv. 1, 5), singing (vv. 6, 7), and a trumpet (v. 5). These are human-initiated praises, and while the psalm does not imagine the nations and peoples sharing in Israel's chosen status, it does invite the peoples of all corners of the earth to praise Israel's God. In keeping with its cosmic themes, Psalm 93 envisions nature, praising God with its sounds: the floods roar and the waters thunder (vv. 3, 4).

The juxtaposition of these two psalms highlights God's sovereign kingship over all creation. Such an image is not without its problems, as human kingship involves exploitative power over both nature and human beings. At Psalm 47:3, God appears to be party to such exploitation; God as triumphant emperor may not be an image we are eager to lift up today. At the same time, when terror and abuse often seem to have the last word, these images of God as powerful ruler can be a source of great hope. If the God who made the world also has charge of all the peoples that inhabit it, then we are bold to imagine a time when God's own power, rather than the brokenness of human institutions, reigns.

D. Mark Davis

http://leftbehindandlovingit.blogspot.com/

Luke 24

The end of Luke's gospel tells of the final post-Resurrection appearance of Christ to his disciples. This story has two important words in play. The first is the word *nous*, typically translated as "mind." It appears three times in verse 45, twice in verbs and once as a noun, which is easily lost in English translations. Literally, verse 45 reads, "Then he (1) made *open-minded* their (2) *mind* (singular) to the (3) *together-mindedness* of the writings." What Luke's readers hear is that the risen Christ is the one who (1) enables disciples to find their (2) unity with the (3) collective meaning of the Scriptures.

The second word is *grapho*, or "writing," which appears three times also—as a participle (v. 45) a noun (v. 46), and a verb (v. 47). Given that the believers, in verses 52 and 53, return to Jerusalem and worship in the temple, the connection between Christ's death and resurrection and the writings in the law and the prophets is crucial. These disciples have a wisdom about the Scriptures that is Christ-given and may not be evident to others who also read those Scriptures in the temple.

The content of the collective meaning of the Scriptures regarding Christ is laid out in verses 46 and 47. It is doctrine and call, about the suffering, death, and resurrection of Christ and about those who proclaim repentance and forgiveness of sins in his name.

The ascension itself gets fairly short attention from Luke. Jesus parted from them and was carried into heaven. The brevity reminds one of the simplicity of the Apostles' Creed, "He ascended into heaven." It is the fact "that," not the descriptions "how" that Luke finds important to communicate—a habit well worth repeating when preaching this text.

May 24, 2015

Pentecost

Acts 2:1-21 or Ezekiel 37:1-14; Psalm 104:24-34, 35b; Romans 8:22-27 or Acts 2:1-21; John 15:26-27; 16:4b-15

Teri Peterson

http://clevertitlehere.blogspot.com

Acts 2

A friend was leading worship one Pentecost when, during the prayers, the gauzy red Communion tablecloth met a candle. After a few moments of shouting, confusion, and frozen uncertainty, someone grabbed the baptismal font and dumped water on the flames. While this was a perfectly practical thing to do, it makes for a strange metaphor. As my friend put it, "In an absurd clash of symbols, the waters of baptism actually extinguished the fires of the Spirit."

We laugh, but the reality in this clash is hard to miss—sometimes entering the church (one of the things baptism symbolizes) is the fastest way to douse the flames of passion: "We've never done it that way before." "That's not what we do here." Working the system to get something done, try something new, or put passion into action can be exhausting. Many give up—why bother? Especially when the world tells us to go with the flow. It's easier to come to worship, or drift away, or find some other place where we can put our passions and gifts to good use. Flames belong in their place— safely contained in fire pits or rule books, not actually burning and heating and lighting and spreading.

But the fire the Spirit can't be contained, any more than the tomb could contain Jesus or the Bible can contain God. God has a way of bursting out of confines we construct. The disciples were, literally, blown out of the house, to speak to the ends of the earth—because the promise is for you, and your children, and everyone who is far away, everyone God calls. Wind and flame will work together to spread God's transforming love, setting the world on fire. Will we fan the flames or dig the trenches?

John Wesley

http://www.ccel.org/ccel/wesley/notes

Ezekiel 37:7

Of all the bones of all those numerous slain, not one was missing, not one missed its way, not one missed its place, but each knew and found its fellow. Thus in the resurrection of the dead, the scattered atoms shall be arranged in their proper place and order, and every bone come to his bone, by the same wisdom and power by which they were first formed in the womb of her that is with child.

Acts 2:4

And they began to speak with other tongues—The miracle was not in the ears of the hearers (as some have unaccountably supposed), but in the mouth of the speakers. And this family praising God together, with the tongues of all the world, was an earnest that the whole world should in due time praise God in their various tongues.

Sharron Blezard

Ezekiel 37; Acts 2

Congregations sometimes act more like the dry, dusty bones of Ezekiel's vision than the fired-up folk in the Pentecost story. Instead of burning with zeal for the gospel and being led by the Spirit, too many Christians waste away in arid committee meetings, fret over shrinking membership and poor stewardship, and pine for those nostalgic "good old days." Fear drives decisions and blocks the visionary work of the Holy Spirit. If your context exhibits none of these traits and habits, then give thanks, praise God, and keep doing what you are doing well. If, however, dried up bones and wasting hope are entirely too familiar, then take heart.

The same Spirit that came with fire and wind and infused the apostles and the early church is still active today and ready to blow new life into tired, discouraged, and struggling faith communities. The same God that animated the bones of Israel in the prophet's vision is still in the business of putting sinews and flesh on the skeletal remains of dying hopes and faded dreams. Jesus still promises to be with the beloved community wherever two or more gather to worship and break bread together, whenever water and word meet in baptism, and when God's people go into the world to share the gospel and serve in the name of Christ.

We are promised the gift of the Holy Spirit to animate our faith, enliven our communities, and even intercede when words fail us. On this Pentecost Sunday, remind one another of this amazing power that can energize us, of the ever-present Advocate, and of the Savior whose love and mercy are stronger than death. Go ahead! Dream big, set a bold vision for mission, and speak on behalf of the marginalized and poor. You are not alone.

Elizabeth Quick

http://bethquick.com

Acts 2

- I don't have experience with speaking in tongues. But early in my ministry, a nine-year old girl read this passage in church on Pentecost, and she whipped through Phrygia and Pamphylia like they were her home-towns. Amazing. When I remember her voice, I can get my head around the idea of speaking in tongues. When an unlikely vessel communicates an even more unlikely message, with unlikely ability? Pentecost.

- This is the moment of truth—Jesus is dead, risen, and ascended. The disciples have been taught, prodded, encouraged, but most of all, entrusted with the good news. Will they carry it on? Will they stand up in the face of opposition and accusations? Yes! The church is born.

- Peter quotes how God's Spirit is poured out on all: son, daughter, young, old, slave, free. Where do we get the idea that God speaks through only *some people*, people of whom we approve?

John 15; 16

- "Because you have been with me from the beginning" (15:27). Those Jesus speaks to know the whole story, or apparently everything Jesus needs them to know to fulfill their roles.

- "It is to your advantage that I go away" (16:7 NRSV). I doubt the disciples saw it this way! Who wants a weird-sounding Advocate instead of the Jesus they know and love?

- "I still have many things to say to you, but you cannot bear them now" (v. 12 NRSV). I think this statement from Jesus still applies to us today. Jesus always wants to fill us in, share more, but we struggle to bear it.

- "When the Spirit of truth comes, [it] will guide you into *all the truth*" (v. 13 NRSV). What a unique way of phrasing this—"all the truth" (emphasis added). What is all the truth?

Linda Lee

The Truth of the Matter (John 15; 16)

Jesus said, "When the Companion comes, whom I will send from the Father—the Spirit of Truth, who proceeds from the Father—he will testify about me" (John 15:26).

This was a word to encourage the disciples when the hard times came. It was a word of comfort, because those who were not yet followers of Christ could not understand the upside-down teachings of Jesus. They certainly would not get it any better when the disciples went out after Jesus' departure from the earth. It would not be by their human effort that people would come to follow Jesus, but by the Companion's revelation of the truth. The truth is that God forgives sin, heals the sick, and cares for the poor. The truth is that God can give sight to the blind and new legs to the lame.

As twenty-first–century Christ followers, our willingness to focus first on what we know to be true because of Christ Jesus can mean the difference between life and death. It can mean the difference between the life or death of relationship with one another and with God, the life or death of nations, and even the life and death of God's good creation. The resurrection power of the love of God redeems our souls from the pits that estrange us and isolate us and restores us to unity with God, ourselves, and one another. The Holy Spirit meets us in our weak places, so we can be faithful to God's command to prophesy to the power of God's love, which "the world" tends to misunderstand or reject. As we prophesy, through our actions, our witness, and our love, God moves, right before our eyes, revealing that the love of God is still the greatest power in the universe.

John Petty

http://progressiveinvolvement.com

John 16

The first thing the *parakletos* does is convict the world "concerning sin." The antidote for sin is "faith" (*pisteuein*) in Christ.

The parakletos will also convict the world regarding justice (*dikaiosyne*), often translated as "righteousness," but more properly translated as "justice."

For the world to need convicting regarding justice is to say that what the world considers "just" is not, in fact, justice. The world's "justice" issues in inequality and poverty. The world's "justice" issues in oppression and want. That is not just, says the Fourth Gospel.

Finally, the parakletos will convict the world concerning "judgment" (*kriseos*), which means "separating," or derivatively, in English, "crisis."

Again, the normal processes of the world are judged and found wanting. The world does not understand its own situation. The reality of the situation is that the rulers of this world already have been judged. Things are different than the "powers" think. There is a "judgment."

When the parakletos comes, he "will guide [*hodegesei*] you in all truth" (v. 13). Hodgesei includes within it the word *hodos*, or "way." The Fourth Gospel, quoting Isaiah, says right off the bat: "Make straight the way [*hodos*] of the Lord." In chapter 14, Jesus himself is "the way" (v. 6). The parakletos will guide the people into Christ and onto his "way."

The phrase "he will announce to you" is used three times (vv. 13-15; CEB has "proclaim"). Thus, the parakletos will not only "convict" the world of sin, justice, and judgment, but will also "announce" God's truth to the disciples. They are not able to do this without the parakletos, but, with the parakletos, the one "called alongside" to help, they will.

Thom M. Shuman
http://lectionaryliturgies.blogspot.com/

Call to Worship
The Day of Pentecost is here:
the day when the flames of faith dance in our hearts.
The Day of Pentecost is here:
the day when our babbling speech becomes the Good News for the world.
The Day of Pentecost is here:
the day when compassion is seared into our souls.
The Day of Pentecost is here:
let the people of God rejoice. Alleluia!

Prayer of the Day
Spirit of the Living God,
dance with us on this day.
Come, Whirlwind of Wonder!
Sing to the groaning of creation.
Come, still small voice of Hope!
Enflame us with your passion for justice.
Come, Liberator of the Least!
Purify us of our grasping greediness.
Come, Advocate of selfless living!
Silence our gossiping tongues.
Come, Harmony of God's Heart!
Wind of God, blow through us;
Fire of God, burn within us;
Tongue of God, speak to us
on this day of renewal and birth,
even as we pray as Jesus teaches us,
Our Father...

Blessing
God's glory has filled our hearts!
We will go to empty ourselves for others.
Christ has given himself for us!
We will go to give ourselves to everyone in need.
The Spirit gifts us with new life!
We go to be a blessing to everyone we meet.

May 31, 2015
Trinity Sunday

Isaiah 6:1-8; Psalm 29; Romans 8:12-17; John 3:1-17

Julie Craig

http://winsomelearnsome.com

Isaiah 6

Holiness—it is a matter of opinion what qualifies. To some people it is going to church; to some it might mean avoiding certain bad habits or adopting certain outward religious practices. Some think clergy are, by default, some kind of holy person. Trust me when I say that idea is patently false!

Growing up, I knew people who adhered to so called "holiness traditions." They willingly and consistently lived the mundane, everyday aspects of their lives according to a strict interpretation of Scripture. It was a willing setting aside of any aspects of humanity in order to be more like what the Bible called for in a follower of Jesus.

In this text, the prophet finds himself utterly, inescapably human in the presence of his vision of God. The death of the king is no mere historical marker, but a sign that things are about to change in Judah. Although Uzziah, in his fifty-two years of reign brought Judah to new heights in terms of prosperity, influence, and power, he forgot that he was an earthly king and not a divine one.

Isaiah's experience of soaking in the presence of absolute holiness brought about a visceral reminder of his own humanity. It's as if he looked around at the angels and the smoke and the trembling temple and the songs and the tongs and concluded, "One of these things is not like the others."

And even though he was made guiltless, and that flaming, searing coal of mercy and forgiveness blotted out his sin, the whole episode is an object lesson in this one unavoidable, undeniable truth: God is holy. We are not. We are human. Or as we like to say, "We're only human."

Paul Bellan-Boyer

Ascribe to the Lord (Isaiah 6; Psalm 29)

Since earliest days, humans have tried to know the nature of God. An impossible task, we know, to put the ocean into a paper cup. But we are human. We are curious and passionate, and we desire this God-ness, this goodness, because we want to go beyond who and where we are.

It's hard to talk about the Trinity without falling into something the church has declared heresy. A doctrine of the Trinity may not be in the Bible, but the biblical authors *give testimony* to the Trinity in the life of the faithful.

We start with the "God is one" confession of our Jewish ancestors (Deuteronomy 6:4). Yet this God has been known in different ways, from the awesome God of nature who led the people Israel, to the humble servant Jesus the reconciler, to the powerful wind of the Spirit that breathes new life into the world.

Knowing God in a triune way gives gifts for spiritual and community life. Father, Son, Holy Spirit are distinct, yet undivided. Take as an example a sports team. The players have a common purpose and work together to achieve a goal and a victory. Or consider a marriage, where two are joined as one, hopefully in love, and hopefully working throughout their lives to form a more perfect union.

So much more is God imaged in this way, a union of three persons who fit so completely together that they *are* One.

The metaphors, though, carry us only so far. The community of faith has consistently turned to praise as the most suitable response to encounters with this God. "Holy, Holy, Holy!" cry the six-winged seraphim. Whatever tales theologians tell about life in the Trinity, our experience is rooted more in awe, in wonder, in holy Mystery than in understanding. In the Lord's temple, all say "Glory!" (Psalm 29:9).

John Wesley

http://www.ccel.org/ccel/wesley/notes

Isaiah 6:2

Seraphim—An order of holy angels, thus called from fire and burning, which this word properly signifies; to represent either their nature, which is bright and glorious, subtle, and pure; or their property, of fervent zeal for God's service and glory.

Romans 8:15

Abba, Father—The latter word explains the former. By using both the Syriac and the Greek word, St. Paul seems to point out the joint cry both of the Jewish and Gentile believers. The spirit of bondage here seems directly to mean, those operations of the Holy Spirit by which the soul, on its first conviction, feels itself in bondage to sin, to the world, to Satan, and obnoxious to the wrath of God. This, therefore, and the Spirit of adoption, are one and the same Spirit, only manifesting itself in various operations, according to the various circumstances of the persons.

Safiyah Fosua

Isaiah 6; Romans 8; John 3

There they are, the Trinity, in this week's readings: God the Father in Isaiah, God the Son in John, and God the Holy Spirit in Romans. They are there as plain as the noses on our faces and as elusive as the wind.

God the Father, elusive for Isaiah until one day in the temple he realized that God was there in majesty that defied description. God was there invoking awe and issuing a call to ministry and service. How many times has God eluded us?

God the Son, elusive again, as Nicodemus tries to make sense of the Son of God in the room with him. Elusive as he, Nicodemus, is sidetracked by semantics, as we often are in our conversations about faith.

God the Holy Spirit obscured from our view in Paul's conversation about being led, as sons and daughters, by the Spirit of God. Obscured from our view as we try to follow Paul's theological arguments about *adoption* and the witness of the *Spirit*.

We are surrounded by the dance of the Trinity.

The heavens scream the majesty of God while we, like Isaiah, sit years without end in places of worship wishing that God would visit us.

The redemptive Son of God stands knocking at every door around us seeking to reconcile each individual with God, longing for devoted disciples who would transform the world, while our heads remained buried in *The Art of War*.

And, the Spirit of God, who has promised that we would never be apart from God's presence, whispers thousands of "I love yous" as we insult her by calling God's guidance *chance* or *good fortune*.

There they are in the readings; here they are in our lives—Father, Son, and Spirit—as plain as the noses on our faces, and as elusive as the wind.

Liz Crumlish
http://somethingtostandon.blogspot.co.uk/

The Voice of God (Psalm 29)
Strumming across the rainbow
with crescendo and diminuendo
as the colors fade in and out.
Rippling through the treetops
with trills and turns
as the leaves catch the rhythm
swaying in and out of the stave
or floating untethered on the wind,
freestyle, unfettered by rules and forms.
God's voice refuses to be pinned down
but weaves around us
in beauty and majesty,
in oceans of calm,
in tempest and storm
lulling us into pausing,
ensuring our rapt attention
before compelling us to act
in response to words of wisdom
so beautifully spoken.
Compelled to take up the cry
for justice and sharing,
compelled to act
until all God's children
hear the voice of God
as wonderfully loving and affirming
and splendid as creation.

Lowell E. Grisham
http://lowellsblog.blogspot.com/

Prayers of the People
Presider: Holy Trinity, One God, the whole world is filled with your glory: Hear the prayers of your children as we say: Ascribe due honor to God's holy Name; worship the Most High in the beauty of holiness.

Litanist: Abba! Father! You have filled your church with your Spirit and adopted us as your own children: Inspire us to speak of what we know and testify to what we have seen. Ascribe due honor to God's holy Name;

worship the Most High in the beauty of holiness.

Jesus, the Son of Man who was lifted up to give the whole world eternal life: Send the spirit of your compassion and understanding unto the leaders of our nation and all others in authority, that they may be led by the Spirit of God in the ways of justice and peace. Ascribe due honor to God's holy Name;

worship the Most High in the beauty of holiness.

Ever present and energizing Spirit: Enable our community to be born from above, born of water and Spirit, that we may manifest your loving compassion and peace toward all. Ascribe due honor to God's holy Name;

worship the Most High in the beauty of holiness.

Glorious Trinity, One God, your presence sustains the world and brings all life into being: Protect, comfort, and heal all who live with illness, threat, poverty, or oppression throughout the world, that they may enjoy the goodness of your blessing. Ascribe due honor to God's holy Name;

worship the Most High in the beauty of holiness.

Your children, O God, have not received a spirit of slavery to fall back into fear, but we have received a spirit of
adoption, through which we ask for your aid:
Hear our prayers for ___.
Accept our praise and thanksgiving for ___.
Embrace with your eternal life those who have died, especially ___.
For you did not send the Son into the world to condemn the world, but in order that the world might be saved
through him.
Ascribe due honor to God's holy Name;

worship the Most High in the beauty of holiness.

Presider: Let our prayers and praises fill your temple, O Father, as you send forth your Spirit into the world to empower your children to do the deeds of your Son and to be signs of your divine presence, in the name of our Savior Jesus Christ who lives and reigns with you, in the unity of the Holy Spirit, one God, now and forever. Amen.

Editor's Insights

Daily Discussion with Jesus (John 3)

I'm in this story with Nicodemus—in this dialectical discussion with Jesus. I have this discussion, sometimes daily, it seems. It would be so good to start again, to have a do-over with the knowledge I have now, with the character I've built up now, after having seen what happens. Of course, I can be "born from above" and see it new ways. Perhaps that happens often for many of us. And it makes me want, even more, to know what I'm actually up against before I act.

On the one hand, being born from above gives us a new point of view, one that helps us see things in ways that are more helpful to others and in how we see God working in the world. On the other hand, being born from above is torturous, as we look back at what we would have or should have been or done. I'm not sure that's bad. I'm not sure it's bad to have a long talk with Jesus about the way things are and about our own contributions to that state of being. It's hard, but I don't think it's bad.

God loved *the world* so much. I like that. I am a part of God loving the world. I am a part of God giving his Son, of believing in Christ, of doing things that make a difference in the world around me. God has given us this privilege, I think, in birthing us once more, from above. For me this passage is not about what God gives to me but what God gives *through* me, to the world, when I have the eyes to see anew.

Carolyn Winfrey Gillette

http://www.carolynshymns.com/

Nicodemus Sought Out Jesus (John 3)

NETTLETON 8.7.8.7.D "Come, Thou Fount of Every Blessing")
Nicodemus sought out Jesus at a lonely, quiet hour.
He said, "Teacher, God is with you! For in you we see God's power."
Jesus turned and gave an answer filled with challenge and with love:
"You can never see God's kingdom till you're born from heav'n above."

"Born again!" said Nicodemus. "Is that something one can do?"
Jesus said, "Don't be surprised now that you must be born anew.
And it's not by your own doing; wind and Spirit both blow free!
They are not for your controlling; trust in God for what will be."

God, your Spirit still surprises like an ever-changing wind,
Bringing life and love and justice where despair and death have been.
May we see your Spirit working as a gift from heav'n above.
Blessed, may we then be a blessing to this world that you so love.

Biblical reference: John 3:1-17

June 7, 2015

2nd Sunday after Pentecost, Proper 5

1 Samuel 8:4-11, (12-15), 16-20, (11:14-15); Psalm 138; 2 Corinthians 4:13–5:1; Mark 3:20-35; Genesis 3:8-15; Psalm 130

Rick Morley

1 Samuel 8

The elders of Israel wanted a king. On the outside this sounds reasonable enough. Samuel was getting old. His sons weren't particularly holy men or fair rulers. And the system of rule-by-judge had its shortcomings.

But the real reason they wanted a king was because all of the other nations had kings, and they wanted to be like them. And therein lies the rub. Israel was called to be different. They were called to be unique among all the nations on earth. They were God's chosen, and as such they were to be set apart in the manner of their living, their governance, and their worship of God Almighty.

This unique calling was meant to be, in more modern parlance, evangelical. Their manner of life was to be a living testament to the holiness and greatness of the God who made the heavens and the earth. From the Pentateuch we see that they were to eat differently, dress differently, they were to circumcise their men, and they were to worship without idols.

And, God was to be their King, not a man on a throne.

But it's hard to be different. It takes courage and strength of character. And sometimes it's just easier to succumb and swim in the same direction as everyone else. The lie we tell ourselves when we decide to go with the flow is that things have to get better. That isn't always the case. It certainly wasn't the case for Israel, whose kingdom would be divided, north and south, in a matter of decades.

True discernment, seeking God's will above our own desires, takes faith and fortitude. Going against the current isn't always the faithful thing to do, but discerning God's great desires for us is.

Mary J. Scifres

Buildings That Last (1 Samuel 8; 2 Corinthians 4–5; Mark 3)

Creating a legacy, building something that will last—I hear these yearnings from church members and church leaders. As the church struggles to adapt and change, facing decline and demise in the twenty-first century, people call out "Give us a king!" (1 Samuel 8:6). The Israelites want to build a kingdom, complete with a monarch, but God yearns to be their only ruler and king. Churches want the perfect pastor or bishop to solve all their problems and create a perfect solution to build a church that will last and a legacy that will endure. But God's Spirit is the perfect solution, when we allow the Spirit to move in our being as we build our ministries on the foundation of Christ and Christ's teachings.

When churches and their leaders reach out to new and different people, welcoming the least and the last, our churches get messy and messed up. Our leaders don't hold office hours or attend church meetings, because they're spending time with drinkers at the local bar or immigrants at the day labor parking lot. The people cry out, as Jesus' family did, "He's out of his mind!" (Mark 3:21b). Jesus' mother and siblings want to protect Jesus within the family, but Jesus yearns to minister to the world, inviting all who would follow Christ into the family. Churches do want to minister to the world, but we want to protect the church family and are nervous with crazy change and unfamiliar paths. Jesus yearns for us to follow into the crazy, unfamiliar mess of service and love, which is the path of discipleship.

Paul knew these struggles well, for the early church struggled in similar ways. But we are reminded that God has a bigger plan for us, an eternal legacy that will endure and outlast kings, rulers, pastors, bishops, and even churches. "We know that if the tent we live in is torn down, we have a building from God. It's a house that isn't handmade, which is eternal and located in heaven" (2 Corinthians 5:1). God's realm will prevail. God's plan will come to fruition.

Building churches, creating a legacy of faith to hand on, and growing the body of Christ are all worthy goals. Still, today's scriptures remind us that the call of Christ often leads to different goals: inclusion and diversity, humility and partnership, spirituality and faith. God calls us to build things that truly last, to build structures that welcome one and all, and to provide foundations and shelter for all of creation. In doing so, we may discover that the legacy takes care of itself.

John van de Laar
http://www.sacredise.com/

1 Samuel 8; Mark 3

After a season of peace and prosperity, Samuel is getting old. Like Eli before him (1 Samuel 3:11-14), he appoints his corrupt sons as judges, and the people are afraid. They have no faith in Samuel's sons, and their trust in God is failing, so, they seek a human king. They ignore Samuel's warnings and set their nation on a course that divides the kingdom, leaves them at the mercy of their leaders, and ultimately drives them into exile.

In a contrasting way, Jesus brings out the fear of both the religious leaders and his family. As his popularity grows, Jesus' family becomes concerned about his sanity; or perhaps that's what they tell themselves to avoid confronting the possibility that he is the Messiah. Either way they have a lot to lose, so in their fear, they seek to take him home.

For the religious leaders Jesus' popularity is a threat to their status, their control, and the purity of their faith. But most frightening, it is a threat to the stability of their nation. So, in their fear, they write him off as demon possessed.

This is the destructive power of fear. It teaches us to reject faith, wage war, hunt witches, hate the "other," and close our hearts to the new. But Jesus is an example of another way. He can challenge the religious leaders, in spite of the danger, because he has given his life for something bigger than his own security. He can refuse to entertain his family's fearful demand to see him, because his loyalty is to something that would ultimately heal and liberate them, along with many others. Jesus consistently and courageously chooses faith instead of fear, and it carries him through the ultimate sacrifice to the ultimate victory.

For more detail: http://sacredise.com/blog/?p=1157

John Wesley
http://www.ccel.org/ccel/wesley/notes

2 Corinthians 4:18

The things that are seen—Men, money, things of earth. The things that are not seen—God, grace, heaven.

Mark 3:30

Because they said, He hath an unclean spirit—Is it not astonishing, that men who have ever read these words, should doubt, what is the blasphemy against the Holy Ghost? Can any words declare more plainly, that it is "the ascribing those miracles to the power of the devil which Christ wrought by the power of the Holy Ghost?"

Two Bubbas and a Bible
http://lectionarylab.com

Mark 3

"That boy done lost his mind!"

Theories varied as to exactly why Ray Skinner (not his real name, by the way) was crazy—or if he even was really mentally unbalanced—but none of us kids was ever brave enough to actually talk to him and find out. He was sort of our local Boo Radley, I suppose. (For a nice synopsis of the characters in *To Kill a Mockingbird* and the figure of Boo Radley, catch the article on Wikepedia [http://en.wikipedia.org/wiki/List_of_To_Kill_a_Mockingbird_characters].)

The setting for today's Gospel reading is a very Boo Radley-like experience that Jesus has with his own family—those who should have been best-positioned to know him.

Jesus is, of course, talking about his "kingdom," his favorite subject. He really believes that God has sent him to establish a kingdom that is sort of, kind of, on this earth—but isn't really exactly like the other kingdoms of the earth.

Yeah, that was some crazy-sounding stuff right there! No wonder his momma and them came to try to talk him into coming home with them.

We may have to be willing to ask ourselves just how crazy are the demands of the kingdom of God for those who would claim to follow Christ today? Are we "brothers and sisters" of our Lord Jesus?

Would we show up to help Jem and Scout—so to speak—even if people thought us strange and absurd?

Suzanne Guthrie
http://www.edgeofenclosure.org

Mark 3

The sin against the Holy Spirit is *willful* despair.

Sometimes I get into moods of darkness thinking about how I've wasted, ruined, and frittered my life away. I confront myself with my mistakes, recklessness, and recurring sins. I fall easily into despair. But I know that in these moods I'm sinning against the Holy Spirit. Because I've observed that no matter how I've wasted, ruined, and frittered away my time and how my mistakes, reckless behavior, and sins have wrecked my hopes, the Holy Spirit has always made a nice shepherd's pie out of my mince and scraps. Every wrong turn yields a creative path toward something good in spite of me. When I forget the work of the Holy Spirit in my life, or doubt that the Spirit can get me out of my latest scrape, I'm sinning willfully.

Maybe the sin against the Holy Spirit is sheer lack of imagination. In light of past evidence, can I willfully forget the power of the Holy Spirit to transform a dead end into a new beginning? And if I complain about the late hour, the parable of the laborers confronts me: those hired at the end of the day earn the same wages as those working from the early morning (Matthew 20:1-16). Ha ! The good news won't take any excuse for stubborn negativity.

You can't change the past. But you can change the future by breathing in the Spirit's transforming Eternal Present.

Todd Weir
http://bloomingcactus.typepad.com/

Mark 3

If you start casting out demons, expect a counterreaction, sometimes even from your own family. Insert the word *dysfunction* for *demon*, and it makes more sense to the modern mind. Murray Bowen, founder of family systems theory, observed that when one person within an emotional system (say a church or family) changes behavior, it affects the whole system (for more information see http://www.thebowencenter.org/pages/theory.html. Everyone else is likely to react and try to force a change back to the status quo. So if you name a pattern of behavior as dysfunctional, and try to cast it out, not everyone will applaud you. Healing and growth seem like a threat when someone is in the grip and logic of dysfunction.

My biggest errors as a pastor have been when I thought I was being a bold or prophetic leader by naming the demonic or dysfunctional in the church. Even when I was right, it was not helpful to the community as a stand-alone intervention. Who among us would want to hear, "I see your problem. Change and you will then be fine"? Real change happens when we get the people in the system to ask, "What is happening here? Is this the way we want to act together? Is there a different way of being together?"

Jesus speaks in a way that allows this to happen. "'Who is my mother? Who are my brothers?' Looking around at those seated around him in a circle, he said, 'Look, here are my mother and brothers. Whoever does God's will is my brother, sister, and mother'" (vv. 33-35). Jesus redefines what a healthy human system looks like. It is not merely a bond of blood and kinship, or of nation, politics, or theology. It is people who choose to live in covenant together. In Christian terms, it then becomes a "beloved community."

June 14, 2015

3rd Sunday after Pentecost, Proper 6

1 Samuel 15:34–16:13; Psalm 20; 2 Corinthians 5:6-10, (11-13), 14-17; Mark 4:26-34; Ezekiel 17:22-24; Psalm 92:1-4, 12-15

Lowell E. Grisham

http://lowellsblog.blogspot.com/

Prayers of the People (1 Samuel 15–16; Psalm 20)

Presider: You have planted the kingdom of God among us like seeds scattered on the ground, O God: Let your creation flourish and grow into the fullness of your abundant life, as we pray: If anyone is in Christ, there is a new creation.

Litanist: Gracious One, the love of Christ urges us on: Lead your church to walk by faith and live for him who died and was raised for us. If anyone is in Christ,

there is a new creation.

Mighty One, we will shout for joy at your victory and triumph in your Name: Guide the nations of the earth to put not their trust in chariots and horses, in tanks and in planes, but rather to call upon the Name of God and to listen to your direction. If anyone is in Christ,

[For use with alternate readings Ezekiel 17; Psalm 92: Almighty One, inspire your loving-kindness and justice among the leaders of the nations, that your righteousness may flourish like a palm tree and spread abroad like a cedar of Lebanon. If anyone is in Christ,]

there is a new creation.

Mysterious One, let your quiet strength work in our sleep and in our rising, night and day, to nurture your purpose for all people, that new life may sprout and grow, we do not know how, and produce a harvest of abundant life for all your creatures. If anyone is in Christ,

there is a new creation.

Loving One, you have planted your Spirit into all humanity: Let us regard no one from a human point of view any longer, but open our eyes to see Christ's presence in all humanity. If anyone is in Christ,

there is a new creation.

Compassionate One, you plant hope in our hearts and you bring newness to life.
Hear our prayers for those for whom we intercede, especially ___.
Hear our grateful thanks for the abundance of your grace, especially for ___.
Raise into your eternal life those who have died, especially ___, because we are convinced that one has died for all,
    therefore all have died and will be raised to newness of life. If anyone is in Christ,

there is a new creation.

Presider: We are always confident, O God, whether we are at home or away, for our life is hidden in you: Nourish our growth in you that we may become mature and fruitful disciples who produce an abundant harvest for the sake of your Name, through Jesus Christ our Savior, who with you and the Holy Spirit, live and reign, one God, forever and ever. Amen.

Ann Scull

http://seedstuff.blogspot.com

Listening Songs

The Allies, "Looking on the Outside" on *Shoulder to Shoulder* (Waco, Texas: Word, 1987) CD edition. Jennifer Knapp, "Into You" on *Lay It Down* (Brentwood, Tenn.: Gotee Records, 2000) CD Edition.

Film Clips

Legally Blond (2001): This film has many clips about judging people by what we think we see.

Swing Vote (2008): When Bud and Molly think that Child Services have come to check on them, they try to appear as religious as possible. I downloaded this film clip from those brilliant blokes at www.wingclips.com (accessed 22 April 2013). Film Clip Discussion: 1. Why do you think Bud and Molly think it will help to appear religious? 2. Are there times in our lives when we think it will help to appear religious? 3. What matters most?

Drama: Keeping Up Appearances

Man: Well, this suit looks OK on me. Think it makes me look a bit thinner too—never a bad thing. The tie—not too bright, not too somber—just subtle enough to make me look the part. If I want this job, I've got to look the part.

Woman: I just hate working with her. She's perfect—clothes, makeup, hair, face! I feel big and fat and clumsy every time I'm near her.

Boy: I'm gonna bust a gut if I do any more weights. But I just have to! At school last week, everybody laughed at me because I look skinny in my P.E. gear.

Teenage girl: Oh no! More pimples! I couldn't look any uglier if I tried! The kids at school will call me crater face for sure.

© Ann Scull

Congregational Discussion: What inner qualities do you hope people see shining out of you?

Response Activity

Perfume (anointing): This great idea is by Sue Wallace, *Multi-Sensory Prayer* (Bletchley: Scripture Union, 2000), 55.

Cynthia Weems

1 Samuel 15–16; Mark 4; 2 Corinthians 5

Appreciating the small and surprising are themes from this week's texts. The text from 1 Samuel reminds us that God uses different criteria for greatness. The world looks on appearances, but God has eyes that see more deeply. When Samuel goes looking for Saul's successor, God enables him to see things in David that no one else can see. By calling David, God reveals David's hidden potential for greatness. The Gospel lesson reminds us of the same greatness, which rests in the tiniest of objects, a mustard seed. God sees the hidden potential in the mustard seed that is difficult for humans to fathom. The parable of Jesus compares the mustard seed to the kingdom of God, something that would be difficult for us to fathom without the help of a parable.

Both David and the mustard seed flourish with a few key ingredients. They both are creations of God. They both receive nurture by human or natural care. Both also face trials. David faces an angry Saul and his own self-imposed disgrace. Imagine the natural calamities a mustard bush encounters over the years it takes to become full grown. Yet the Lord clearly marks their growth as a sign of the Spirit among the people, bringing to life the potential that God knew was always present, even if doubted by humans.

Paul, addressing the young church in Corinth, reflects this same theme of surprise. He, too, knows the futility of focusing on outward appearance and proclaims, "We regard no one from a human point of view" (2 Cor 5:16 NRSV). God sees us differently, as a "new creation" (v.17 NRSV). The Lord has plans for the small and surprising elements among us and within us.

Mark Stamm

1 Samuel 15–16; 2 Corinthians 5; Mark 4

This is my first opportunity to comment in this resource on one of the Sundays during Ordinary Time. By the way, *ordinary* refers to Sundays "in order," and not to something boring. As an Ordinary Time discipline, I commend preaching on the semicontinuous narrative in 1 and 2 Samuel, which covers ten Sundays until mid-August. Samuel offers a narrative of both tragedy and grace, of rivalries and intense loyalty, but most of all it is the story of God's work—albeit sometimes hard to discern—in the midst of God's people. As you read this mixed narrative, remember that David and Jesus are family, and God insists that it is so (Matthew 1:1-17). Can you believe that your local church is the family of God? Do they believe it? God chose David, perhaps ruddy and handsome, but by "outward appearance" the least likely choice (1 Samuel 16:7 NRSV, compare 2 Corinthians 5:12). As to God's call, by whose standards do we evaluate?

Paul insists that Christians must no longer regard others "from a human point of view," that is according to our cultural standards of excellence or comeliness. In Christ each is a new creation (2 Corinthians 5:16-17). Making such assertions often requires holy imagination: *That* argumentative person? *That* oddball? *These* apathetic youth and their exhausted parents? Yes, insists the text, them. Communities that preach and believe this good news can help persons manifest their giftedness.

Jesus calls us to believe in the dynamic expressed in these parables. In the kingdom of God, small seeds can become great shrubs. So again, we must remember that we are dealing with the people of God, that we are living within the grace of God. That makes them (and us) persons of great dignity, even if we can't quite see it yet.

Marci Auld Glass

http://www.marciglass.com

2 Corinthians 5

In the Corinthians passage, Paul sets up a dichotomy between God's eternity, which cannot be seen, and our mortal existence, which we can see, touch, and hold. Interestingly, all of the descriptions of permanence, weightiness, and stability belong to God's realm, which our society would describe as "ethereal." In last week's lesson, he said that this world is "preparing us for an *eternal weight of glory* beyond all measure" (4:17 NRSV). Eternal weight of glory: God is making us a building "not made with hands, eternal in the heavens" while we live in here on earth in a flimsy tent (5:1 NRSV).

What the revelation of Christ crucified does is change where we place our permanence. The world tells us we are safe when we take proper precautions: when we lock our doors, when we stay home. But Christ crucified tells us that is not the point, *because this world is not our home.*

We, who have received the revelation of Christ crucified, no longer place our security in the powers of this world. Sure, I still will wear my seatbelt and look both ways before I cross the street, but I am no longer under the illusion that any power of this age is my protection or my home. I was hit with anxiety because, in my attempt to keep myself and family safe, I was crashing into the reality that I am not in control. I cannot keep myself safe. I cannot keep my kids safe. I cannot control world politics.

Paul's words to the Corinthians reminded me how this is good news, and not reason for anxiety. My attempts at control end only in anxiety and frustration—it is like trying to keep sand from falling through your fingers. Trusting in God's control, on the other hand, allows me to leave my home.

Excerpt from http://marciglass.com/2013/04/18/home-body/.

John Wesley

http://www.ccel.org/ccel/wesley/notes

2 Corinthians 5:7

For we cannot clearly see him in this life, wherein we walk by faith only: an evidence, indeed, that necessarily implies a kind of "seeing him who is invisible;" yet as far beneath what we shall have in eternity, as it is above that of bare, unassisted reason.

Mark 4:26

So is the kingdom of God—The inward kingdom is like seed which a man casts into the ground—This a preacher of the Gospel casts into the heart. And he sleeps and rises night and day—That is, he has it continually in his thoughts. Meantime it springs and grows up he knows not how—Even he that sowed it cannot explain how it grows. For as the earth by a curious kind of mechanism, which the greatest philosophers cannot comprehend, does as it were spontaneously bring forth first the blade, then the ear, then the full corn in the ear: so the soul, in an inexplicable manner, brings forth, first weak graces, then stronger, then full holiness: and all this of itself, as a machine, whose spring of motion is within itself. Yet observe the amazing exactness of the comparison. The earth brings forth no corn (as the soul no holiness) without both the care and toil of man, and the benign influence of heaven.

Editor's Insights

Mustard Is a Creeper (Mark 4)

Whenever I think I've got my ducks in a row, I remind myself that mustard is a creeper. It's a weed like Creeping Charlie, which makes its way into the fields of our lives, at times spreading as rapidly and thoroughly as a cancer. Why is the kingdom of God like this, laced throughout with creeper?

On February 17, 1992, I gave birth to a severely autistic son. On that day I had no idea that my life had changed profoundly. I had no idea that I was no longer the "good mother" I seemed to be while parenting my "well-behaved," typical daughter. I had no idea that what I had always considered my call was about to be challenged and threatened by a persistent creeper—caring for someone with a disability, who needed me with an intensity I couldn't understand, with the threat of losing myself in the process constantly hovering over. For a period, this mustard seed, this creeper that entered my life and altered my ability to see things the way most people see them, swallowed me up.

Caring for my son influences everything about me. I am not the same person I was before he arrived and began his work in my life, before God began working in me through a newborn boy, bringing both joy and, at times, anguish.

Our faith—our entire way of thinking about God and the sacred—is influenced by creepers. Our own participation in the kingdom of God is not always a pleasant choice. Sometimes it overtakes us, and we become something we never dreamed we would or could be. Good? Bad? Those terms don't even have meaning when "the biggies" hit. And they come to all of us, those mustard seeds, and grow. How is the kingdom of God like this? How do we read the texts this Ordinary Time, keeping in mind how we are changed—continually, almost ominously—by the Spirit for the sake of the kingdom?

Teri Peterson

http://clevertitlehere.blogspot.com

Mark 4

I have a friend who used to joke about the first line of the Magnificat, "My soul magnifies the Lord," by saying, "Well, I suppose infinitely large is actually infinitely small. Why else would you need to magnify?"

The kingdom of God is like a mustard seed. And the earth makes seeds to grow, we know not how.

Often we think we are called to create the already-large bush, offering shelter to all creatures, as if we could simply transplant the fully grown kingdom of God into our gardens. But Jesus doesn't say that the kingdom of God is like the *mustard bush*, he says it's like the mustard seed, and for all our scientific advances, we still don't see or know *exactly how* a seed grows while it's buried in the dark fertile earth: infinitely small yet infinitely large.

What would our calling look like if it was about that tiny mustard seed, not about the bush?

June 21, 2015

4th Sunday after Pentecost, Proper 7

1 Samuel 17:(1a, 4-11, 19-23), 32-49 or 1 Samuel 17:57–18:5, 10-16; Psalm 9:9-20 or Psalm 133; 2 Corinthians 6:1-13; Mark 4:35-41; Job 38:1-11; Psalm 107:1-3, 23-32

Elizabeth Quick

http://bethquick.com

1 Samuel 17

What's your Goliath? I read this passage and see such a cartoon/childhood-Bible-story image. But for the Israelites: terror. What would be a comparable image of terror for you?

David removing the armor reminds me of a scene from the movie *Contact*. Jodie Foster's character, Ellie, is traveling in a spaceship of sorts, and is strapped to a chair that wasn't in the original blueprint for the ship, out of concern for her safety. But eventually she realizes that the chair is only holding her back, and once she unstraps herself from it, she floats calmly and safely in the ship. What kind of things do we try to add into our lives that are only holding us back?

Goliath thinks he knows what David is all about because of how he looks, because of appearances. What would your appearance say about you? Is that who you are? When do you let appearances influence what you think about others?

2 Corinthians 6

God's time and our time don't always seem to mesh. We're so rushed; we rarely seem able to wait for God's action. But when the acceptable time comes, when God acts, we don't always seem ready to respond! Jesus preached that the time was now—the kingdom of God has arrived. Do we miss the message? Are we late?

What a description from Paul in verses 4-10 of how he has sought to mold himself and his ministry. Can you apply these descriptors to yourself? What would your "list" look like?

Paul says he and his cohorts have had "no restriction in our affection" for the Corinthians, and calls them to "open wide your hearts also" (vv. 12-13 NRSV). It is hard to live without putting conditions on our love of others. How open are your hearts?

Cynthia Weems

1 Samuel 17; Mark 4

Goliath is the most well-known giant in the Bible. Today, even those totally unfamiliar with the Bible will recognize an allusion to "David and Goliath." We assume the simplest interpretation of the reference: God saves the little guy and defeats the bully.

The Gospel lesson introduces a new set of bullies. The wind and the sea roar up to bring a scare upon the disciples. Anyone who lives in the path of hurricanes knows well the fear that a nasty set of waves can bring. Natural disasters press in like an angry Goliath, ready to pounce on what lies in their path.

David and Jesus respond to these "giants" in similar ways. We often assume God gives David, with pint size and small frame, the physical ability to slay the giant. We often assume that when we root for David, we are rooting for God to produce a miracle in us when we face the "giants" in our lives.

What we forget is what David and Jesus both knew. The powers they used to tackle the giants before them are not temporary steroids or super powers. David and Jesus both know their power comes from God. David knows full well he cannot take on Goliath with his own powers. That is why he is the only one among his brothers not paralyzed with fear. David knows he can take Goliath down because the strength of the Lord is with him. Jesus calms the waters in the same way. Their faith in the power of God allows them to slay their giants. Their faith also demonstrates to those seized by fear and doubt that faith in God is a primary weapon in slaying giants of all kinds, including the modern-day giants we face.

John Wesley

http://www.ccel.org/ccel/wesley/notes

2 Corinthians 6:6

By prudence—Spiritual divine; not what the world terms so. Worldly prudence is the practical use of worldly wisdom: divine prudence is the due exercise of grace, making spiritual understanding go as far as possible. By love unfeigned—The chief fruit of the Spirit.

Mark 4:39

Peace—Cease thy tossing: Be still—Cease thy roaring; literally, Be thou gagged.

Liz Crumlish

http://somethingtostandon.blogspot.co.uk/

Mark 4

In Scotland, we have many superstitions surrounding boats. In many of the northeast fishing villages, it used to be considered unlucky for the fishermen to catch sight of any womenfolk on their way to the harbor in the early morning. It is said that some would turn around and go home rather than take their boat out after such a bad omen.

A few years ago, as chaplain to a local shipbuilding yard, I was asked to bless a ship before her launching ceremony, which was performed by Her Majesty the Queen. While Her Majesty's part in the proceedings was an honor for those who had commissioned the vessel, the woman minister's contribution caused some murmurs of amusement and wonder. I was, of course, delighted to have caused even such a minor storm in a teacup, and took the comments in the spirit of good humor in which they were offered.

I have a deep respect for the sea, alongside which I was born and close by which I have always lived. The power and energy of water is immense and commands respect. I have witnessed the calm mirrorlike surface of the river becoming a boiling cauldron without warning. So I can understand how a tired out Jesus could sleep easily in the stern of a boat, cradled, rocked, and nurtured by the sea. From such a slumber, it seems natural that he, so at one with the elements, should be able to rebuke them and bring calm. This is the same Lord, so in tune with us, children of his creation, that he brings the same peace into our stormy lives. Jesus, who entered the boat "just as he was," continues to demonstrate his sufficiency for us just as he is—at one with all creation.

D. Mark Davis

http://leftbehindandlovingit.blogspot.com/

Mark 4

In this text, Jesus rebukes the wind and speaks to the sea. It is great storytelling but troubling reality for a twenty-first-century worldview. Do we really think the wind and the sea have any sort of agency, whereby a command to them can be obeyed or not? A responsible preacher is compelled to ask these sorts of questions. Even if one has hermeneutical apparatus for letting a story speak in literal language and believing it in symbolic language, some listeners will simply hear this story in literal language. They are faced, then, with either denying what seems evidently true to them as modern persons or denying the "truth" of the Scriptures. It is better for the preacher of this text to address these kinds of issues responsibly out loud rather than to pretend they do not exist. It is even more beneficial to find the creative tension between our contemporary scientism regarding nature and this compelling story.

It may be helpful to see this story as pointing beyond itself to something else. A storm at sea is the most expressive depiction of chaos that seafaring people know. There is literally nothing stable to grasp when one's entire ship is engulfed in wind and waves. Anything that might offer stability—like a large stone cropping out of the sea—is a threat more than a help in this kind of trouble. Truly, everything is in flux. Hence, a storm at sea is perfectly illustrative of a situation when it seems that all of our possible moorings are far away, and we are helpless against the elements.

By taking this story out of a literal reading, it raises pertinent questions about believing, not in a mythological construct, but in God's steadfast love, even in the midst of unimaginable chaos.

Carolyn Winfrey Gillette

http://www.carolynshymns.com/

"O Teacher, Don't You Care?" (Mark 4)

LEONI 6.6.8.4 ("The God of Abraham Praise")

"O Teacher, don't you care?" the Lord's disciples cried.
"The waves are beating everywhere—We'll surely die!"
They called to him in dread, for mighty storms could kill.
Then Jesus spoke into the fury, "Peace! Be still!"

Lord, still the storm winds blow, and still we cry in fear:
We too are sinking, don't you know? Lord, are you here?
We seek to live your way, yet sorrows beat us down.
We feel alone and wonder: Where can peace be found?

Your church, your little boat, is struggling in the seas.
We question if we'll stay afloat in times like these.
The world is raging round; there's trouble everywhere.
When we are facing mighty storms, Lord, hear our prayer.

What awesome strength you've shown! So calm your church's fear.
Remind us that we're not alone, for you are here.
And though the winds are strong and sometimes even kill,
Your loving presence in our lives is greater still.

Biblical references: Matthew 8:23-26; Mark 4:35-41; Luke 8:22-25 and Romans 8:31-39

Kwasi Kena

Mark 4

Storms. Who hasn't experienced nature's fury? After living through enough storms, two things may occur. First, you might develop the assurance that when storms hit, you will get through it. Second, you may develop a somber respect for nature's ability to wreak havoc on life and limb in a flash.

In Mark 4, the disciples find themselves in the middle of a violent storm while crossing the Sea of Galilee. They have crossed this sea before, but on this evening the storm seems demonically driven such that the disciples frantically cry out, "Teacher, do you not care that we are perishing" (v. 38c NRSV)? Yet, Jesus, who was also on board, lies sleeping.

The psalmist notes, "He who keeps you will not slumber" (Ps 121:3 NRSV). What a contrast between that vigilant God and this sleeping Jesus. Doesn't Jesus care?

The prevailing worldview of the day held various beliefs about the sea and storms. In near-Eastern narratives, the sea symbolizes chaos, evil, and demonic power. Jewish apocalyptic literature likens the raging sea to the conflict between God and Satan. The stormy sea equals the power of death, which means powerlessness in Jewish thought. Could the disciples have avoided such thoughts that night?

Despite the disciples' angst, Jesus sleeps. Why? To him, the storm was not a crisis. He obviously believes the situation is not beyond control. In ancient Eastern theology, the Creator God can "sleep" because God fears no challenger to his authority. Resting is a divine choice.

Once awakened, Jesus commands the storm to be quiet. The storm, violent enough to scare seasoned fishermen, ceases. Jesus' stilling of the storm shows the disciples that storms—demonic or otherwise—remain subject to God's authority. What storms have you allowed to usurp God's authority in your mind? As an act of faith—rest.

June 28, 2015
5th Sunday after Pentecost, Proper 8

2 Samuel 1:1, 17-27; Psalm 130; 2 Corinthians 8:7-15; Mark 5:21-43; Wisdom of Solomon 1:13-15; 2:23-24 or Lamentations 3:23-33; Psalm 30

Cameron Howard

2 Samuel 1

It may seem curious that David would compose a lament for the man who had been trying to kill him. Then again, the story of David, Saul, and Jonathan is full of tragic absurdity. Saul once loved David and was comforted by his music and companionship (16:21-23). Plagued by jealousy (1 Samuel 18:7-9), fear (v. 12), and perhaps mental illness (vv. 10-11), Saul began to pursue David in order to kill him. Meanwhile, Jonathan loved David deeply, such that he assisted David in his flight and betrayed his father, Saul, in the process (20:30-42). Twice, David had the opportunity to kill Saul, but he did not, lest he incur guilt by killing the Lord's anointed (24:6, 10; 26:10-11). Both of those incidents appeared to end in reconciliation (vv. 16-22; 26:17-25), yet David continued to flee in fear until after Saul's death (27:1; 2 Samuel 2:1).

The lament's famous refrain, "How the mighty warriors have fallen" (2 Samuel 1:19, 25, 27), underscores the wartime ethos that pervades the books of Samuel. Saul and Jonathan are remembered as warriors with great military prowess; the song praises their shield, bow, and sword. The lament for these departed warriors could read like political propaganda from David, a man who would want to win over factions loyal to the previous king in his own bid to take the throne.

Yet David's grief takes a more personal turn at verse 26, the only verse in the lament in which David uses first-person speech. David is described as the object of much affection in 1 Samuel: Saul loved David (16:21); Jonathan loved David (18:1); Michal, daughter of Saul, loved David (v. 20); all of Israel and Judah loved David (v. 16). Never, though, is David the subject of the verb love ('hb). Yet in 2 Samuel 1:26, David expresses his profound sense of loss, particularly with regard to Jonathan. Beyond the political machinations they recount, the grief plaguing the wartime narratives of 1 Samuel may also prompt reflection on the tragic losses wrought by war in any age, as in the lament of 2 Samuel 1.

Two Bubbas and a Bible

http://lectionarylab.com

Lamentations 3; Psalm 130; 2 Corinthians 8; Mark 5

Fear and faith. The woman touched Jesus; he stopped and asked, "Who touched me?" She came in "fear and trembling," fell down before him, and told him the truth. He said to her, "Daughter, your faith has healed you" (Mark 5:31-34).

In the wraparound story of Jairus' daughter, at this very point, some people come from the leader's house to say, "Your daughter has died. Why bother the teacher any longer?" But Jesus says to the man, "Don't be afraid; just keep trusting [have faith]" (vv. 35-36).

As a child, I had a lot of faith; I also had a lot of fear. My faith was in the reality of God, not trust in the goodness or compassion of God. As I have grown older, faith and fear have remained in dynamic tension in my life. Just as my faith has matured and become more sophisticated, my fears have grown less generalized and more realistic.

So the question is—as we face these realistic fears, where do we place our faith, our assurance, our hope for the future? In governments? In armies? In secret agents?

The scriptures call us to trust in God. First, Lamentations reminds us "that the steadfast love of the Lord never ceases, / [God's] mercies never come to an end" (3:22 NRSV), then goes on to talk about those times when one feels abandoned by God. This is a realistic look at faith in the face of fear.

The psalm is a dialogue between faith and fear, first saying "you hid your presence. / I was terrified" (Psalm 30:7), while also exclaiming, "Lord, my God, I will give thanks to you forever" (v. 12).

Second Corinthians encourages people to be generous in the face of want, an act of faith over worry. As Jesus said, "Do not fear, only believe" (Mark 5:36).

Cynthia Weems

2 Corinthians 8; Mark 5

The two stories presented in the Gospel lesson pull on our heartstrings. One refers to long suffering, such as that of the hemorrhaging woman. One refers to the physical battles of an innocent child and the emotional trials of her parents. Pastors and parishioners alike will find both of these stories painfully familiar.

In their pain and desperation, both the woman and Jairus know where to turn in their time of need. Jairus has the advantage of being a leader in the synagogue. He can publicly fall before Jesus and beg for his help. The woman has no such advantage. She is seen as unclean, and knows that. She has to beg for Jesus' help in a different way. Jesus, however, does not differentiate in his response. Both ill females are made well because, we are told, of their faith.

Paul encourages the church in Corinth to be generous as he requests their assistance with a special offering. Christ is the model for the eager generosity Paul invokes. This is a challenging example for all Christians. How often are we eagerly generous? How often do we welcome a tug on our cloaks? How often do we respond positively to a desperate plea for attention in the midst of our busy schedules?

Paul reminds his audience that the most acceptable gifts are those that reflect what the individual or community possesses, not what they do not possess. A common focus in our modern context on what we do not have often leads to a less than generous response to the requests that come our way. Our generosity is to reflect that of Christ himself, a generosity that eagerly awaits those whose faith leads them to call on him.

John Wesley

http://www.ccel.org/ccel/wesley/notes

2 Corinthians 8:12

A man—Every believer. Is accepted—With God. According to what he hath—And the same rule holds universally. Whoever acknowledges himself to be a vile, guilty sinner, and, in consequence of this acknowledgment, flies for refuge to the wounds of a crucified saviour, and relies on his merits alone for salvation, may in every circumstance of life apply this indulgent declaration to himself.

Mark 5:22

One of the rulers of the synagogue—To regulate the affairs of every synagogue, there was a council of grave men. Over these was a president, who was termed the ruler of the synagogue. Sometimes there was no more than one ruler in a synagogue.

Julie Craig

http://winsomelearnsome.com

Mark 5

The first time I was ushered into a room where a person was on life-support, I had been a CPE chaplain for all of two weeks. When you're on life support, and machines are breathing for you—circulating your blood, removing your wastes, and causing your heart to beat artificially in order to keep some electrical pulses firing—your presenting problem is that you're mostly dead. Some parts of you are more dead than others, depending on how you got into this situation, but the upshot is this: It doesn't look good. You need a miracle.

Today's story presents two people who are half dead. The woman who reaches out to touch Jesus may have walked there on her own steam, but to the culture and the society and the religious community of the day, she is at least half dead and probably considered by many to be completely dead. Ritualistically impure by the cleanliness standards of that time, she could not worship, could not be in close community with anyone, could not touch anyone or be touched. She was an utter outcast, and she has been for as long as Jairus's daughter has been alive. So there is half dead that looks half dead, and then there is half dead that can fool the casual observer.

These two stories of the half dead wrap intricately into one another. And when Jesus shows up, the miracles start happening. Because that's how Jesus works.

There is currently a lot of hand wringing about the fate of the church. Some think the church is dead, and some think it is dying. Perhaps it is half dead. As far as the miracle healing we're all waiting for, I'm counting on Jesus—the one for whom half dead is no obstacle.

John Petty

http://progressiveinvolvement.com

Mark 5

Mark does not explicitly mention violations of the "purity code," but there are two of them in this reading. First, the woman with the hemorrhage touches Jesus, rendering him unclean. Second, Jesus touches the dead young woman, which also would have rendered him unclean.

That Mark does not mention this, even though it would have been obvious to a first-century audience, is a way of saying that Jesus took no notice of these purity violations. For Jesus, human need always trumps technical rules.

He takes the young woman's hand and says, in Aramaic, "Talitha koum." This is the first of only four instances of the use of Aramaic in Mark's gospel.

The next use of Aramaic is ephphatha, which means "be opened," and is used in the context of healing a blind man in 7:34. ("Be opened" also relates thematically to what happens following the healing.) Abba, the Aramaic word for "father," is used in Jesus' prayer in the Garden of Gethsemane in 14:36, expressing the intimacy of Jesus' relationship with his Father, and, finally, Jesus' "cry of dereliction" from the cross (15:34) is spoken in Aramaic as well: Eloi, eloi, lama sabachthani.

Talitha koum means "little girl, rise up," a word of resurrection, whereupon follows Jesus' greatest miracle in Mark's gospel, the raising of a dead person to life. The little girl gets up, walks around, and the people are astonished and in "great ecstasy"—ekstasis. The only other time the word ekstasis is used in Mark's gospel is at the resurrection of Jesus (16:8).

Incidentally, Peter, James, and John have no excuse for not having faith in the rest of Mark's gospel. They witness Jesus' greatest miracle, and still, they don't get it.

Julia Seymour

http://lutheranjulia.blogspot.com

Mark 5

Jesus is not magic. It is not simply a wave of his wand, a sip of his water, or a touch of his garment that heals. At first, the woman in Mark 5 may not have understood that. Once Jesus understands what has happened, however, he does not ask her to keep it secret. Jesus clearly announces to the crowd that her faith has healed her. Somehow, God brought her to faith and spurred her to action.

Mark is concerned that, once readers see Jesus raise the little girl from the dead, they will believe Jesus is magic. The gospel writer stresses that it is not so. Healing comes to those who have faith to approach God in Christ and seek what they need. Where does that faith originate?

Who moves first between humans and God? Not unlike the comedy routine with a similar name (the classic "Who's on first?" of Abbott and Costello), it is confusing to understand human-divine interaction. If we believe humans cannot automatically choose the good of their own accord, then God always moves first. God draws us in and gives the gift of the Holy Spirit to gift us with faith and to nourish that faith.

Perhaps there was divine prompt that urged the woman on to see Jesus. It could have been words heard in the marketplace or rumors at the well. She believed going to Jesus would heal her. Whether a last-ditch attempt or her first attempt at supernatural healing, God responded to her as one who had faith in the power of Christ. In a mystery that cannot fully be explained, God moved first and last. God always does.

July 5, 2015

6th Sunday after Pentecost, Proper 9

2 Samuel 5:1-5, 9-10; Psalm 48; 2 Corinthians 12:2-10; Mark 6:1-13; Ezekiel 2:1-5; Psalm 123

Lowell E. Grisham

http://lowellsblog.blogspot.com/

Prayers of the People (Ezekiel 2; Psalm 123)

Presider: Ever-present God, you come to us through the teaching of your Son Jesus Christ, risen and manifest in every place and time: Grant that our eyes and ears may be open to his wisdom and his healing, that we may be sent forth in his name to do the work that he calls us to, as we pray: To you we lift up our eyes, for your power is made perfect in our weakness.

Litanist: Gracious God, you have given authority to your church over many things that threaten your creation: Grant us the grace of your Spirit that we may teach with Christ's wisdom and perform his deeds of power for the healing of the world. To you we lift up our eyes,

for your power is made perfect in our weakness.

Let our nation hear the words of your prophets to reveal our impudence and stubbornness and to change our hearts: Give us just and compassionate leaders and protect our nation, that we may be a people of hospitality, welcoming your work of reconciliation and obeying your right hand of justice. To you we lift up our eyes,

for your power is made perfect in our weakness.

Enable this community to see and to hear heavenly things and to treasure the mystery of your revelation so dearly that we may recognize and accept the unexpected gifts offered to us by our neighbors, family, and friends. To you we lift up our eyes,

for your power is made perfect in our weakness.

Let your compassionate spirit go forth throughout the world to comfort and uphold all who suffer any form of weaknesses, insults, hardships, persecutions, and calamities, that they may be upheld by your strength and justice. To you we lift up our eyes,

for your power is made perfect in our weakness.

Strengthen us humbly to persevere through our tribulations, O God, and heal all who need your gift of mercy,
     especially ___.
We thank you for your goodness revealed in all the blessings of life, especially for ___.
Receive into Paradise all who have died, especially ___.
To you we lift up our eyes,

for your power is made perfect in our weakness.

Presider: Let your infinite grace, O God, free us from all attachment, cynicism, and fear, that we may participate in your universal mission of teaching and healing through the reconciling spirit of your Son, Jesus Christ our Lord. Amen.

Julie Craig

http://winsomelearnsome.com

Ezekiel 2; Mark 6

    I can't help but think that one of the ways that God keeps us moving in a divine direction is by shaking up our world once in a while. Both of these texts launch new things. In the Gospel lesson, Jesus has gone back to his people,

119

and they have received him like a stray dog—muttering at his less-than-glamorous pedigree and doubting his authority to do much of anything good or noble or worthy of mention. So Jesus gives his authority over to the twelve, and sends them out two by two. He reassures them that they already have everything they will need. All they need is to move their feet and go; oh, and to remember that some people will not like what they have to say. Some unclean spirits can be very tenacious.

Ezekiel's call to prophetic ministry takes place during the exile, displaced from the homeland, a stranger in a strange place, living under strange new rules. But the divine message is one of reassurance: "Get up on your feet, and I will tell you what to say. Oh, and by the way—some people will not like what you say and will be openly hostile towards you. Tell them what I said anyway. Don't be afraid."

It is indeed a scary thing to set out to do a new thing. It helps, I think, to hear of ancient stories of prophets setting out with the message of God's mercy and of God's highest intentions for our lives. Jesus was more than Mary and Joseph's oldest kid, no matter what the townspeople thought. And we are, each of us, because of him, more than just the sum of our parts.

Marci Auld Glass

http://www.marciglass.com

Ezekiel 2; Mark 6

When I get weary in my work, I turn to Ezekiel. His life always makes mine seem easier by comparison. I've never had to eat a divine scroll (3:3). I've never had to lie on my side for 390 days to make a point to Israel (4:5). The list is long for why I am glad to not be Ezekiel. But that isn't the primary reason I turn to him when weary.

When he is sent to prophesy to the people of Israel, God reminds Ezekiel that his job is only to speak the divine word. Whether people respond *or not* is not his job.

There is something freeing about separating the job from the response. "Whether they listen or whether they refuse, . . . they will know that a prophet has been among them" (v. 5).

I'm no Ezekiel, I try not to equate myself with the prophets of old—*most days*—but surely we are meant to remember Ezekiel when we hear how it went for Jesus in his hometown. Because there was a prophet among them, and they showed him nothing but contempt. "Isn't this the carpenter? Isn't he Mary's son?" (Mark 6:3).

The "impudent and stubborn" people Ezekiel warned about are the same people whose disbelief keeps Jesus from getting anything done in his hometown.

There are times when it seems our small, little voice is not enough to be heard over the din of negativity, cynicism, and vitriol in our society. And we think, "Why do I bother?" But then we remember the call to speak the divine word of love, good news, and mercy. And we turn to God for the Spirit to enter us and set us on our feet, as it did for Ezekiel. And we shake the dust off our feet and move on with the message.

Online at http://marciglass.com/2013/04/30/not-my-job/

John Wesley

http://www.ccel.org/ccel/wesley/notes

2 Corinthians 12:9

My grace is sufficient for thee—How tender a repulse! We see there may be grace where there is the quickest sense of pain. My strength is more illustriously displayed by the weakness of the instrument. Therefore I will glory in my weaknesses rather than my Revelations, that the strength of Christ may rest upon me—The Greek word properly means, may cover me all over like a tent. We ought most willingly to accept whatever tends to this end, however contrary to flesh and blood.

Mark 6:5

He could do no miracle there—Not consistently with his wisdom and goodness. It being inconsistent with his wisdom to work them there, where it could not promote his great end; and with his goodness, seeing he well knew his countrymen would reject whatever evidence could be given them. And therefore to have given them more evidence, would only have increased their damnation.

Carolyn Winfrey Gillette

http://www.carolynshymns.com/

We Hear, Lord, Your Promise (2 Corinthians 12)

ASH GROVE 6.6.11.6.6.11 D ("Let All Things Now Living")
We hear, Lord, your promise: "My grace is sufficient!"
Those few simple words brought such comfort to Paul;
And though every thorn in the flesh may be different,
We find in your message good news for us all.
Your strength is made perfect in times of our weakness,
When hardships assail us and pain comes along;
For you dwell within us, and we learn your goodness—
And when we are weakest, in you we are strong.

Through all that we suffer, your grace is a blessing;
O Christ, you are with us to carry us through.
What hope you still offer when life is distressing!
You heal and forgive us, so we turn to you.
When pain is so great that we hardly can bear it,
We call on your name and we hear your love's song;
You send us the comfort and peace of your Spirit,
And when we are weakest, in you we are strong.

Biblical reference: 2 Corinthians 12:5-10

Tune: Welsh folk melody, harmony by Gerald H. Knight (1908–1979). Text: Copyright © 2007 by Carolyn Winfrey Gillette. All rights reserved. Copied from *Songs of Grace: New Hymns for God and Neighbor* by Carolyn Winfrey Gillette (Upper Room Books, 2009). Email: bcgillette@comcast.net New Hymns: www.carolynshymns.com

Chuck Aaron

2 Corinthians 12; Mark 6

The theme of people who do not experience healing creates a link between the Paul passage and the Gospel lesson. The lack of healing comes for different reasons and teaches different things.

In the *Corinthians* passage, Paul recounts a mystical (near death?) experience in which he enters paradise. Initially, he uses circumlocution to avoid saying that he experienced this, but he clearly intends to describe his own vision or out-of-body moment. He purposely eschews giving details about the experience, because he received instruction to do so. Paul uses the experience not for its own sake but to set up the discussion of his "thorn" in his body. Again, he does not give details about the thorn, leading to much speculation over the centuries. Whatever the thorn, it tormented him. Despite his prayers for its removal, the Lord denied his request. Paul learned instead to bear up with the thorn in place. God's grace enabled him to endure the thorn and continue his ministry despite it.

In the Mark passage, Jesus cannot perform healing because of the lack of faith of the people in his hometown. The narrative gives the preacher the opportunity to examine the role of faith in receiving God's grace. God does not refuse to act until we have faith. Yet a lack of faith can hinder the flow of God's grace and power.

Jesus then sends the twelve out in a ministry of proclamation and healing. They too might encounter resistance and a lack of faith. Even so, their ministry bears fruit. The church continues its ministry despite opposition and doubt.

Faith can open us to healing, but faith also enables endurance when healing doesn't mean a cure. Grace and faith can produce strength, serenity, and perseverance.

Cynthia Weems

2 Corinthians 12; Mark 6

There are people in our lives who know us best. We have lived with them, worked with them, and in many cases, we are like them. They know our flaws and our failings, because ours are much like their own. During political races, candidates always take pride in their hometowns, and the hometowns take pride in them. However, it is often from this same hometown that the past foibles of a candidate get dredged up and shared publicly. It is hard for us to believe in a hero from our own ranks. We love heroes, but are suspicious of those who carry with them traits that too closely resemble our own.

Jesus had a hard time being himself in his hometown of Nazareth. He had already shown himself to be capable of healings and powerful deeds but could not accomplish many in Nazareth. We are told that the unbelief of the people there was great. Jesus spoke in the synagogue, and the people were astounded, but they quickly began to question his credentials, because he appeared to be just like their own. Surely, a hero, the Messiah, wouldn't come from Nazareth.

Paul provides us with words that balance our unrealistic need for hero worship. "My grace is sufficient for you, for power is made perfect in weakness" (2 Corinthians 12:9a NRSV). Paul hears from the Lord the same word Jesus must have known deep within. It is a call to lay aside all presumptions about strength, might, and persuasion in order for power to rise up through God's grace, calling forth a faithful response. We need not rely on our own strength alone when the Lord is at work through us.

July 12, 2015

7th Sunday after Pentecost, Proper 10

2 Samuel 6:1-5, 12b-19; Psalm 24; Ephesians 1:3-14; Mark 6:14-29; Amos 7:7-15; Psalm 85:8-13

Elizabeth Quick

http://bethquick.com

2 Samuel 6

- This is a strange passage. Michal, one of David's wives, and daughter of deceased King Saul, looks whiny and moody. But make sure you know her whole story. She was in love with David, and he married her, but eventually when he and Saul came into conflict, Saul gave Michal to another man to be married. When David wanted Michal back, he had to tear her away from her new husband, who followed after them crying. It is not surprising that she isn't thrilled to see David prancing around in his ephod (decorative ritual underwear!).

- Chapter 6 unfortunately ends with the note that Michal remains barren, not able to continue her family bloodline. I think she gets a bad deal.

- All that aside, the heart of the text today is in David's full body, soul, and heart dance before the Lord. He puts his whole self into giving thanks to God, dancing "with all his might." We are rarely so free and uninhibited when it comes to putting ourselves before God. What's holding you back?

Mark 6

- This text is another one that has dancing in it—a strange connection for texts.

- Foolishness—King Herod, walking the line with a chance of making a right or at least better decision, perhaps even somewhat intrigued by John, winds up, as the result of a drunken promise, beheading him. What is the most foolish thing you've ever done? How might things have been different in the long run if Herod had not been so foolish?

- How do you think John's disciples felt? The Gospels tell us that they interacted, of course, with Jesus' disciples. Do you think they were disillusioned? Did they go to follow Jesus? What do you think they did, after losing John?

Cynthia Weems

2 Samuel 6; Ephesians 1

At middle school dances, few actually dance. Many of us have memories of standing along the wall, wishing we had the guts to get out there and let loose. Typically, the young men and women who do dance at middle school dances are the ones possessing inner confidence, in themselves and their dancing ability. They make their way onto the dance floor with that confidence in tow.

David dances. Of course, David does not lack confidence. Yet we see David dancing even at a time when most of us would be more reserved. It is a procession into Jerusalem of great religious pomp and circumstance. David's confidence abounds. It is confidence in the Lord.

Throughout the course of David's life, his deep relationship with and reliance on the Lord continually amazes us. David, as a young man, wrestled with lions and bears and giants. As an adult, Saul hunts him. David knew the source of his strength was the Lord. His confidence in this gave him the ability to dance "with all his might" as he led the way into Jerusalem (v.14 NRSV).

Paul describes what happens to those who believe in Christ. They are "marked with the seal of the promised Holy Spirit; this is the pledge of our inheritance toward redemption as God's own people, to the praise of his glory" (Ephesians 1:13c-14 NRSV). The images of a seal, a promise, and an inheritance are reminders of the confidence that rests deep within us all, originating not from personal abilities but from God. David danced with a passion that showed the true center of his being and the foundation of his leadership among the people. Do we live with that same confidence and passion?

John Wesley

http://www.ccel.org/ccel/wesley/notes

Ephesians 1:13

Ye were sealed by that Holy Spirit of promise—Holy both in his nature and in his operations, and promised to all the children of God. The sealing seems to imply,

1. A full impression of the image of God on their souls.
2. A full assurance of receiving all the promises, whether relating to time or eternity.

Mark 6:20

And preserved him—Against all the malice and contrivances of Herodias. And when he heard him—probably sending for him, at times, during his imprisonment, which continued a year and a half. He heard him gladly—Delusive joy! While Herodias lay in his bosom.

Eric D. Barreto

Mark 6

John the Baptist was an irritant in Herod's life. John's preaching was a disruptive force in the wilderness and not welcome among the powerful, among those unwilling to search out a wild-eyed prophet in the wilderness and ask forgiveness.

Although John is arrested in chapter 1, Mark only here notes his demise in light of the success of Jesus' disciples in preaching repentance, exorcising demons, and healing the sick. The power of Jesus is refracted through his commissioning of the twelve, causing many to wonder who this Jesus is. Herod wonders too, because he becomes convinced that rumors about John's reappearance are true. The man he had killed, he believes, has returned in a blaze of prophetic power.

Mark reports that Herod's twisted family life became the object of John's scorn. John's critiques led to his own arrest. These same bizarre family dynamics would lead to John's execution as well. Somehow, revelry, manipulative relatives, and weak leadership conspire to cause John's death. This brief scenario is a mockery of Herod's purported might.

He feels so bound by a public oath voiced in foolishness, among guests he seems oddly dependent on, that he beheads a man he knows to be righteous. This decision comes back to haunt him and reveals the frailties and illusions of Herod's hold on power.

Why does Mark tell this story in between two stories about the success of the disciples in fulfilling Jesus' commission? The episode augurs Jesus' own cruel and unjust execution. His crucifixion may not involve family relationships worthy of a soap opera, but they are no less tied to corrupt authority. Moreover, the episode is a reminder that the path of the prophet is dangerous. Even in the midst of doing God's work, escape from suffering is not assured.

Editor's Insights

Whose Earth Is It? (Psalm 24)

"The earth is the LORD's and all that is in it, / the world, and those who live in it" (v. 1 NRSV).

Reading this psalm responsively in a congregation could be a very powerful experience. These words flow from religious tongues easily, especially from my own. It is tempting for me, perhaps for all of us, to divide the world into "us" and "them," with ourselves on God's side (of course)—I believe *this way*, as a liberal Christian, as an educated environmentalist; and "they don't."

Sometimes I wonder what it would mean to give the "other side" the benefit of the doubt that they, too, have read this scripture, and they, too, believe it, and they, too, read it mechanically, just as I do, believing that the consequence of their belief shows in their own way of life.

I wonder what it would mean truly to listen to these words as I say them. It all belongs to God. All of it. None of it is mine. And none of it belongs to anyone else. I go on reading, about the gates opening and the King of Glory, victorious, entering the city. (We can deal with the battle imagery another time!), I wonder: What must we do to cause this event? Must we believe with all of our heart that "the earth is the LORD's and all that is in it, the worlds and those who live in it?"

Some days I can't imagine what it would mean to *live* as if this scripture actually is so, as an individual and in community. Yet these words so easily escape my mouth, as if they mean very little. How do I stop and listen? How do I help those I lead in worship actually stop and listen?

Julia Seymour

http://lutheranjulia.blogspot.com

Mark 6

After Jesus' baptism, the Spirit drives him into the desert. After he has resisted temptation, we read, "Now after John was arrested, Jesus came to Galilee, proclaiming the good news of God" (Mark 1:14 NRSV). Then all of a sudden, five chapters later, John's fate is recounted in the middle of the stories of the works that Jesus is doing.

This is deliberate placement by Mark. Just as Jesus emphasizes the importance of faith and relationship with God, Mark also wants to keep the hearers of the gospel from dwelling on the miracle aspect of Jesus and to be drawn to the truth of God within Christ.

When we think of following Christ, we often think of the life of faith as truth or consequences. Jesus is the truth (and the way and the life), and if you don't believe it, there are consequences. Seems simple enough, but that's not the message to which the whole Bible points us. The life lessons of John the Baptizer and Jesus the Christ show us that there is truth *and* there are consequences. Eternally, there might be an "or," but in the here and now, it's an "and."

There are consequences for our faith: time, money, and spiritual wear and tear. When we lose someone we love, we struggle with the balance of grief and hope. When we know of a neighbor who needs care, we have to yield to the Spirit's motivation to help that person, regardless of how we feel about him or her. When we see injustice in our communities, we are not allowed to rest and believe that someone else will take care of it.

D. Mark Davis

http://leftbehindandlovingit.blogspot.com/

Mark 6

Mark offers a long and unusually detailed story of the death of John the Baptizer using intertextual elements of the stories of King Ahasuerus, Queen Vashti, and Queen Esther. Vashti was Ahasuerus' first wife, whom he commanded to expose her beauty to all of his consorts at a feast. She refused and was banished—and later beheaded with her head on a platter, according to Midrash texts. Esther was Ahasuerus' second wife, who pleased him among all the other virgins of his harem, and to whom he made the promise to give her anything she wanted. We find most of the structural elements of Mark's telling of John's death in the Vashti/Esther stories.

Yet Mark weaves this story well, offering profoundly complex characters. Herod likes to hear John, but is condemned for political adultery by John; he protects John, he kills John; he is boastful, he is afraid and sorrowful. First commanded and then promised, the daughter asks her mother for guidance and then hastily complies. Herodias seems to be the only one-dimensional character, despising John and scheming for his death.

What prompts Mark's recounting the death of John is that Jesus has sent the twelve on a successful mission, Herod has heard of it and, as a result, he knows the name of Jesus. Something about the twelve's successful mission has reawakened Herod's worst nightmares. Within Mark's gospel, this is a resurrection story, where the death of one gives rise to the emergence of new life and ministry. Just as Jesus came preaching when John was first arrested, and just as the disciples are to go to Galilee to continue Jesus' work after his death, Herod's senseless killing of John is now part of a new story of ministry and life.

Suzanne Guthrie

http://www.edgeofenclosure.org

Mark 6

I feel an uncomfortable affinity to Herod in this story, not over the creepy lust for his stepdaughter, obviously, but in his being torn between truth and self-interest. What draws Herod Antipas, the power-hungry ruler, tetrarch of Galilee, son of Herod the Great, to the preaching of repentance, forgiveness of sins, turning in conversion toward God? Something inside of him must resonate with John's message.

Herod also wants to meet Jesus (see Luke 23:8-12). The long-anticipated meeting ends in fury and frustration. Jesus simply refuses to speak to him. Herod sends Jesus back to Pilate in a purple robe. Herod and Pilate bond over the joke.

These encounters with John the Baptist and Jesus become mere footnotes to Herod's life and the passionate love story of Herod and Herodias. Here is where my awkward sympathy lies with Herod. Are Jesus and John the Baptist footnotes to my own passions and the dramas of my own personal history?

Do I not make choices every day like Pilate and Herod, appeasing others, acquiescing to my culture, societal expectations, and to maintain my standard of living? Do I accept the way things are with such studied ignorance and self-interest? Is my love for God, for justice, for the kingdom, as powerful as my devotion to distractions, glittering things, and self-preservation?

Will I end my days torn between two loves—one worldly and the other drawing me toward the eternal heart of the universe? Sacred love calls to me into the wilderness of my soul: repent, forsake my sins, and prepare the way for the Holy One of God.

Is my love for God as strong as death?

July 19, 2015

8th Sunday after Pentecost, Proper 11

2 Samuel 7:1-14a; Psalm 89:20-37; Ephesians 2:11-22; Mark 6:30-34, 53-56; Jeremiah 23:1-6; Psalm 23

Julie Craig

http://winsomelearnsome.com

2 Samuel 7; Psalm 89

My favorite image of God in this text is God moving about in a tent and a tabernacle. I think of God as a moving target, always on the go, hard to pin down in one place, and always going exactly where needed. Or sometimes like the saying of Desiderius Erasmus (that Carl Jung had inscribed over the front door of his house) goes, "Bidden or unbidden, God is present."

And a God like that, always on the move, out among God's people, staying beside us, moving where we move and dwelling where we dwell and being worshiped where we choose to worship—well, that's not the kind of God who fits in a box, or the kind of Creator who needs walls, or the kind of Savior who responds well to efforts at containment. The temple couldn't box God in, and the grave couldn't contain the risen Jesus, and the Upper Room was no match for the Holy Spirit.

The God of the Old Testament dwelt among the people, with them wherever they went, and promised to build them a house, a house not made of cedar or mud or gold or adorned with any precious gem. No, the house of the promise of YHWH is made of the very family of God, and its cornerstone is Jesus Christ.

We are that house. We are the place where God's mercy and generosity and creative energy and grace and love are manifest. May the God who moves about among God's people, going with us wherever we go, making a place for us and planting us and giving us rest, may that God find in us a church without boundaries, a kingdom without end, a home without walls.

Thom M. Shuman

http://lectionaryliturgies.blogspot.com/

Great Prayer of Thanksgiving (2 Samuel 7; Psalm 89)

You built a house for us,
Architect of Steadfast Love,
and called it creation,
full of all we needed as your children.
Yet, we took the temptations sin offered us,
building our shaky foundations on death.
When we misread the covenant you made with us,
you sent the prophets to spell out each word for us.
When our hostility and anger increased,
you sent your Child, Jesus, to proclaim peace.

So with all who are near, and all who seem so far away,
we lift our voices in joy to you:

Holy, holy, holy! God of faithfulness and love.
All creation sings praises to you.
Hosanna in the highest!
Blessed is the One who is our peace.
Hosanna in the highest!

You placed your hand over your holiness,
pledging your faithful and steadfast love
made flesh in Jesus Christ, our Redeemer.
Everywhere,
he tore down those thick-headed
walls we build around us.
Everyone he met,
he welcomed as a sister and brother.
To those gathered around him,
he took the anger they felt towards others,
healing them with his grace.
Forever, he destroyed the power of death.

As we remember his life, death, and resurrection,
we speak of that mystery we call faith:

Christ came, to break down all barriers;
Christ died, to bring peace to all;
Christ rose, to offer new life to all;
Christ will return, to take all home.

As you will not renege on your promises,
pour out your Spirit on those who have gathered
to share the gifts of the Table.
Saints and sinners pass
the broken bread and,
hearing the echoes of your whispers,
serve those whom the world considers as strangers.
Native born and immigrants
drink deeply of grace
and together rush to minister to the sick,
to the dying, to the hurt, to the lost.

And when we no longer strangers but family
by your steadfast love,
we will join together,
warming your heart with our glad songs,
God in Community, Holy in One. Amen.

John Wesley

http://www.ccel.org/ccel/wesley/notes

Ephesians 2:20

And are built upon the foundation of the apostles and prophets—As the foundation sustains the building, so the word of God, declared by the apostles and prophets, sustains the faith of all believers. God laid the foundation by them; but Christ himself is the chief cornerstone of the foundation. Elsewhere he is termed the foundation itself.

Mark 6:40

They sat down in ranks—The word properly signifies a parterre or bed in a garden; by a metaphor, a company of men ranged in order, by hundreds and by fifties—That is, fifty in rank, and a hundred in file. So a hundred multiplied by fifty, make just five thousand.

Paul Bellan-Boyer

He Is Our Peace (Ephesians 2)

Communities often define themselves by belief. If you believe in a certain idea or set of words, you are included in the community of faith. These words are a brief statement about the God that is building this community.

The early church had confessions that preceded the creeds. "Jesus is Lord" may be the most famous and edgy. Jesus is Lord: not Caesar, not me, not any other authority. Jesus, the one Caesar tortured and killed; the one his disciples betrayed, denied, and abandoned, is Lord.

In Ephesians 2:14, we have another confession, central to Jesus' identity. His followers have called him many names: savior, shepherd, redeemer.

But he is also our peace. A bit abstract, perhaps, unless you have the experience of warfare, enmity, cruelty, injustice, poverty, deception, or fear. Then peace becomes tangible, a living hope. And its incarnation is sweet beyond belief.

The apostle knows Christ Jesus as peace for his new community. Christ is the reconciler, the one who has healed divisions between groups: Jew from Gentile, slave from free, man from woman (see Galatians 3:37). The same process is still at work. We see non-Godly divisions being broken down—black from white, immigrant from native-born (notice the apostolic language of aliens into citizens), gay from straight, poor from rich.

Think not that this peace is easy or idyllic. The apostle uses architectural terms to indicate that God's peace is built through struggle: with tradition, with privilege, with injustice, with greed, with fear. The peace of Christ is persecution and death transformed into the resurrection of reconciliation.

Christ's peace, our peace, does not bless the world order; it transforms it by breaking down one last dividing wall: human from divine. In the household built with Christ as cornerstone, no member's high status depends on another being brought low.

Sharron Blezard

Ephesians 2

On October 13, 2010, one-hundred-one-year-old Eulalia Garcia Maturey became a naturalized citizen of the United States of America. She entered the U.S. as a baby in the arms of her young, single mother, who settled in Brownsville, Texas. After the passage of the Alien Registration Act in 1940, Eulalia registered with the government and received a Certificate of Lawful Entry a year later. For decades, she lived unsure of her status, keeping her entry document pristine, yet fearful of making waves that might cause her to have to leave the country. Finally, more than one hundred years after crossing the border from Mexico, through the help of relatives and immigration officials, Eulalia became a legal citizen of the United States, saying she wanted to feel "libre" or "free."

Imagine how it must feel to live your entire life without a sense of full incorporation, always knowing you do not fully belong and that your status can be questioned at any moment. In today's epistle lesson, Paul tells the Christians at Ephesus that because of Christ they are unsettled no more: "So now you are no longer strangers and aliens. Rather, you are fellow citizens with God's people, and you belong to God's household" (2:19). We, dear friends, are free in Christ. We have our citizenship, and we never have to worry or wonder about whether we are "legal" or whether we "belong."

Christ has bridged the chasm between life and death, between alien and citizen, making a way and extending full status and membership in the household of God to all people. No more do we have to wander or wonder. We have a place, you and I, and no one can take that away from us. This is good news worth sharing and celebrating!

Source: http://www.usimmigrationsupport.org/mexican-immigrant-naturalized-101.html

John Petty

http://progressiveinvolvement.com

Mark 6

For "sheep without a shepherd" (v. 34), the reference is to Numbers 27:16-17: "Let the Lord . . . appoint someone over the community who will go out before them and return before them, someone who shall lead them out and bring them back, so that the Lord's community won't be like sheep without their shepherd."

The one appointed in Numbers is Joshua—yeshua, in Hebrew, the same name as Jesus, a serendipity that, in my view, Mark fully intends.

Similarly, Ezekiel 34 speaks of shepherds who do not feed the sheep, and Zechariah 11:5 says, "Their own shepherds won't spare them." Thus, drawing from the prophetic tradition, "sheep without a shepherd" is a critique of a ruling religious class that does not care about the people.

Moreover, the subsequent feeding prepares the people for that time when Jesus will be killed and "the sheep go off in all directions" (Mark 14:27). The feeding of the five thousand, with its strong eucharistic overtones, is one way that Jesus will continue to be present with the community even after his death. The open table fellowship of the Jesus movement, with food for all, is yet another.

After the feeding, Jesus and the disciples went to Gennesaret, a town just west of Capernaum, also on the Sea of Galilee. Again the people "recognized" (knew) Jesus. Their response is to comb the countryside for sick people in order to bring them "wherever they heard he was" (6:54-55).

Word about Jesus seems to be spreading through an informal, grassroots communications network. Also, in the original Greek, Mark uses the present tense in verse 55; the people "were hearing" where "he is." Writing circa 70 CE, Mark wants the people to know that Jesus is presently available.

Ann Scull

http://seedstuff.blogspot.com

A Useful Image

For a bridge-building theme: Hampden Bridge, Australia's oldest suspension bridge is found at http://seedstuff. blogspot.com.au/2012/07/proper-11-ordinary-16-b-july-22.html (accessed April 27, 2013, scroll down).

Listening Song

Third Day, "Come Together" on *Come Together* (Franklin, Tenn.: Essential Records, USA, 2001) CD Edition. This matches the Ephesians reading.

Children's Story

"God Is Never too Busy." The Gospel reading stands alone as a great story to show that God is never too busy. But don't just read it; use a good storyteller. It makes all the difference!

Film Clip

Burst is a brilliant seven-minute film about reconciliation, forgiveness, and freedom. View it at http://www.youtube.com/watch?v=hXdtNswjL_k (accessed April 27, 2013). For copyright details and permission, contact www.tropfest.com. Discussion Questions: 1. Who is the peacemaker, reconciler, forgiver? 2. Who does the God things?

Film Clip

One Cross, One Body: based on the Ephesians reading, this is available, for a small cost, from http://www.worshiphousemedia.com/mini-movies/5256/One-Cross-One-Body (accessed August 2, 2013).

Drama

"The Bridge" in Verena Johnson (ed.), Mega Drama 4 (Adelaide: Open Book Publishers, 2002), 14. This is based on the Ephesians reading. Discussion Starter: Share an experience of being excluded. Share an experience of being included.

Response Activity and/or Prayer of Confession

"The Wall" found in Sue Wallace, Multi-Sensory Prayer (Bletchley, UK: Scripture Union, 2000), 51. This goes well with any of the readings as a confession, but is particularly relevant to the Ephesians reading, in any context.

Meditation

(Source unknown but probably me). Ask people to sit comfortably, relaxed, with their eyes shut. Read the following slowly:

Think about God. Think about the places in your life where bridges need to be built—maybe a personal relationship that has gone wrong, maybe an injustice in your local community or the world, maybe a disagreement within your congregation. Whatever it is, talk to God about it....ask God what your role is in healing the situation.

July 26, 2015

9th Sunday after Pentecost, Proper 12

2 Samuel 11:1-15; Psalm 14; Ephesians 3:14-21; John 6:1-21; 2 Kings 4:42-44; Psalm 145:10-18

Cynthia Weems

2 Samuel 11; Psalm 145; Ephesians 3

The eleventh chapter of 2 Samuel tops the list of high drama in the Bible. This story of deception and arrogance is familiar. Readers are disappointed in the David here. Yet this David is, in many ways, more recognizable than he is elsewhere because of the common human flaws he exhibits.

The trouble begins for David the minute he decides to go to the roof of his house and lounge on a couch. Perhaps that is where the trouble begins for many of us. During a time of the year when David would normally be occupied, he finds himself relaxed and unoccupied. The trouble begins when David mistakes his human solitude and idleness for divine absence.

There is no mention of God in the story. It is better this way for David, as God's overt presence would only complicate things for him. But Scripture assures us the Lord is near, even when we assume otherwise. The question that hangs over this passage is, how do we live when we are under the false impression that the Lord is not present?

Believed to have been written by David, the psalm for this day issues a word of hope, "The Lord upholds all who are falling" (145:14a NRSV). This is good news, as David and all of us know. Yet perhaps the falls would be less frequent if we could address our human tendency to stray in times of idleness. Paul proclaims that the power that lies within us "is able to accomplish abundantly far more than all we can ask or imagine" (Ephesians 3:20 NRSV). Our lives are meant to show evidence of that power, a power that fills idle time with accomplishments of good and demonstrations of faith.

John van de Laar

http://www.sacredise.com/

2 Samuel 11; John 6

David was finally on the throne. All he wanted was his—until he spied the beautiful Bathsheba. But, since God had given him an unassailable authority, he summoned her to his palace and satisfied his lust. When Bathsheba became pregnant, and David's attempts to get her husband to sleep with her failed, he had Uriah killed. It was a tragic failure of David's faith in God's ways, and his reign was never without strife after this.

Fast forward to a hungry crowd receiving a miraculous feast at Jesus' hands. For the gospel writer, this was not just a miracle. It was a sign of God's glory manifest in Jesus. John's gospel spends a lot of time comparing Jesus to Moses, which makes the twelve baskets of leftovers significant. As Moses fed the twelve tribes in the wilderness, so Jesus fed the crowds such that everyone had more than enough. The message is clear—Jesus is not just like Moses; Jesus is Moses' God in the flesh. The question was whether the people would believe this or stop at the miracle.

John's gospel calls readers beyond the self-interested faith of David and the miracle-focused faith of the crowds. Such shallow "faith" destroys and separates. It leads kings to take by force the wives of their subjects. It makes the world a place of division, competing ideologies, and violence.

Rather, John calls us to the faith of the boy who willingly shared his small lunch. It's a faith that knows that self-interest never satisfies. It's rooted in the person of Jesus, and gladly follows his way of life-giving sacrifice. Only this faith can save our economies and our planet, stop the guns and violence, and ensure that every hungry mouth is fed with plenty left over.

For more detail: http://sacredise.com/blog/?p=1165

Two Bubbas and a Bible

http://lectionarylab.com

2 Samuel 11; John 6

My, oh, my! What can we say about King David and his wandering eyes?

There are any number of approaches possible for preaching this text; certainly, "be sure your sins will find you out" is a tried-and-true message. The futility of trying to hide from God (a la the story of the Fall in the garden of Eden) might be another. Finding somebody else to take the fall for you ("go on down to your house, Uriah, and 'wash your feet' [wink, wink]") is another fool's errand.

I am struck by the depth of desperation that ensues as David seeks any remedy other than honest confession for his sin. Those in the recovery community learn—at a price, to be sure—that responsibility must be accepted and amends must be made. You can't send Joab to do your dirty work for you.

No rest for the weary—and, on this occasion, no food, either. John's telling has Jesus slyly testing the disciples. They are excellent foils for his plans to illustrate what faith in God looks like. Working with very little, Jesus leads the disciples to see that God does not give just enough—but, in fact, provides much more than they ever could have imagined.

For the disciples, it's personal. When the lesson has ended, they each have their own basket to carry away—a reminder of God's sufficiency.

The second episode, with Jesus walking on water in the midst of a storm, illustrates even further how little we need fear when God is the strength of our lives. It is tough in the midst of our own storms. But let the words of Christ dwell richly in us: "It is I; do not be afraid" (v. 20 NRSV).

John Wesley

http://www.ccel.org/ccel/wesley/notes

Ephesians 3:20

Now to him—This doxology is admirably adapted to strengthen our faith, that we may not stagger at the great things the apostle has been praying for, as if they were too much for God to give, or for us to expect from him. That is able—Here is a most beautiful gradation. When he has given us exceeding, yea, abundant blessings, still we may ask for more. And he is able to do it. But we may think of more than we have asked. He is able to do this also. Yea, and above all this. Above all we ask—Above all we can think. Nay, exceedingly, abundantly above all that we can either ask or think.

John 6:5

Jesus saith to Philip—Perhaps he had the care of providing victuals for the family of the apostles.

Liz Crumlish

http://somethingtostandon.blogspot.co.uk/

Ephesians 3

Toward the end of my second pregnancy, I can recall the terror I felt when it hit me that soon I would be responsible for another tiny bundle of humanity. I simply couldn't conceive how I could possibly love two little human beings. Would my love for this new arrival somehow rob my firstborn of something that was rightfully his? I had no concept, no experience of how love can grow and be all-encompassing. And still, it is something that can't be explained but that happens nonetheless.

In hindsight, I did know it then, even if I couldn't articulate it. I had experienced it in the amazing love of God. But, even if I had been able to make the connection, it is unlikely that I would have believed that humans are capable of such love—or anything near it.

This passage, in Ephesians, speaks of the blessings God showers on us by adopting us, by loving us, by making us family, rooting and grounding us in love.

> Not because we are deserving
> but because God loves.
> Not because we are attractive or intelligent or even amusing
> but because God delights in calling us beloved.
> before time began, before the clay was dry
> God decreed that we would be his children.
> You and me.
> There's no end to God's love, no limits
> We can never be too dull
> or too smart
> too handsome
> or too gross
> In fact, there's no escape
> God loves us
> and calls us family.
> Blessed are we.

Dan R. Dick

Ephesians 3

Many Christians have a love-hate relationship with the Apostle Paul. Paul, and those who write in Paul's name throughout the Christian scriptures, is all over the theological and philosophical map. Some teachings are deeply insightful and display an amazing wisdom. Some are a bit narrow-minded and judgmental. Many teachings are speculative, while some are laser-focused and incredibly specific. Paul's thinking evolves and matures across the years, and occasionally he strikes a perfect note, offering the very best of the best. The prayer in Ephesians 3:14-21 is one such example. This is a prayer among prayers—an example of perception and grace. Here is gratitude and blessing and benediction. Here is intercession and petition and adoration. Here is humility and hope and thanksgiving. Rarely is a word from Paul more grace-filled or visionary. In a few short, simple sentences, the author provides a model of healthy piety and deep faith.

We pray "about" a lot of things. In our Western culture, prayer generally is viewed as a personal and private practice of faith. We may pray for others, but we rarely pray with others outside of church. We pray about problems and concerns more frequently than we pray from a foundation of adoration and thanksgiving. We all too often forget to end our prayers with "your will be done." We fill our prayer time with what we want to say to God, and often we give God very little time to say anything to us. In many ways, we have lost our faith in prayer. The prayer in Ephesians is a wonderful reminder of the way we should pray, not just on our own, but together in Christian community. It is a prayer of faith and hope, love and promise—the very things our world so desperately needs today.

Todd Weir

http://bloomingcactus.typepad.com/

John 6

Do you think five thousand people would venture from home and the only person to make any provision was a small boy with his five loaves and two fish? The author of John tells us the people were following Jesus for healing, not because they were starving. They were likely poor and in need of their daily bread, but that doesn't preclude people carrying some provisions, if they are walking a few hours from home. I am making the case that the real miracle here isn't necessarily creating lox and bagels without preexisting matter, but rather—it is a wonder that a wary crowd of strangers could come together in trust and community and share what they had. They moved from a sense of scarcity and selfishness to a spirit of sharing and abundance. This miracle should, perhaps, be renamed the miracle of a small boy's openhearted sharing.

We can't go back to the security footage to see what really happened, and even John's gospel is vague as to the precise moment of the miracle. If Jesus defied the laws of science, I'm fine with that. (After all, doesn't Wonder Bread defy nature by never molding?!) But he remains my Christ, if he did not magically produce bread. What miracle does the world really need now? The miracle we really need is for people to stop living as if their neighbors are just part of the crowd. We need communal ideals that don't leave some starving and others hoarding. We need a biblical faith that challenges excessive inequality and upholds a wise stewardship of our resources. That would be a miracle worthy of a messiah. The feeding of the five thousand is the symbolic act of communion, the living out what Martin Luther King, Jr. called "the beloved community."

August 2, 2015

10th Sunday after Pentecost, Proper 13

2 Samuel 11:26–12:13a; Psalm 51:1-12; Ephesians 4:1-16; John 6:24-35; Exodus 16:2-4, 9-15; Psalm 78:23-29

Safiyah Fosua

2 Samuel 11–12

"If you see something, say something." Nathan the prophet could easily have coined the saying. Of interest in today's passage is the length of time between King David's sin and Nathan's confrontation. Using the chronology of the text, this conversation took place long after the arranged death of Bathsheba's husband, Uriah, long after Bathsheba's period of mourning, after David and Bathsheba were wed, and after the birth of their first child. This long gap between David's sin and God's rebuke through Nathan raises several questions: Did God orchestrate the delay in order to give David an opportunity to repent without Nathan's prompting? How long was Nathan aware of (and troubled by) the impropriety of the king's behavior before he mustered enough courage to speak?

The text does not tell us what went on inside Nathan before he used a parable to confront the king, but human nature suggests that there are several probable stages to consider: awareness, discomfort, wisdom, and courage. We can easily imagine Nathan becoming aware of the story by hearing bits and pieces of it whispered in the palace or community. His journey from awareness to discomfort to wisdom to courage is less easy to imagine. It is equally difficult to chart our own progression through those stages. When we hear of the outrageous things that are happening around us, are we outraged or numb to moral issues when they are in the public area? Are we more *numb* or *more* outraged when moral transgressions are discovered closer to home? Do we eventually speak out? Or do we remain silent? Perhaps a more relevant issue raised by the text is the time and effort needed to move any one of us from awareness to discomfort to wise action when similar situations take place around us.

Natalie Ann Sims

http://lectionarysong.blogspot.com

2 Samuel 11–12 (Nathan Confronts David about His Greed. David Confesses.)

- "Forgive Us Now" (David Brown)—This is one of the best songs seeking forgiveness that I know. "Forgive us now, O mother love for all the idols we have built, / For all the time we've worshiped there in company of dark despair." (lyrics, sound sample, songbook: http://www.wholenote.com.au/songs/forgiveusnow.html)

- "For the Hurt I Create" (Shirley Murray)—Beautiful tunes and words. Tune (ii) is most simple, so use that if you will sing it as a congregation. Tune (i) is also good if you have musicians who can sing it for your congregation. If using tune (ii), you may suggest to your congregation that they simply join in on the "forgive me, Lord, forgive" line, but make sure you teach it to them first.

- "Forgive, Forgive Us, Holy God" (Shirley Murray / Colin Gibson)—Very easy tune for a congregation. The words focus on our desensitization to violence and our greed. The final verse has a focus on communion, yet still makes sense if you are not celebrating it this week. (lyrics: http://www.musiklus.com/anthology/item/1078/forgive-forgive-us-holy-god)

- "Come as You Are, That's How I Want You" (Diedre Browne)—This song is beautiful, gentle, simple, and very well known. A good song to start the service. (lyrics: http://laughingnome.blogspot.com.au/2007/02/come-as-you-are-thats-how-i-want-you.html; slow and mushy sound sample: http://www.paulgurr.com/products.html)
- "God Is Forgiveness" / "*Bóg jest miłością*" (Jacques Berthier): "God is forgiveness, love and do not fear." This simple chant will be good if you choose to focus on the theme of forgiveness. (lyrics in many languages, music and sound samples: http://www.taize.fr/spip.php?page=chant&song=257&lang=en)

Linda Lee

Grace to Grow (Ephesians 4)

"His purpose was to equip God's people for the work of serving and building up the body of Christ until we all reach the unity of faith and knowledge of God's Son" (vv. 12-13a).

Christ knows us, and calls us anyway. We are called because he believes in us. Christ bestows us with the gifts needed by the world. In unity with Christ, we are part of building up his body in the world. We ordinary people become the divine conduit of healing, ministry with the poor, justice, and peace.

How do we do this? We build ourselves up with love, and we do our part (v. 16).

This is often easier said than done. When we encounter persons difficult to love, when we have gotten too busy and don't want to do our part anymore, when we feel as if we need to be the one *being* built up, the Spirit of Christ within is a source to which we can go. The Spirit of Christ is within us individually and collectively. When we can remember to turn to Christ within as the people and world around us are whipping around like a mid-summer storm, we gain strength to go on. Each time one of its "parts" grows stronger, the whole body strengthens. One member's new wholeness strengthens the family. Each family that becomes more mature in faith builds up our congregations. Our communities are made new by the faithful service of those equipped by Christ through the gifts given to each of us.

Christ chooses us, not because of our accomplishments or by our perfection or imperfection, but according to his grace-filled gifting of us. Through this grace, we grow and participate in possibilities beyond what we can ask or imagine.

John Wesley

http://www.ccel.org/ccel/wesley/notes

Ephesians 4:3

Endeavouring to keep the unity of the Spirit—That mutual union and harmony, which is a fruit of the Spirit. The bond of peace is love.

John 6:26

Our Lord does not satisfy their curiosity, but corrects the wrong motive they had in seeking him: because ye did eat—Merely for temporal advantage. Hitherto Christ had been gathering hearers: he now begins to try their sincerity, by a figurative discourse concerning his passion, and the fruit of it, to be received by faith.

D. Mark Davis

http://leftbehindandlovingit.blogspot.com/

John 6

Evangelism and church growth emphases often leave the impression that the more people who follow Jesus, the better. This text will challenge the easy correlation between popularity and discipleship, when Jesus observes that the crowd seeks him, not as the sign sent from heaven, but as a provider of bread. Seeking "food that perishes" is to see the feeding story as a way of filling one's belly. Seeking "food that endures to eternal life" is to see the feeding as a sign that Jesus is the one sent from heaven.

A key term in this story and throughout John's gospel is "eternal life." It is different from the Greek concept of the immortality of the soul (which would include preexistence as well as post-bodily-death existence). The phrase literally reads "life of the ages," and has much to do with life of the present, but life in a way that has lasting, nonperishable value.

Some commenters suggest that this text from John is an example of an early Christian homily, replete with (1) an argument over how to read the Scriptures (i.e., the Old Testament) and (2) how those Scriptures are fulfilled in Christ. In the first case, Jesus clarifies that it is "God" and not "Moses" who provides the bread from heaven to eat. In the second case, Jesus points to himself (or the gospel writer points to Jesus) as the sign that is sent from heaven, resulting in the "I AM" saying, "I AM the bread of life."

In the end, the "work" that the crowd is to do (v. 29, CEB has "what God requires") is to believe that Jesus is God's provision for life and sustenance.

Martha Spong

http://marthaspong.com/

John 6

We live in a fast-food world. We can buy just about anything between two pieces of bread or two halves of a roll. Few of us have ground wheat by hand; a few more have baked bread. Most go right to the store. The people Jesus met knew the complex and time-consuming process of making bread and the never-ending chore of drawing water. This man claimed to be the one who would eliminate not only hunger and thirst but the effort required to relieve them.

I know this is a metaphor. I cannot understand not understanding him—except when I can.

"Lucy, have you found your college yet?"

Her seatmate in the back of the van asked this question all through vacation, as often as "Are we there yet?" He is seven and interested in her, and he wants to understand. We tried to explain that you can like some colleges, but then you have to be sure they like you before you can decide which one you like the best. That answer was too complicated, so he asked the question again.

"Lucy, have you found your college yet?"

Finally, she said, "It's the same answer as the last time you asked me."

Are we there yet? We should be. We're two thousand years past the people following Jesus, pushing closer to ask him who in the world he is. We understand the metaphor.

Well, we understand that there is such a "thing" as a metaphor, that Jesus isn't actually bread or water.

But are we there yet? I think we're still asking him, a little desperately, "Who are you?"

It's the same answer as the last time we asked. He is the Living Bread. Come to him and never be hungry.

August 9, 2015
11th Sunday after Pentecost, Proper 14

2 Samuel 18:5-9, 15, 31-33; Psalm 130; Ephesians 4:24–5:2; John 6:35, 41-51; 1 Kings 19:4-8; Psalm 34:1-8

Thom M. Shuman
http://lectionaryliturgies.blogspot.com/

Canticle 130

i dangle my toes over
the curb of my heart,
my toes washed in
those tears racing
toward the storm drain,
my keening words
echoing through the
empty streets;

if you wrote all my sins
on the blackboard
you would run out of schools,
but the Spirit stays after class,
banging dusty death out of the
erasers
begging your pardon
for Crossing
out your work;

more than those
who watch the clock
on the graveyard shift,
i wait (we wait!) for hope
to be the lyrics of
the music of your heart,
more than a rooster
scanning the horizon
for that first glimpse of dawn –

we hope
for you . . .

David Lose

1 Kings 19; Psalm 34; John 6

There is an earthy, even visceral element of Israel's faith and worship that is easy for us to overlook. Consider the psalmist who sings not, "*Look* and see how good the Lord is," but "*Taste* and see how good the Lord is" (v. 8, emphasis added). Food is not more visual or aural information, it is life itself—nourishment, health, and strength. So when journeying to freedom through the wilderness, Israel didn't want to *see* their destination or hear stories of their victory; They wanted food. And when Elijah was at death's door, fleeing Jezebel, the angel didn't bring him a message but rather food and drink that he might be nourished for the road still ahead of him.

Although John's gospel is known for its sophisticated theology and developed Christology, in this passage Jesus invites a similarly tangible, earthy, and even visceral relationship to him. "I am the bread of life," Jesus says, contrasting the eternal life he gives with the important but limited nourishment provided by the manna given in the wilderness.

It is preposterous, of course. How can any man—let alone one so common that those in attendance knew his father—possibly be bread that gives life?

Yet Jesus does just that. He is, as John's larger narrative makes clear, the new Passover lamb whose body and blood are given so that all who believe may have life.

Jesus as the bread of life. Jesus as the Passover lamb. The bread and wine of Communion that mediate Jesus' body and blood given for us. All of it can seem too much, too difficult to understand. Yet we have in this passage the promise that God in Jesus seeks to meet us in our physical as well as spiritual lives so that God might nourish us for the journey ahead.

John Wesley

http://www.ccel.org/ccel/wesley/notes

Ephesians 4:26

Be ye angry, and sin not—That is, if ye are angry, take heed ye sin not. Anger at sin is not evil; but we should feel only pity to the sinner. If we are angry at the person, as well as the fault, we sin. And how hardly do we avoid it. Let not the sun go down upon your wrath—Reprove your brother, and be reconciled immediately. Lose not one day. A clear, express command. Reader, do you keep it?

John 6:51

If any eat of this bread—That is, believe in me: he shall live forever—In other words, he that believeth to the end shall be saved. My flesh which I will give you—This whole discourse concerning his flesh and blood refers directly to his passion, and but remotely, if at all, to the Lord's Supper.

Suzanne Guthrie

http://www.edgeofenclosure.org

John 6

I've sat inside a monastery rotunda to good profit in my soul, contemplating a golden starburst monstrance enclosing a pale host. Sacramental objects teach me to see sacramentally. Sacristans, altar guild members, and priests handle chalices and fair linens as an almost remedial lesson in caring for ordinary things. Architects create beautiful orderly spaces of worship to open people's hearts to beauty in a disorderly world. Devout men and women eat the bread of Holy Communion in order to help awaken their consciousness to recognizing the bread of life everywhere.

If God lived in a tabernacle in a church only, I would never leave church. Liturgy lets me linger with the thought of Presence, then pushes me out the door with the insistent dismissal to seek and recognize God elsewhere, that is, in the places most difficult to perceive Divine Love. When I'm weary, I come back to renew the process, each Eucharist giving me, hopefully, a deeper and wider insight into the next adventure.

And so, liturgy at its best simulates deep play—like a child testing a hypothesis, letting imagination extend freely into possibility, the pretending a world you might, with maturity, make real. What if this little host is so sacred, it can be touched only with great respect and delicacy? What if it contains the universe and reveals the union of the sacred and the divine, of interconnected, inseparable matter? What if there were really a universal bread of life that satisfied hunger and a drink that quenched thirst? What if everybody on earth is this little host—so sacred, so loved, so revered? What if the whole earth is sacred, the way we play Communion? And what if we lived as if that were so?

Karoline Lewis

John 6

The third section in the five-part series of the Bread of Life Discourse has a unique claim that sets it apart from the other sections. It is the statement of Jesus, "I am the bread that came down from heaven" to which the Jewish leaders take issue (v. 41), not just that Jesus said, "I am the bread of life." By putting these two things together, "the bread" and "coming from heaven," Jesus is revealing not only what he *does* (provide life), but who he *is* (God incarnate and from God). The offense of Jesus is not just that he is able to secure daily sustenance but that he seems to have an "in" with the source of this provision of life. Isn't this just the little boy we watched playing ball in the street? The son of Mary and Joseph, our neighbors, who never put his bike away but left it on the front lawn? Whose backyard we had picnics in and played croquet? This portion of the discourse represents the heart of the irony and even poignancy of the meaning of the feeding of the five thousand. Jesus' interpretation of this miraculous sign is more important than the sign itself. Yes, it is truly incredible that Jesus can feed five thousand people with five loaves of bread and two fish. But even more extraordinary is what it reveals about Jesus' identity, Jesus' origin, and the abundance of life that Jesus can offer. It is not enough to bask in the glory of Jesus' miracles. For the gospel of John, interpretation, recognition, and affirmation must follow. One cannot simply be the recipient of life abundant. There is a called for response that acknowledges who Jesus is: the Word made flesh, the very dwelling of God among us.

Martha Spong

http://marthaspong.com/

John 6

They often turn up at churches, charismatic, with a touch of grandiosity. Frequently he carries a perfume of alcohol and the aroma of smoke. She tells a story of complexity and tragedy and sometimes homelessness, and in my last church, which ran a pet pantry, the dire need for a bag of kitty litter.

I think the people who knew his parents put Jesus in that category. He makes it easy for them. "I don't care," he says. "You only understand me if my Father wants you to understand." Still, he goes on explaining.

I once spent an hour in my office with a tattooed guy in a leather cowboy hat who wanted the church to give away some money, but only by his rules. More than once, I have had lunch with men in neckties who wanted the same thing. I have been guilty of wanting to go along with the latter and hoping the former will leave and never come back, because I am thinking, "I know his Mama. I know his odd and terrible story. What can he possibly have to tell me that matters?"

Leather Cowboy Hat showed up at church one night at 6:00 p.m. Alone in the building, I begged off, excusing myself with a meeting at 7:00 (true) and work to finish (somewhat true). Yes, it's sensible not to meet with people when I am alone in the building. Yes.

But I am guilty. I'm not sure I would have put the other type off that way.

Leather Cowboy Hat Jesus, I confess. Forgive my cynicism, my sense that I know it all, and my fear of men who show up at the back door unannounced with an important message. I hope it wasn't you this time. I hope it wasn't you.

August 16, 2015
12th Sunday after Pentecost, Proper 15

1 Kings 2:10-12; 3:3-14; Psalm 111; Ephesians 5:15-20; John 6:51-58; Proverbs 9:1-6; Psalm 34:9-14

Lowell E. Grisham
http://lowellsblog.blogspot.com/

Prayers of the People (1 Kings 2; 3; Psalm 111)

Presider: Living Father, Holy Wisdom, you have come to us in Jesus as the living bread given for the life of the world: Accept our prayers on behalf of the whole human family, that all may abide in you, and live, and walk in your ways, as we pray: Feed your creation with your eternal life; abide in us, O Christ.

Intercessor: Nurture your church, O Christ, with the food and drink of eternal life as we celebrate our Eucharist on this feast day of your resurrection: Fill us with your Spirit as we sing psalms and hymns and spiritual songs, giving thanks to God the Father at all times and for everything in the name of our Lord Jesus Christ. Feed your creation with your eternal life;

abide in us, O Christ.

Guide the leaders of our nation and all who wield power and authority in the world that they may have wisdom and understanding to discern between good and evil. Feed your creation with your eternal life;

Use with alternate readings, Proverbs 9; Psalm 34. Guide the leaders of our nation and all who wield power and authority in the world, that they may turn from evil and do good; seek peace and pursue it. Feed your creation with your eternal life;]

abide in us, O Christ.

Invite our community to the banquet of your divine life, where we may know the works of your hands, which are faithfulness and justice, full of majesty and splendor. Feed your creation with your eternal life;

Use with alternate readings. Invite our community to the banquet of your divine life, where all may live and walk in the way of insight. Feed your creation with your eternal life;]

abide in us, O Christ.

Be the bread of life for those who lack and suffer hunger throughout the world, that all who suffer may know the nourishment of your love. Feed your creation with your eternal life;

abide in us, O Christ.

Let your nurturing life renew and strengthen those for whom we pray, especially ___.
We thank you for the living bread that came down from heaven; hear our prayers of gratitude, especially for ___.
We commit to your never failing heart those who have died, especially ___. May they abide in you and rejoice at the
      banquet of your heavenly feast.
Feed your creation with your eternal life;

abide in us, O Christ.

Presider: Generous God, you call all people into your banquet to eat and drink of the true food and true drink that you give for the life of the world: Bless our celebration with the power of your presence, that we may grow in wisdom and faithfulness all our days, through Jesus Christ our Savior.

Amen.

Marci Auld Glass

http://www.marciglass.com

1 Kings 2; 3

For the writer of 1 Kings, the legitimacy of Solomon's reign is beyond question. True, he was not born of David's *first* wife. True, he was not the *eldest* son of David. Yet, it is to Solomon that the wisdom and understanding of God are given as to no other mortal.

The writer tells this in inhuman terms. Solomon is the Superman of the ancient world because nobody could really emulate him. We could look at him and aspire, but the bar is set too high.

And God appears to Solomon in a dream—"Ask whatever you wish," says God (3:5).

What would we ask for? The ability to fly? Health, wealth, and happiness? A winning lottery ticket so we could build a fellowship hall that was more easily accessible for people with mobility issues? A BCS championship game for Boise State?

But Solomon gives the answer that makes the rest of us look bad. As soon as we hear him say, "Give your servant a discerning mind in order to govern your people and to distinguish good from evil" (v. 9), we think, "Yeah, what he said. That's what I meant to say, God. I was joking about the lottery ticket."

Solomon has answered well. He is King David's son, after all. And God gives him a wise and discerning mind. God also gives him riches and honor, which he did not ask for.

And then Solomon wakes up from his dream.

Do you wonder what he thought as he woke up? *Was it real?* How long will it take until I know?

We aren't told if Solomon's wisdom came upon him immediately, or if he took the more normal course of acquiring wisdom, gradually, and usually after making mistakes. But he acquires wisdom.

Excerpt from http://marciglass.com/2009/10/20/wisdom/

John Wesley

http://www.ccel.org/ccel/wesley/notes

Ephesians 5:16

With all possible care redeeming the time—Saving all you can for the best purposes; buying every possible moment out of the hands of sin and Satan; out of the hands of sloth, ease, pleasure, worldly business; the more diligently, because the present are evil days, days of the grossest ignorance, immorality, and profaneness.

John 6:57

I live by the Father—Being one with him. He shall live by me -Being one with me. Amazing union!

Rick Morley

John 6

Of all the things that Jesus teaches during his earthly ministry, this is apparently one of the most explosive. John tells us that many people who had begun to follow Jesus came to the conclusion that they could no longer associate with him because of what he says here. Like a congregation dispersing because of a controversial statement by the clergy, people pick up and leave because they are scandalized.

The heart of the scandal, I think, comes from Jesus' persistent admonishment to drink his blood. Leviticus 17 makes it crystal clear that absolutely no one is to ever, for any reason whatsoever, consume blood. The consequence of violating this commandment is being "cut off" from God.

Of course, Jesus isn't ignorant of Leviticus, and neither is he ignorant of how his words grate on the ears of his listeners. No, Jesus doesn't speak out of ignorance, but rather with Leviticus in mind. Blood was not prohibited food because blood is unclean or dirty. Quite the opposite; blood was regarded as sacred because it contains the very life of the creature.

So when Jesus gathers crowds of people around him, and he tells them to "eat my flesh" and "drink my blood," what he's really saying to them is to take his life and pour it into their lives. His blood does indeed contain his very life, and he wants God's people to have it coursing in their veins—his life in our lives.

Jesus could have probably found a gentler way to say this and saved himself from a mass desertion. However, his point, and the point of the gospel is extreme: Jesus' life is a gift for us.

Natalie Ann Sims
http://lectionarysong.blogspot.com

John 6 ("I Am the Living Bread." Bread Becomes Flesh)
- "Hallelujah! We Sing Your Praises" / "*Haleluyah! Pelo Tsa Rona*" (South African)—Joyous and simple song; "Christ the Lord to us said 'I am wine I am bread.'" Good for kids.
- "Eat This Bread Drink This Cup" (Taize Community)—Excellent, particularly if you have a capable cantor. Some resources say, "Come to him and never be hungry," but others have "come to me / trust in me."
- "You're Like the Sun That Warms Me" / "Bread of Angels" (Robin Mann)—This is a nice ballad, a favorite of many in our congregation. It may not be easy for a congregation without some introduction because the structure is a little tricky.
- "As We Walk Along beside You" (Shirley Murray)—Excellent words recognizing Christ in the word, the bread, the resurrection. A simple tune.
- "Bread of Life Our Consolation" (Daniel Poirier)—A nice gentle song. Would be good for distribution of Communion.
- "Feed Us Now" (Robin Mann)—One of my favorite Communion songs. Simple to sing and beautiful, simple theology. "Piece of bread, cup of wine, Lord this food is good." Good for kids. (lyrics: http://www.vailchurch.com/worship/Worship/archive/2007/worship090207.txt; search for "Feed Us Now")
- "Bread for the World a World of Hunger" (Bernadette Farrell)—Very nice words. Tune a bit schmaltzy, but the words save it. A bit gutsy really. Good for a soloist during distribution of Communion.
- "We Will Take What You Offer" (John Bell)—An excellent, simple short song that works well either as an upbeat chorus or as a reflective chant. (sample: http://www.giamusic.com/search_details.cfm?title_id=8379)

August 23, 2015

13th Sunday after Pentecost, Proper 16

1 Kings 8:(1, 6, 10-11), 22-30, 41-43; Psalm 84; Ephesians 6:10-20; John 6:56-69; Joshua 24:1-2a, 14-18; Psalm 34:15-22

Elizabeth Quick

http://bethquick.com

1 Kings 8

- "The priests could not stand to minister because of the cloud; for the glory of the Lord filled the house of the Lord" (v. 11 NRSV). Sometimes I think we feel something similar as pastors—so overwhelmed by God or underwhelmed by ourselves that we find it hard to be pastors. I felt this way during the first baptism I celebrated.

- This passage makes me think about public leaders and expressions of faith. In a nonchurch state society, what kinds of expressions of faith of public leaders are authentic?

- Solomon, despite his power and position, still seems to have a good sense about God. We so often want to box God in. Solomon builds a dwelling for God with a wise amount of hesitation.

- In the midst of ongoing conversations about immigration and border control, the biblical witness on treatment of foreigners is pretty clear. Here, Solomon talks about foreigners and residents united by faith.

Ephesians 6

- What are your strengths? How are you strong in God?

- Paul subverts all these war images in this passage and turns them into non-violent images so effectively, much like Isaiah's "beating swords into plowshares" (Isaiah 2:4 NRSV), only in a more subtle way.

- Compare this passage to Colossians 3:12, where we find more clothing imagery.

- "Make known with boldness the mystery of the gospel" (v. 19 NRSV). What mixed images: We dare to be bold about something that is still shrouded in mystery. That's how God moves in our lives!

John van de Laar

http://www.sacredise.com/

1 Kings 8; Ephesians 6

The account of Solomon's prayer probably was written a few centuries after his reign to explain why Israel had been conquered and the temple destroyed. After briefly celebrating God's grace and majesty, the prayer moves on to seven petitions that are mostly concerned with issues that undermine kingdoms. Solomon is probably sincere, but he is also seeking God's endorsement for his reign.

God's response (recorded in the following chapter) includes a promise to watch over God's people, and a warning that, should they be unfaithful, they will be uprooted and the temple will be rejected. The writer of this account gives

Solomon's disobedience, and the apostasy of most of his successors, as the reason for Israel's downfall. And we find the seeds of this disaster in Solomon's prayer, which is focused on self-protection, not obedience.

Centuries later, Paul teaches the Ephesian believers that evil systems and power structures are the product of human hearts. The weapons of our defense, then, are also of the heart: truth; God's righteousness (or justice); readiness to proclaim the gospel of peace, faith, and salvation; God's word; and finally, prayer, which brings them all together. Prayer teaches us to release our need for control and to destroy our own little kingdoms before they destroy us (like the faithless kings of Israel). Prayer reveals that the problem is not outside of us, but in our own rebellious hearts—which is where we must fight the battle.

These stories describe two kinds of prayer. Solomon's prayer seeks only to change what is outside of us in our favor. Paul's prayer, however, refuses to blame either people or outside circumstances, but opens the heart to change by God's Spirit. Now we, too, must choose which prayer we will practice in our own lives.

For more detail: http://sacredise.com/blog/?p=1177

Kwasi Kena

Joshua 24; John 6

When looking at the central messages of today's passages the phrase "decision day" comes to mind. During Joshua's farewell address, he issues an urgent plea the people "put aside the gods that your ancestors served" (v. 14b).

We have to remember that it took many years for the Hebrews to embrace monotheistic belief. The first commandment given to Joshua's predecessor, Moses, was "You must have no other gods before me" (Exodus 20:3). Decades later, monotheism still had not gained full acceptance. So Joshua urged the people to revere God and put away their idols.

Joshua's plea signals a decision day. In the preceding verses, Joshua rehearses the great deeds God did: prospered Abraham with many offspring, delivered the Israelites from Egyptian bondage, parted the Red Sea, and finally led the Hebrews into the promised land. With that as his preamble, Joshua calls his people to account "But if it seems wrong in your opinion to serve the Lord, then choose today whom you will serve" (v. 15a). Put up or shut up.

Fast forward to John's gospel and you find another decision day in the making. Jesus tells the people that they must eat his flesh and drink his blood if they want to have life. Unfortunately, the people Jesus spoke to could not understand that he was speaking about the Eucharist and abiding in him.

The disciples responded as many of us do when we can't understand spiritual sayings, they grumbled. Jesus fired back, "Does this offend you?" Then he says some of you do not believe. At that, many of his disciples turned and no longer followed him.

How much of current church practice avoids "decision days"—those honest conversations in which we declare our intentions to follow Christ—or not. How might decision-day conversation affect your relationship with Jesus Christ?

John Wesley

http://www.ccel.org/ccel/wesley/notes

Ephesians 6:10

Brethren—This is the only place in this epistle where he uses this compellation. Soldiers frequently use it to each other in the field. Be strong—Nothing less will suffice for such a fight: to be weak, and remain so, is the way to perish. In the power of his might—A very uncommon expression, plainly denoting what great assistance we need as if his might would not do, it must be the powerful exertion of his might.

John 6:63

It is the Spirit—The spiritual meaning of these words, by which God giveth life. The flesh—The bare, carnal, literal meaning, profiteth nothing. The words which I have spoken, they are spirit—Are to be taken in a spiritual sense and, when they are so understood, they are life—That is, a means of spiritual life to the hearers.

Editor's Insights

Longing (Psalm 84)

This is a responsive prayer. It's easy to read or sing it in worship yet not hear what it's saying. I wonder how often we long for God. In our rhetoric, of course, we long for God. We long for justice. We long for "home." We long for the kind of world that "is God's." But in reality, do we truly long for God?

Despite our claims about the wealthy, and the fact that we are not them, we *are* them. Any leveling of that playing field would affect most of the people who are reading this volume in a way that they probably would not consider positive. Is it enough that this "leveling," this arrival of God in a reality other than the spiritual one, would place us in the presence of God in a clearer way? Is it true that this would be "enough"? And for how long?

I especially ponder the words "I would rather be a doorkeeper in the house of my God than live in the tents of wickedness" (v. 10b NRSV). I really don't want to admit my complicity with the wicked, my absorption in a world that profits me at the expense of others, my utter contentment with that arrangement. I don't live in the "tents of the wicked." But, of course, in this equation, in the final judgment, I do. The world runs on fairly nicely for me because others suffer.

I'm not sure what to do about that. I can think of a lot of ways to approach it. But in this apocalyptic image of what it would mean for God to "show up" and be "in charge," the thing I would gain would be the Presence of God. Am I willing to give up the rest of it for that alone? Am I even able, honestly, to pray that it become so?

Amy Persons Parkes

Ephesians 6

The armor is no armor. The belt of truth will not repel the sinking feeling in your gut; truth will reveal the vulnerability not conceal it. The breastplate of righteousness does not keep your heart from breaking; rather, righteousness will break open your heart to expose all the ulterior motives and manipulations of self-righteousness. The shoes of peace dare not crush the stones of conflict beneath your feet. Instead, peace will seek out the jagged edges of anger, pain, and fear to pinpoint and overturn the protruding stones violence and discord. The shield of faith neither deflects nor blunts the piercing arrows of doubt and chaos. Faith gathers in and includes our misgivings and our wayward thoughts and covers them with assurance and hospitality. The helmet of salvation never kept one mind from delving into the darkness of our wounds; on the contrary, salvation unmasks our defenses, unsettling our enthroned egos with the threat of integration and holy healing. And the sword of the Spirit, the Word of God—no matter how many days you have wielded her in battle, she will surprise you with a new twist, a different weight, or an adjusted heft when you least expect it. On an occasional morning when you gingerly pick her up and sift through her pages, you could swear someone else raised her in battle and changed the words in the middle of the night.

The armor of God is no armor at all. You might as well come to battle naked, bare, vulnerable, weak, and humble if you would defeat the powers of darkness.

Todd Weir

http://bloomingcactus.typepad.com/

John 6

Why is this teaching so difficult that many disciples stop following Jesus? Is the image of eating his body and drinking his blood too distasteful? Do they not believe in the message of heaven and eternal life? Or is it because Jesus talks about the manna in the wilderness as lacking something essential to faith?

Perhaps the context of the synagogue of Capernaum sheds some light. It is the city said to be home of the first disciples, including Peter. Jesus taught there many times, and it is the sight of his first sermon in Mark's gospel, where he concludes by healing a man with an unclean devil (1:21-28). It is the site of many healings, including the servant of a Roman centurion (Luke 7:1-10), and a paralytic man who was lowered through the roof in order to get him to Jesus through the crowds (Mark 2:1-12). This healing sparks great controversy because Jesus forgives the man his sins, and some say it is blasphemous, for only God can forgive sins. Mark 2 is a series of controversies over calling Matthew the tax collector, eating with sinners, and picking grain on the Sabbath.

It seems that the controversy in Capernaum is over law and custom on the surface, but also about authority and power. To abide in Jesus, to eat his flesh and drink his blood, means eating and drinking with lepers, tax collectors, centurions, and those once possessed by demons. It is not just sharing with the ancestors who ate manna in the wilderness. "This message is harsh. Who can hear it?" (v. 60). Jesus pushes his disciples to the margins of society, and not all can go. Can I say with Peter, "Lord, where would we go? You have the words of eternal life. We believe and know that you are God's holy one" (vv. 68-69)?

August 30, 2015
14th Sunday after Pentecost, Proper 17

Song of Songs 2:8-13; Psalm 45:1-2, 6-9; James 1:17-27; Mark 7:1-8, 14-15, 21-23; Deuteronomy 4:1-2, 6-9; Psalm 15

Ann Scull
http://seedstuff.blogspot.com

Just a Note
These resources, based on the Song of Songs, probably work best in the Southern Hemisphere where winter is ending—however, in of the world where there are no seasons or the seasons are in reverse, this still seems to be a time of the year where particular things (like holidays) are finishing and there are new beginnings so use the following resources either as analogies or adapt them to your particular situation. Have fun, anyway!

Listening Song
Evanescence, "Bring Me to Life" on *Fallen* (Hollywood: Epic, 2003) CD Edition.

Film Clip/Story
Either use the book: C. S. Lewis, *The Lion, the Witch and the Wardrobe* (London: HarperCollins, 1950) or the film *The Lion, the Witch and the Wardrobe* (2005) to illustrate how, under Aslan, winter gives way to spring. For example: "Wrong will be right, when Aslan comes in sight, / At the sound of his roar, sorrows will be no more."

Discussion Questions
What are examples of the winter times in our lives, in our churches, in our communities, in our world? How can we, with God, turn these winters into springs?

Response Activity
Give out a card: on one side, print the words from Song of Songs 2:10-11: "Rise up, my dearest, / my fairest, and go. / Here, the winter is past; / the rains have come and gone." On the other side, print a wintery image with room enough to write about the person's personal winter. See http://seedstuff.blogspot.com.au/2012_08_01_archive.html (accessed 27 April 2013) for a useful image. Give people time to write and then encourage them to staple a sprig of blossom over the top of their winter as a sign of God's promise to them.

Julia Seymour
http://lutheranjulia.blogspot.com

Song of Songs 2
The painful human tradition around Song of Songs is that it is an allegory about God and the church. We cannot seem to handle the truth of this book that exposes the depth of human love and human sexuality. Most of us have

absorbed and internalized negative ideas about bodies, about sex, and about our physical selves, and we are unable to separate those feelings from what we think about God. That's the devil's temptation with regard to our physical selves. If we can be made to believe that God is interested only in our souls, we will either ignore our bodies to their detriment or think that what we do with them doesn't matter.

If God didn't want us to have bodies, God wouldn't have given them to us. If our physical selves didn't matter, then God would not have sent the Son, *in the flesh*, so that we might know more fully God's love. Jesus wouldn't matter because we would have nothing to gain from knowing God's body was hungry, tired, or bruised. Furthermore, if God had no interest in our bodies, then we would be able to do God's work with our minds.

Song of Songs deserves our attention as the deep, erotic hymn to human love that it is. This hymn of hymns keeps us from ghettoizing our sexual selves, keeps our bodies at the forefront among our gifts from God, reminds us of women's voices in Scripture and in the world, and serves as resistor to temptations from the forces that oppose God.

John Wesley
http://www.ccel.org/ccel/wesley/notes

James 1:17
No evil, but every good gift—Whatever tends to holiness. And every perfect gift—Whatever tends to glory. Descendeth from the Father of lights—The appellation of Father is here used with peculiar propriety. It follows, "he begat us." He is the Father of all light, material or spiritual, in the kingdom of grace and of glory. With whom is no variableness—No change in his understanding. Or shadow of turning—in his will. He infallibly discerns all good and evil; and invariably loves one, and hates the other. There is, in both the Greek words, a metaphor taken from the stars, particularly proper where the Father of lights is mentioned. Both are applicable to any celestial body, which has a daily vicissitude of day and night, and sometimes longer days, sometimes longer nights. In God is nothing of this kind. He is mere light. If there Is any such vicissitude, it is in ourselves, not in him.

Mark 7:4
Washing of cups and pots and brazen vessels and couches—The Greek word (baptisms) means indifferently either washing or sprinkling. The cups, pots, and vessels were washed; the couches sprinkled.

Teri Peterson
http://clevertitlehere.blogspot.com

James 1
One of the difficulties with practicing generosity is that we really enjoy being appreciated. We want to be thanked, for people to notice that we have been generous. Too often, it becomes an opportunity to congratulate ourselves for our contributions.

But James says, "Every generous act of giving…is from above" (v. 17 NRSV). In other words, while we're applauding our latest big gift, we're missing the fact that it's *not we who* give, but *God* who gives through us. None of this wealth was ever really ours to begin with, because "the earth is the LORD's and all that is in it" (Psalm 24:1 NRSV). When we are generous, it's God at work in us—not something to applaud in ourselves, but rather yet another thing for which to be grateful.

This reality that we are not faithful under our own power, but God's, plays out further when we contemplate being "doers of the word, not merely hearers" (James 1:22 NRSV). Hearing without acting is a way of hindering God's work, keeping God from fulfilling God's plans. When we are doers of the word, we are conduits for God's grace on the move in the world, pathways of generous love. We do not "do" in order to be noticed or to earn the favor of God or neighbor, but rather to incarnate God's word yet again in a world that needs some good news.

John Petty

http://progressiveinvolvement.com

Mark 7

For the second time (see v. 3), the phrase, "the tradition of the elders" is used, this time by the Pharisees: "Why do your disciples not live according to the tradition of the elders, but eat with defiled hands?" (v. 5 NRSV).

Jesus responds to this question with an attack on the authority of the Pharisees and scribes. The Pharisees derived their authority from the "oral law." Where the Sadducees recognized the Torah as only the books of Moses, the Pharisees also included "oral law" within Torah, the pharisaic tradition of interpretation which, they claimed, was also given by God to Moses on Mount Sinai.

Jesus calls them "hypocrites." They "let go" the command of God and "hold fast" to human traditions (*ten paradosin ton anthropon*). In other words, they subvert true Torah with their "oral law," which Jesus dismisses as mere "human tradition."

Verses 9-13 are not part of this Sunday's lection. It is there, however, that Jesus makes his argument. In verse 10, Jesus draws an unfavorable comparison between the pharisaic tradition, or "oral law," and what "Moses said." In doing so, he seriously deflates and devalues their unique source of authority. Their vaunted "oral law," supposedly given to them (and them alone) by Moses, is really only "human tradition."

His critique accused the Pharisees of disobeying the fourth commandment—"honor your father and mother"—on the issue of *korban*. *Korban* was money or assets willed to the temple. The family could no longer use these assets, and one could not be released from a vow of korban even if one's parents were indigent.

Thus, the human tradition of korban involved breaking the commandment of God to honor one's parents. Their human tradition, korban, opposes Moses' law. They do not stand for Moses; Moses opposes them.

The scribes, paid by the temple, had an economic interest in korban, but the Pharisees did not. By lumping the two groups together on this issue, Jesus associates the Pharisees with the temple establishment in the public mind and uses that connection to undermine their credibility. This is a nice example of Jesus' political *jiu jitsu*.

Mary J. Scifres

All Good Gifts (James 1)

One of my favorite songs, "All Good Gifts," from the musical *Godspell*, is a paraphrase of James 1:17: "Every good gift, every perfect gift, comes from above." Songwriter Stephen Schwartz goes on to call us to gratitude, "so thank the Lord for all his love." But James actually calls us to *live* our gratitude. Responding to the wonderful gifts of our lives provides an opportunity to live into God's purpose by being "doers of the word, and not merely hearers" (v. 22a NRSV).

Jesus often loses patience with the scribes and Pharisees, primarily when they aren't living the Law that they want to preserve. We all run this risk when we try to hold onto the gifts we have been given or when we are quick to speak and slow to act. All of the good gifts we have been given are gifted to us to fulfill God's purpose in the world, to bring God's realm into being, to share God's love with the world.

Matthew L. Skinner

Mark 7

Although the conversation begins there, hand washing and diet are not this passage's primary concerns. Jesus' main point focuses on the source of defiling and destructive things: not from impurities entering the body but from within the body itself, emanating from "the human heart." In Jesus' day, the heart represented rationality and will. Unholiness comes from how we are wired to think and act.

To make his point, in verses 6b-7, Jesus refers to the Septuagint (Greek) version of Isaiah 29:13. He compares the "rules handed down by the elders" (v. 5) to "human words" (v. 7) that obscure God's "commandment[s]" (v. 8). Jesus does not reject the law of Moses. Rather, some interpretations of the law, he claims, have obscured the law's true purpose: to promote holiness and purity. What the lips do matters little if the heart is corrupt. This anatomy lesson continues in verse 14 and beyond; defilement does not slip in through the mouth, it contaminates us from the inside out.

Preachers should note how far Jesus' words extend. He criticizes more than opinions represented by a sampling of scribes and Pharisees. The words "human" and "person" appear repeatedly in these verses, indicting all humanity. Do not blame the devil or the most dastardly members of the human race for the wickedness that wrecks our lives. All of us play some part; our social, familial, and economic systems perpetuate our sinfulness. Sermons should acknowledge how evil roams throughout our collective existence, yet they must not veer into "blame the victim" territory.

Fortunately, the gospel's overall message promises deliverance from our heart's (and our neighbor's heart's) mischief. Allow this passage to announce its bad news about the human condition. Do not neglect to guide a congregation also toward discovering the renewal that God makes possible for all people.

September 6, 2015

15th Sunday after Pentecost, Proper 18

Proverbs 22:1-2, 8-9, 22-23; Psalm 125; James 2:1-10, (11-13), 14-17; Mark 7:24-37; Isaiah 35:4-7a; Psalm 146

Mark Stamm

Isaiah 35; Mark 7

Jesus didn't want anyone to notice him (Mark 7:24), but there wasn't much chance of that happening, was there? The great parade of those in need continued, and we're part of that procession. Given contemporary emphasis on inclusivity, we can admit that his insulting response to the Syrophoenician woman (i.e., "the dogs..." v. 27) shocks us. She didn't, of course, go away quietly. Given a first-century context, her impertinent response may have been even more shocking. It stands as model for our praying.

One way to receive this text is to join her in offering equally scandalous intercessions. Bowing with her, we could plead God's mercy for those on death row and those they have harmed, for prostitutes and those who use their services, for drug dealers and addicts. We could intercede for victims of domestic abuse and their abusers, for illegal immigrants and those who employ them, and so on. We will do well to remember the classic Prayer of Humble Access ("We are not worthy so much as to gather up the crumbs under thy table" *The Book of Common Prayer* [New York: Church Publishing, 1979], 337). Many unjustly view that prayer as too negative, and thus it is used sparingly in the contemporary church. Given today's gospel, it is worth using, especially if the Eucharist is celebrated.

Note that verse 37, "He does everything well! He even makes the deaf to hear," reflects the Isaiah 35 text, and is meant as evidence that the Messianic reign has appeared in Jesus. "Everything well" may intimidate us, especially given contemporary emphasis on excellence. Remember, however, that ours is not to create the reign of God by our cleverness and hard work, but rather to discern its presence and cooperate with it.

Lowell E. Grisham

http://lowellsblog.blogspot.com/

Prayers of the People

Presider: Ever-present and compassionate God, you care for all persons with your unqualified divine love, and you extend your liberating grace to all peoples: Open our hearts to be strong and fearless in the pursuit of justice and relief, especially on behalf of the poor and the stranger, as we pray: You care for near and far alike; liberate your children from their oppression.

Litanist: You have called your church to follow the royal law to love our neighbors as ourselves: Empower our witness of reconciliation that we may speak gracefully to those whose ears cannot yet hear the good news of God's love and serve generously those whose mouths cannot yet proclaim your grace. You care for near and far alike;

liberate your children from their oppression.

You guide the leaders of the nations to show mercy and to eschew partiality: Free from their bondage those whose lot is only the leftovers and crumbs, and empower those who struggle to live on what falls from their masters' tables. You care for near and far alike;

liberate your children from their oppression.

154

You have chosen the poor in the world to be rich in faith and heirs of the kingdom: Reconcile our community that we may be people of radical hospitality, welcoming native and foreigner, rich and poor, without distinction or partiality. You care for near and far alike;

liberate your children from their oppression.

You embrace with your compassion, O God, those whom some call dogs and others who are poor or dishonored: Heal and comfort all who are in weakness or in need throughout the world. You care for near and far alike;

liberate your children from their oppression.

You withhold your healing presence from no one: Honor our prayers for all who are in need, especially ___.
You call us to share in your work of reconciliation and freedom. We thank you for the many ministries of this
      congregation: our work of worship, outreach, education, service, and fellowship. Hear our joy as we give
      you thanks, especially for ___.
You keep your promise forever; hear our prayers for those who have died, especially ___. You care for near and far alike;

liberate your children from their oppression.

Presider: Gracious and living God, your loving care reaches to the ends of the earth, rescuing those who live in bondage and fear: Open our eyes and ears to your call of compassion, that we may joyfully share in your eternal life, and bring all humanity into the goodness of your Spirit, through Jesus Christ our Lord.

Amen.

Carolyn Winfrey Gillette

http://www.carolynshymns.com/

O Lord, May All We Say and Do (James 2)

TALLIS CANON LM ("All Praise to Thee, My God, This Night")

O Lord, may all we say and do
Reflect the faith we have in you;
For faith is meant to change the way
We live our lives from day to day.

Lord, keep us humble! Keep us free
From showing partiality;
And may we give the poor our bread,
For faith without good works is dead.

Just as a spark can start a fire,
Our words can damage or inspire;
We pray for wisdom from above
To speak and act in gentle love.

May we not covet earthly things
Or seek the riches this world brings;
May we not boast of all our plans,
For all our lives are in your hands.

O Lord, possessions rust away,
But people matter every day.

Through prayer and service in your name,
May we live out the faith we claim.

Biblical reference: James 1:25; 2:1, 15

Tune: Thomas Tallis, Adapt. Parker's *Whole Psalter*, c. 1561. Text: Carolyn Winfrey Gillette © 2012 The Center for Christian Ethics at Baylor University, Waco, Texas. Used with Permission. Email: bcgillette@comcast.net New Hymns: www.carolynshymns.com

John Wesley

http://www.ccel.org/ccel/wesley/notes

James 2:7

Do not they blaspheme that worthy name—Of God and of Christ. The apostle speaks chiefly of rich heathens: but are Christians, so called, a whit behind them?

Mark 7:33

He put his fingers into his ears—Perhaps intending to teach us, that we are not to prescribe to him (as they who brought this man attempted to do) but to expect his blessing by whatsoever means he pleases: even though there should be no proportion or resemblance between the means used, and the benefit to be conveyed thereby.

D. Mark Davis

http://leftbehindandlovingit.blogspot.com/

Mark 7

Mark's story has one of the most challenging verses one will ever read out of the mouth of Jesus, when he likens a woman to a dog. In many cultures, dogs are more pests than pets—scavengers lurking around the edges constantly looking for food, defecating, or procreating. It is a horrible thing to compare a person to a dog—much less a distraught mother, who has fallen down at one's feet begging mercy for her little child. Certainly, one can point out that the woman's daughter is eventually healed. One can show that Mark is using this challenge by Jesus as a way for the woman to parry the remark and say something wonderful, to which Jesus relents. One can contextualize the comment within whatever prejudices and real enmity were at play in the first century between Jews and their Gentile neighbors to the north. One can say "All's well that ends well." But, it is still a horrible thing for Jesus to call a person a dog. One must start with that.

When we recoil at Jesus' words, two things happen. First, we challenge the easy assumption that Jesus was always perfect, in lieu of an appreciation of how the Synoptic Gospels speak of Jesus more dynamically—growing in wisdom while growing in stature, hungering and thirsting, getting weary or frustrated. This text provides a place where Jesus outgrows prejudices that were part of his social fabric. Second, the woman of this story reveals how suffering can produce a kind of defiant faith. Defiant faith cries out in horror at the suffering of others. Defiant faith is undeterred by restrictive social constructs and demands a loving God to respond to suffering. Jesus grows into that kind of love in this story.

Peter Woods

Mark 7

I am surprised when people get angry at me for suggesting that Jesus learned as well as taught during his ministry. There is a common misconception that Jesus dropped fully enlightened and educated into the manger at Bethlehem. I don't think so, and it isn't helpful for our understanding of Jesus to think this.

The life of Jesus makes the most sense as incarnation when we allow the humanity of the savior to shine through. I remind myself that Jesus was crucified, not for being too holy but for being too human. His companionships and engagements with the marginalized are what scandalized him in the eyes of the religious establishment.

Seeing Jesus converted in his programmed cultural bias against Syrophoenicians by a desperate woman tells me more about the nature of God than any puritanical sermon.

In the epistle, James pleads with his hearers to show their faith in acts of kindness (2:14-17). This appeal is a continuation of what Jesus did both with the Syrophoenician woman and then later in the Decapolis with the deaf man who had a speech impediment.

Every encounter that Jesus had with suffering shaped him and the sufferer, and a synergy of healing and salvation was the result.

Isn't it interesting that Jesus' appeal of "Open up" (Mark 7:34) follows directly after he has been challenged to be open to the needs of the desperate Syrophoenician?

It is also not clear to whom Jesus directed the prayer of "*Ephphatha*." Was he addressing the man's deaf ears or was he, looking at heaven, sharing with his parent in the divine domain his realization that heaven's gates are wider than even he had imagined?

No one will be excluded if we also can be opened by the words and touch of Jesus.

September 13, 2015

16th Sunday after Pentecost, Proper 19

Proverbs 1:20-33; Psalm 19 or Wisdom of Solomon 7:26–8:1; James 3:1-12; Mark 8:27-38; Isaiah 50:4-9a; Psalm 116:1-9

Thom M. Shuman

http://lectionaryliturgies.blogspot.com/

Call to Worship

We are not our own:

so, neither our will nor our wisdom should get in the way of God's hopes for us.

We are not on our own:

so, we should not choose what is easiest or the most gratifying way to live.

We are not our own, we are God's:

so, let us choose to live for God and serve all of God's children.

We are not on our own, as we walk the streets of God's kingdom:

so, as far as is possible, we will forget ourselves and follow Jesus Christ.

Prayer of the Day

All around us, O God,
creation preaches a silent sermon
about your glory.
The full, orange moon
declares your constant watchfulness;
the early morning mist over a schoolyard
speaks of your steadfast love;
the cool breeze through slowly changing leaves
whispers of your grace.

Holy Jesus,
you ask questions
that turn us speechless;
you tell us things about yourself
we imagine we need to correct;
you offer us a way of life
we dare not refuse.

Spirit of Wisdom,
you stand in the midst
of rush hour traffic
crying out to us
about our fascination with foolishness

158

and stretch out your hand
to point to the One
who walks towards us
offering a cross.

God in Community, Holy in One,
in this time together,
may we hear you in the silence
and the songs,
and discover you in the people around us,
even as we pray as Jesus teaches us, saying,
Our Father...

John Wesley
http://www.ccel.org/ccel/wesley/notes

James 3:1

Be not many teachers—Let no more of you take this upon you than God thrusts out; seeing it is so hard not to offend in speaking much. Knowing that we—That all who thrust themselves into the office. Shall receive greater condemnation—For more offenses. St. James here, as in several of the following verses, by a common figure of speech, includes himself: we shall receive,—we offend,—we put bits,—we curse—None of which, as common sense shows, are to be interpreted either of him or of the other apostles.

Mark 8:34

And take up his cross—Embrace the will of God, however painful, daily, hourly, continually. Thus only can he follow me in holiness to glory.

Julie Craig
http://winsomelearnsome.com

James 3

Perhaps you, like me, hung onto every positive, affirming word from a beloved teacher's lips and carried them around like precious treasure. Perhaps you, like me, found the smallest criticism or rebuke from that teacher to cut like a well-sharpened knife.

My earliest memory of the powers of my own speech to hurt someone else involved a teacher, in fact. I was seven years old, and I dreaded show and tell. Showing was one thing. Telling was torture. I don't know why I chose a magic trick, but I did. I can't even remember the trick. What I do remember, however, is that as soon as I finished, another little girl, named Linda, told the class the secret of the trick. All I can remember is my blind rage. At recess, I marched up to her, and said the most scathing, awful thing I could imagine saying. I blurted out, "I hate you." She looked at me and said "Okay." I'd flung the most awful, nasty thing I could possibly fling; I'd spent my whole arsenal of animosity on that one moment with Linda. And she'd simply taken it and walked away.

Linda walked straight to my beloved teacher and ratted me out. And as soon as she did, I saw the full impact fall, right on Mrs. S.'s face. And I knew that I had changed in her eyes. Maybe not forever, but changed, for sure. The person who I counted on to see how smart I was, how good I was, how special I was, knew what I really was: an ordinary, common, little trashy-mouthed girl.

I wish I'd known this passage then.

Paul Bellan-Boyer

Taming the Untamable (James 3)

James is one of the more difficult letters to read, if for no other reason than its focus on what followers of Jesus ought to be practicing. It's one thing to confess that Jesus is Lord. It's another to love your neighbor, and carry that love through in everything we do. *And say.*

To speak in a way that always shows forth God's love seems beyond us. Daily we confront our anger, envy, and fears, expressed through our words and deeds. Keeping your mouth shut hardly helps. God sees what is going on in our hearts, which is every bit as troublesome as what comes out of us (see Matthew 5:21-22).

We might think this is hopeless. These words judge us, and we are very wanting. We are in a hole deeper than we can climb out of. We need a word of grace, and James has one: "All of us make many mistakes" (v. 2 NRSV). Yes, this is grace. *All of us*... make *many*... mistakes. None of us can feel too superior on this point.

God knows this. God knows the evil to which we succumb. God knows our faults and those of our neighbors, and God loves us. With God, love precedes judgment, and love endures *through judgment*.

Love and care for another is its own reward. But it has a practical benefit in community. Is there anything else that can tame our tongues and our other members? James knows that, left to our own devices, we careen from blessing to curse. Without love, we are subject to the prevailing winds of our desires. James knew a better guide, the Holy Spirit, God's gift to the Church and its people. It is God's Spirit, living in us, which is our only bridle (James 4:5-10).

Julia Seymour

http://lutheranjulia.blogspot.com

James 3

Many people have difficulty keeping a conversation positive, even (especially) in the church. Complaining is so much easier and sometimes seems more fun. We know that we should not share that "little story" or what we overheard or speculate beyond the facts we have. Yet, when we're in the middle of it, stopping ourselves can seem rude or prudish. It's what we have to do, however.

We know that words hurt more than most sticks and stones. We remember words long beyond when a bruise would have healed. And many of us hold onto hurtful words far longer than we do compliments, which we hesitate to accept.

Church should be a place where words do not hurt, where we use phrases to build up and to heal. Our tongues should be instruments of peace, joy, and reconciliation, not tools of destruction and discord. Words travel quickly in a community. We must all work together and pray for one another to be sure that our words are part of the work God is doing here. If they are not part of community building, then they are joining with the forces that oppose God. We are called to renounce those forces and their activities!

Let us resolve to speak well of one another, to refrain from complaining, and to use our words to build and support one another. Let us also work on accepting compliments and hearing good things about ourselves. Let our lives be practice and proof of the way we are called to love one another through Christ.

Chuck Aaron

Mark 8

The Mark passage raises a question with which the church, and each individual Christian, must contend. Jesus confronts the disciples with the question of his identity. In the case of the disciples, they had traveled with Jesus, had seen his healings, and heard his teachings. Does the narrative suggest that despite these experiences, only Peter had drawn the correct conclusion? Only he speaks up in the narrative.

The contemporary church continues to seek a proper understanding of Jesus' identity. How well does the title "Christ" or "Messiah," the anointed one, work for contemporary Christians? The ancient title draws on the role of the king of Israel, and the restoration of the Davidic monarchy. These do not represent burning issues for the modern church. Without losing the tradition of Jesus as the Christ, the church can offer help to people to find ways to identify Jesus. As the Messiah, Jesus comes as one who heals, liberates, and challenges. A proper understanding of Jesus includes his confrontation of evil in the world. Jesus enables the church to recognize appropriate uses of power. This passage speaks to the importance of continuing theological reflection for the church. The church faces the temptation to receive the healing and the grace of God without doing the hard intellectual work of theology.

The passage also calls the church to risk and sacrifice. God does not call the church to glorify suffering for its own sake, to devalue itself. Mark recognizes the power of the demonic forces. Whether one understands that language metaphorically or more concretely, no one can deny the strength and intractability of evil. The risk and sacrifice to which this passage calls the church results from confronting that strong, tenacious evil.

Todd Weir

http://bloomingcactus.typepad.com/

Mark 8

"Who do you say that I am?" How might I go about answering this question? I have empathy for Peter, for I can be quick with the correct theological answer, but stubbornly slow at realizing the implications. Some questions require more of us than the correct answer; they require a reassessment and rearranging of our lives. I wish the Christian faith could be an intellectual journey; then I could comfortably do my research and write about who Jesus is. I could even put together a list of important moral imperatives and ethical implications of Christ's life. I wish the Christian faith could be an assurance of happiness and success. I like the clarity of the Protestant work ethic—I am one of the chosen and financial security is a sign of God's blessing—which allows me to believe in a cozy home. I wish this journey was therapeutic, so I could talk to a wise counselor who would help me resolve all my issues, and, with some daily yoga and meditation, I would be happy and at peace.

But there is more to answering Jesus than any of these paths. Jesus chose to enter into the fullness of human life, including the immense suffering, agony, and travails of tears. He answered these great trials with his life. I do not mean merely that he died on the cross. Jesus was in agony and filled with compassion for the suffering long before the reality of the cross. Jesus was with the lepers, the hungry, the demon possessed, the widows, orphans, and adulterers long before the cross.

Anyone who has walked among the suffering knows this kind of agony. More sympathies are with Peter's astonishment, but my heart tells me Jesus calls us to move with love toward suffering.

September 20, 2015
17th Sunday after Pentecost, Proper 20

Proverbs 31:10-31; Psalm 1; James 3:13–4:3, 7-8a; Mark 9:30-37; Wisdom of Solmon 1:16–2:1, 12-22 or Jeremiah 11:18-20; Psalm 54

Marci Auld Glass

http://www.marciglass.com

Proverbs 31; James 3–4

I don't like this woman. There. I've said it. She's *that* person. *You know who she is.*

She gets up at 5:00 a.m. each morning for Pilates class and then makes her children chocolate chip waffles for breakfast before she drives them to school in her hybrid SUV with the "My child is an honor roll student at Jericho Elementary School" sticker on it.

Then, in her purple linen outfit that is always pressed, she volunteers in the classroom before she heads to work. She volunteers each week at the homeless shelter. Her house is always clean. Her yard is perfectly manicured. Her roses do not have fungus.

She knits blankets for kids at the children's hospital. The kids in the neighborhood hang out at her house because her kids are cool and have all the right toys and video games. They are polite. Their shirts are tucked in. She cooks a balanced meal each night, which the family eats together before she heads out to her community board meetings.

I don't like her. Do you know why? Because I am not her.

My linen looks wrinkled the moment I put it on. I exercise under duress and only because I know it is good for me. And the "bread of idleness"? It is one of my favorite foods. I do try my best to provide for my family, but sometimes we eat cereal for dinner. She may open her mouth with wisdom, but I often open my mouth with complaints or whining.

I don't like her because I am afraid. Afraid I can't measure up. Afraid people will find out I'm a fraud.

And so, without knowing this woman at all, I dismiss her. I keep her at arm's length, hoping that nobody will notice how much I am not like her.

Excerpt from http://marciglass.com/2012/09/23/laughing-at-the-time-to-come/

John Wesley

http://www.ccel.org/ccel/wesley/notes

James 4:8

Then draw nigh to God in prayer, and he will draw nigh unto you, will hear you; which that nothing may hinder, cleanse your hands—Cease from doing evil. And purify your hearts—From all spiritual adultery. Be no more double minded, vainly endeavoring to serve both God and mammon.

Mark 9:37

One such little child—Either in years or in heart.

Eric D. Barreto

Mark 9

We almost can't help it, can we? When given the opportunity to revel in God's goodness, we still yearn for status and standing. We seek ways to improve our lot at the expense of others, to find a way to cut in line, to be recognized for how great we really are. We can't help it and neither could the disciples.

In Mark, the disciples jockey for position in Jesus' heavenly kingdom, entirely missing that the reign of Jesus does not follow the logics of our political systems. Condemning them even further is the wider context of their disputations. Jesus has just told them that his reign will begin, not with victory or acclamation, but with the pain and shame of death on a cross. The disciples, however, don't understand Jesus. How could they? How can anyone defeat the forces of death and be raised again? Who can resist the rules of a world that too often drives us toward destruction? In the midst of their confusion and fear, the disciples resort to an apostolic ranking system as useful as preseason sports predictions.

"Do you want to be great?" Jesus asks. Then be like this child. Here, ancient ideas of childhood must be at the forefront of our interpretation. Jesus' message is not saccharine. He is not pointing to a child's presumed innocence or even how sweet a precious child can be. In the ancient world, children were a gift but also a burden. They needed to be fed but could scarcely work for their sustenance. Widows and children together represent those most exposed and susceptible to the vicissitudes of ancient life. Do you want to be great? Then be a like child. Be vulnerable. Be a burden. Be on the margins of this world.

Sharron Blezard

Mark 9

Children have a lot to teach us about living, and if you do not find a way to involve youngsters in the worship of your congregation, you are missing a great opportunity. Sure, it takes some risk, a healthy dose of flexibility, and a good sense of humor to work with children, but the abundant rewards and blessings of doing so make it all worthwhile. In fact, we know that Jesus had a special place for children in his ministry.

In today's Gospel lesson from Mark, the disciples are initially clueless about what Jesus is up to and trying to teach them. Worse yet, they are too cowardly to ask him about it. Whether they are afraid of looking stupid or just letting hubris get in the way, they become sidetracked, fussing and fretting about who is top disciple. So Jesus sits them down and explains once again the upside-down and inside-out ways of the reign of God. Power is found in weakness—in being last, in taking less, and in welcoming the most marginalized and powerless.

Children may not have much power and control, but they know how to live in the present moment. They know how to wonder at the marvels of the universe and revel in the delights of creation. They bring honesty and authenticity to the table, too. Jesus is making an important point about how the body of Christ looks, acts, and lives. When we welcome all people without judgment, truly we welcome Jesus into our midst. Pay attention to the children in your context; they are both the future and present church. In them, we find glimmers of God we might otherwise overlook.

Suzanne Guthrie

http://www.edgeofenclosure.org

Mark 9

No doubt a gaggle of children hung around the grandmas, aunties, and mothers supporting Jesus out of their own means (Luke 8:1-3). But the children hold little interest to the Gospel writers except here.

163

Did Jesus play and joke with the children? Did he listen to their dreams and nightmares early in the morning? Did he commiserate with the injustices and frustrations of childhood, and, particularly, life on the road? Did he allow himself to see through their eyes? Did he tell them special stories? Did he allow them to climb into his lap at naptime to fall asleep? Did he slyly reverse the power dynamics over children with a word here, a wink there, a protective or loving gesture? I'd like to think so.

"Whoever welcomes one of these children in my name welcomes me; and whoever welcomes me isn't actually welcoming me but rather the one who sent me" (v. 37).

Perhaps I am one of those children in the chaotic community of travelers. Perhaps Jesus places his hand upon my head, blessing me. But I'm distracted by some movement in the crowd, another child's misbehavior or clowning. Or I'm absorbed in my own daydreaming, usually of more interest than what's happening around me. I'm hungry or sleepy or I've lost track of my mother, away buying bread or washing a sibling's swaddling clothes or helping to pack up camp as we set out for another destination.

Who can blame me for my distraction? The Holy One reaches to me from behind time from the eternal present. How can I possibly know how deeply I am blessed?

Teri Peterson

http://clevertitlehere.blogspot.com

Mark 9

There are some requirements for every youth group lock-in. Snacks. Movie. And "Sardines": a version of hide-and-seek played in the dark. One person hides and everyone looks for them—but when you find the person you hide *with* them, until everyone is together in the same place. You see why it's called Sardines.

One of the key strategies of Sardines is silence. Anyone who's spent the night with sugared-up teenagers knows this strategy is not high on the priority list. So a game of Sardines usually involves lots of running, shrieking, laughing. But eventually the noise level goes down, down, down, until there's just one person left looking for everyone crammed into a closet or under a table.

The growing silence is eerie, a sign you've been looking in all the wrong places.

I wonder if the disciples, or maybe even Jesus, felt that distress in the silence that followed his question, "What were you arguing about during the journey?" (v. 33).

As we walk along, what occupies our thinking and speaking? If we're honest, we're not so different from the disciples. Who is greatest? We humans, especially in our culture, tend to be easily seduced by the ever-addictive success.

Did you notice the story has two silences? The second is most obvious—the embarrassed silence. But first came the confused silence at verse 32. Jesus was teaching and they didn't understand, but were afraid to ask. At the moment the disciples could have directly asked Jesus to say more about his way, they stayed silent.

That fearful, confused moment of silence led directly to the embarrassed moment later on, because they didn't take the opportunity to learn, listen, focus—instead they ended up on their own way, looking in the wrong place, arguing over things that don't matter to the kingdom of God.

John van de Laar

http://www.sacredise.com/

Mark 9

As the threat against Jesus grew, the disciples debated their relative greatness. They may not have understood Jesus' predictions of his death, but they must have sensed that all was not well. Their response was to seek a position of power by which they could fend off any threats and possibly call on God's might as a weapon should they need it. The temptation to use power as a way to security is a universal human condition.

But Jesus denied them this comfort. God's reign, he taught, is not a doorway to power, but a way in which the greatest lay aside their power in service of others. It is a way in which those who seek God's life share it by welcoming those with no status and no way to repay the kindness. Such hospitality must have seemed like insanity to the disciples—the worst defense. But Jesus had no interest in defending himself. He was concerned with ending cycles of violence and with overcoming the strangeness of the "other" through relationship and sharing. What Jesus' words and life proclaim is that our need to defend ourselves only makes the world less safe and more violent. If we really desire a world of peace and love, we must deny our quest for power and security. We must learn to open the doors of our homes and hearts to welcome and serve others, even when it hurts.

We need to know that our hospitality will probably be abused. We will get hurt in the process, and we will face many situations in which we will be tempted to abandon our welcoming attitude. But no amount of power or self-preservation will bring the healing that we seek. Only the life-giving hospitality of Jesus can do that.

For more detail: http://sacredise.com/blog/?p=1190

Editor's Insights

Two Kinds of People? (Psalm 1)

There are thousands of Facebook and Twitter memes that begin: "There are two kinds of people...." Psalm 1 can seem like one of those. There's the righteous, good person and there is the wicked, bad person. We all know these types. We all know which side we're on.

But not so fast. As with any such statement, there is more to the story. First, there are more than two kinds of people. Second, what is supposed to be the reward of the good and the punishment of the bad is not always the case. Third, we're usually not on the side we think we are on.

"Memes" such as this seem to me to be like any dialectic. It's true and it's not true. It's false and it's not false. It's me and it's not me. And somewhere in exploring the most significant of these kinds of statements is a truth. It's not found by reading the statement and going on knowing I/we belong to the right community. It's found by meditating on how we (as individuals and communities) are and are not on the "right" side of the equation, and how, while completely true, the issue is larger than that.

At the same time, there's something to be said for keeping it this simple. What if, today, I made a commitment, a decision, to put myself on the side of this I always thought (and told others, implicitly and explicitly) I was on. How might my life, how might our communities and our world, be different?

September 27, 2015

18th Sunday after Pentecost, Proper 21

Esther 7:1-6, 9-10; 9:20-22; Psalm 124; James 5:13-20; Mark 9:38-50; Numbers 11:4-6, 10-16, 24-29; Psalm 19:7-14

Cameron Howard

Esther 7; 9

Esther is difficult to study or preach on in lectionary-sized passages, since the book is one long, compelling narrative. Most sermons will need to present a synopsis of the storyline in order to orient listeners to the unfolding plot. Even so, the omission of verses 7-8 from the Esther 7 selections offers a particularly difficult problem for this week's presentation of the story. Without these verses, a reader might get the impression that it is either Esther's rhetorical savvy or the king's own sense of righteousness that leads Ahasuerus to execute Haman and thus begin the process of saving the Jews of Susa from annihilation. No, what drives the king out of his angry huff and into action is actually his inability to read the situation in front him. When King Ahasuerus returns from the garden, he sees Haman prostrate on the queen's couch, begging her for his life. Yet the king thinks he sees Haman assaulting Esther, and this misinterpretation compels him to order Haman's hanging.

Verses 7-8 are important because they underscore the farcical nature of the book. Esther lampoons the authority of the Persian Empire and particularly the character of the king, who cannot make a decision without his advisers, who has palace records read to him to combat his insomnia, and who cannot tell when a man is begging a woman for mercy rather than trying to take advantage of her. The character Esther is certainly courageous, and her actions are indeed instrumental in saving her people. At the same time, the book of Esther also testifies powerfully to the futility of earthly kingdoms and rulers. Through its comic portrayal of the king, this story bears witness to the ultimate triumph of God's kingship.

Linda Lee

True to Destiny (Esther 7; 9)

There are times, along this human journey, when the most important thing we can do is be true to our divine destiny. Often, like Ester, that destiny is not that something we have sought for or desired. And just as often, God's plans for us require much more than we thought we had to give. Yet God's grace makes it possible for us to be available at just the right time to accomplish God's purposes.

Sometimes we may consider ourselves handicapped by age (too young or too old), or gender or race or physical or mental condition. Our internal battles can distract us as well from the path God has set before us. But every gift makes room for itself when the bearer of it is willing and ready to give it away. Consider Esther, comfortable in her role and position as queen. She probably never anticipated that things would change the way they did. And certainly not that she would be the instrument of a historical intervention of God. Yet, when God called, she answered, even though it could have meant losing everything she had—even her life. There was a cause bigger than her personal life. This cause was for justice because of the love she possessed for her people. God did not require she give up her life, but she did have to give of herself.

As Christians in the twenty-first century, our task is to stay open to God's call. However daunting the task may appear to us before we begin, we know by faith that it is God who gives us strength and power. Because Jesus was true to his divine destiny, we have both life and hope. The spirit of Christ within empowers us to fulfill our destinies in just such times as these.

Natalie Ann Sims

http://lectionarysong.blogspot.com

Psalm 124 (Strength in the Face of Oppression)

- "We Shall Overcome" (Unknown)—Particularly good if your congregation is facing struggle. Other songs from the civil rights era would also fit well with this psalm. Here's Martin Luther King, Jr. talking about the power of this song: http://www.youtube.com/watch?v=130J-FdZDtY.

- "Guide My Feet while I Run This Race" (African American Spiritual)—An excellent civil rights song. Would work as a meditative prayer for guidance or as an uplifting call to action at the end of the service. Good for kids. (lyrics and clunky sound sample: http://www.hymnsite.com/fws/hymn.cgi?2208)

- "Goodness Is Stronger than Evil" (Desmond Tutu)—"Victory is ours, victory is ours, through him who loves us." Some congregations change "victory" to "compassion," but *victory* isn't necessarily militaristic. Good for kids. (sound sample: http://www.giamusic.com/mp3s/5671.mp3)

- "Our Help Is in the Name of God" (Jane Marshall)—Simple refrain and good paraphrase of the psalm for a cantor, a chant, or to be read with a response.

- "Now Israel May Say and That in Truth" (Scottish Psalter)—This paraphrase is very beautiful, and the language reads well even though it is so old. It may be best if your musicians can sing it to the congregation as a prayer. The tune is not difficult if you would like to use it for the whole congregation. The words are not entirely inclusive, but very close, although this depends on the source.

- "The Snare Is Broken" (Isaac Everett)—A simple psalm refrain with improvised music during the reading.

- "Blessed Be God" (Linnea Good)—This will need to be taught, but won't be too hard. Get one part of the congregation on the chant part ("God before Me") while the others sing the top part, and then add in other parts as you are able.

Liz Crumlish

http://somethingtostandon.blogspot.co.uk/

Numbers 11

In a former parish, my early morning walk took me through a beautiful glen alongside a tumbling brook. I loved the sights and sounds and smells of early morning in that place all through the seasons—except for a brief time toward the end of summer. Because then the wild garlic would be prolific and at its most pungent—not the most welcome accompaniment at the start of the day.

Fragrances can evoke so many memories—of places and people and different times in our lives. Reading of the Israelites craving garlic among all those other evocative foods, transports me back to Daff Glen.

The story of the sharing of the Spirit with the elders (vv. 24-29) also takes me back to that parish where I learned so much about the inimitable Spirit of God that:

- is whimsical, that cannot be contained

- rarely can be predicted but, instead, turns up in the most unlikely places

- contains elements of joy and is rarely evident in those who persistently grumble

- always shows up just when we feel we've gotten to the end of our tether with no reserves left

- takes pleasure in confounding wisdom

- is meant to be shared and cannot be possessed by any one group or body

- stimulates and infuriates

God shares that Spirit with ordinary people so that we can meander the glens and brooks of God's world, aware of the sights and sounds and smells that alert our senses to the presence of God in today's world.

Two Bubbas and a Bible

http://lectionarylab.com

Number 11; James 5; Mark 9

Healing and a return to *shalom*, or wholeness, is a theme in all our texts. In Numbers, there is community dysfunction, a societal rift. The children of Israel turn on their leader, Moses; and Moses in turn shifts the blame to God. God responds quite cleverly (if you can call God clever). The bestowal of the Spirit on the Seventy is a democratization of leadership. Early on, Israel moved away from an authoritarian, Spirit-filled leader model to a "Spirit-dispersed-on-the-people" model of leadership. The Eldad and Medad episode takes the point further by showing that God can work outside the established lines. God's healing power knows no bounds.

James is about both physical healing and spiritual healing, and ultimately about the need for the community to take care of one another. While many may stress the charismatic gift of healing (which I have witnessed and do not deny), it is more important to think about how this passage deals with community cohesion and compassion. This is especially evident in the language about the reconciliation of sinners.

In the Gospel passage, Jesus launches into the plucking and gouging stuff, which, frankly, grosses me out. This is hyperbole, exaggeration for the sake of emphasis. It is a call to the disciples and to us to take following Jesus seriously, to commit ourselves wholly to holy cross bearing.

The important question is not, "What did Jesus mean by this extreme imagery?" Rather, each of us must ask, "What do I need to cut out of my life that keeps me from being complete, the whole person God made and means me to be?"

John Wesley

http://www.ccel.org/ccel/wesley/notes

James 5:14

Having anointed him with oil—This single conspicuous gift, which Christ committed to his apostles, Mark vi, 13, remained in the church long after the other miraculous gifts were withdrawn. Indeed, it seems to have been designed to remain always; and St. James directs the elders, who were the most, if not the only, gifted men, to administer it. This was the whole process of physic in the Christian church, till it was lost through unbelief. That novel invention among the Romanists, extreme unction, practiced not for cure, but where life is despaired of, bears no manner of resemblance to this.

Mark 9:38

And John answered him—As if he had said, But ought we to receive those who follow not us? Master, we saw one casting out devils in thy name—Probably this was one of John the Baptist's disciples, who believed in Jesus, though he did not yet associate with our Lord's disciples. And we forbad him, because he followeth not us—How often is the same temper found in us? How readily do we also lust to envy? But how does that spirit become a disciple, much more a minister of the benevolent Jesus! St. Paul had learnt a better temper, when he rejoiced that Christ was preached, even by those who were his personal enemies. But to confine religion to them that follow us, is a narrowness of spirit which we should avoid and abhor.

Ann Scull

http://seedstuff.blogspot.com

Listening Song

Newsboys, "Shine" on *Shine: The Hits* (Compilation remix, Sparrow Records, USA, 2000) CD Edition. This song goes well with the Gospel reading.

Film Clips

Legally Blonde (2001): Watch the scene where Californian girl Elle Woods arrives at Harvard. She clearly doesn't fit the perceived picture of a Harvard Law student—and she suffers for it!

Thunderpants (2002): Watch the clip where Alan tells Patrick that he could not possibly ever be a spaceman. This clip has the same idea as *Legally Blonde* but is aimed at primary school–aged children.

Discussion: Ask, "What is going on in the film clip (whichever you used)?" Read Mark 9:38-50, repeating verses 38-42. Ask, "What is going on with the disciples in this reading?"

Ask people to compare the two situations. When do you think we act like the disciples or the Harvard students or Alan? According to the disciples, why doesn't the man casting out demons belong?

Put yourself in the shoes of the disciples; how would you feel? What makes us critical of others?

Would the man, or those witnessing what happened, feel that they could join the community of disciples after what the disciples had just said? How does our church today send similar messages to those who might wish to join us?

Response Activity: Give each person a picture of a key on a business card. Encourage them to use the cards as a reminder that God opens up all kinds of possibilities for us to see potential in others. Or, give everyone a piece of self-hardening clay and ask them to make a small goblet as a reminder of Mark 9:41 (project the verse while people are working).

October 4, 2015

19th Sunday after Pentecost, Proper 22

Job 1:1; 2:1-10; Psalm 26; Hebrews 1:1-4; 2:5-12; Mark 10:2-16; Genesis 2:18-24; Psalm 8

Safiyah Fosua

Job 1; 2

Job's suffering has moved to the status of metaphor for most people even remotely acquainted with the Bible. Few dare to take his suffering seriously; it is much easier to regard his story as an exaggeration, like "seventy times seven." Only those who endure unfathomable suffering dare take the story at face value. For us, these words jump off the page: "for no reason" (2:3). Various translations render the phrase "without cause" (KJV) or "without any reason" (NIV), while Peterson's *The Message* avoids the phrase altogether. Job went through a trial that did not even make sense to God! The seemingly unavoidable trap of those who suffer greatly is to look for some reason for their calamity. We prefer to cast our world in cause and effect because surely, if there is a cause, it would be possible to avoid most suffering, wouldn't it? But this disturbing phrase—"for no reason," introduced in 1:9 as "for nothing" and repeated in 2:3—is upsetting for a culture that plans the details of individual life. The phrase implies that there may be times when we cannot avoid the unthinkable. And when the unthinkable happens, there is no one to blame, not ourselves, not our neighbors, not even God!

So where is the good news in this sad story of a man unwittingly caught up in a contest between God and Satan? What good news could possibly exist in the story of a bewildered man and his equally bewildered wife who lose family, status, and health? (Remember that Job's wife also lost her children, a comfortable way of life, and may have feared that she was also about to lose her husband.) The gospel in the story is that Job eventually came to understand that some things happen without cause, that God is beyond blame.

Julie Craig

http://winsomelearnsome.com

Job 1; 2

Job's wife, horrified though she might have been about her husband's appearance, does not expect Job to just put up with his condition and live out a miserable existence. She advises Job to give up entirely and die a miserable death. Job's integrity is the fulcrum on which this passage balances. In his wife's eyes, if Job's integrity is based on conformity to religious norms and customs, if his piety—inward and outward—is at the center of his being, he must bless God, put up with this affliction, and commit an act of deceit regarding his culpability. If, however, Job's integrity is built on honesty, he must curse God and violate social integrity.

Job's reply violates not only the wife's dichotomy of choices, but says more about Job than anything we have learned about him so far. Hear this again, "Will we receive good from God but not also receive bad?" (2:10).

For most of us, receiving the good from God is pretty easy most of the time. In fact, it is so easy, we often go through our lives thinking that the good life is our default setting, if you will. Let's talk about the other side of the spectrum. What about those for whom suffering is the default setting? We probably all know someone like this, someone

170

who—despite their best efforts, despite trying to live as good a life as possible—cannot catch a break. This kind of life is a vortex you can get stuck in, where the same tragedies happen repeatedly. First the donkeys, then the sheep, then the camels…until it's all pretty much gone. How are we able to accept some good when all we have is bad?

Dan R. Dick

Job 1; 2

Job is an incredibly important book for the church today. This ancient allegory answers the question "Why do bad things happen to good people?" though in a way that displeases many. The personification of Satan and God in a tug-of-war with Job as the rope may seem to indicate direct involvement on behalf of the spiritual powers and principalities, but the messages contained within offer a different message. The concern many raise is this: If our God is good and loving, why is there so much evil and pain in the world? The answer from Job is simple: If there is good, there will be bad. We cannot expect only to have good things in our lives. No one is exempt. Faith is not a free pass that rewards believers. Faith is a transformative power that allows us to navigate evil and pain in a new and different way. Belief in God does not raise us above the natural order; it simply means that the natural order has less power over our attitudes, beliefs, and behaviors. In faith, we gain better and stronger coping skills. When tragedy strikes, the bad has less power and influence to push us to hopelessness and despair. God doesn't take the problem away. God gives us everything we need to cope with the problem. And when we stand strong in the face of adversity and loss, we become a powerful witness to the power of God to turn calamity into celebration. Life is no longer a burden to bear but a blessing to share. We do not merely endure. We thrive. In enduring and rising above the hurt and hardship, we grow and become more like Christ—the one who suffered and lost it all that we might ultimately win.

Editor's Insights

Listening for God (Job 1)

I have to confess that I have a great love of dark comedy. The book of Job strikes me as Wisdom, indeed. The absurdity of the chess game between God and Satan, which picks up Job because he happens to be righteous, is close to my heart. Which one of us has not been there? Which one of us has not been Job, almost comically thrown around like a chess piece? Which one of us has not pondered and been misunderstood in the midst of our worst pain and crisis of faith and conscience?

Maybe even more, I think about the contemporary church in connection with this passage. As it goes about its business, being righteous and doing the will of God, the church has been swept up in an upheaval that almost seems, well, like a chess game between God and Satan. And whose side are we on? And how do we weather being seeming pawns in a game between cultural influences much greater than ourselves, when all we want to do is preach the gospel?

I love the ending of Job. I like the part about getting new cows and kids, because certainly we do, all the time! But I like God speaking to Job out of the whirlwind, in great authority and majesty. Heavily paraphrased: "Who do you think you are, church, that *you* have everything figured out about how I will and must work in the world? I was modeling and writing, living and pouring Myself out long before you came on the scene! How dare you talk and not listen! How *dare* you feel sorry for yourself!"

Listening is tough. But, to me, the story of Job is about learning to listen—to really listen to the Voice of God *today*, as the whirlwind moves around us, seeming to destroy everything in its path. The contemporary church is *Job* in some ways, I think. How do we have faith and faithfulness within the reality of the whirlwind?

Martha Spong
http://marthaspong.com/

Job 1; 2

It starts with little red bumps on my forearms, just above the wrists. At first, they are so faint they seem to be beneath the skin. Untreated, they rise above the surface and become dry, red patches.

All my life, I've had eczema. At its worst, in a flare, it spreads all over the place. The last time it was that bad, I found myself quite unconsciously rubbing my shoulder blades up and down a doorjamb.

It felt awful enough that I thought of Job and his potsherds. The terrible itch came up from deep places; it needed digging out and scraping off. The trouble is scratching makes the itch worse.

Before we launch into dozens of chapters of poetry, Job is a short story, a fable about a man coming to grips with undeserved suffering. He scrapes at his sores while sitting on the ash heap. When his wife comes to him and, in her own excruciating grief for the loss of their family, tells him to curse God and die, Job remains faithful.

I want to be that person. I strive to be that person, receiving even suffering with equanimity where God is concerned. But sometimes I still end up rubbing my shoulder blades against the doorjamb.

Here's the thing: Almost all suffering is undeserved; almost all suffering simply arises from the human condition. We have an autoimmune disorder. We lose the baby. The roads were slick. The other driver was drunk, or inexperienced, or simply driving too fast. Life itches, and scratching the itch hurts us more.

I remember Job when the little red bumps reappear. I smooth salve on my forearm. I breathe. I take the bad with the good. I pray for patience. I breathe again and try not to make things worse.

John Wesley
http://www.ccel.org/ccel/wesley/notes

Hebrews 1:4

So much higher than the angels—It was extremely proper to observe this, because the Jews gloried in their law, as it was delivered by the ministration of angels. How much more may we glory in the gospel, which was given, not by the ministry of angels, but of the very Son of God! As he hath by inheritance a more excellent name—Because he is the Son of God, he inherits that name, in right whereof he inherits all things His inheriting that name is more ancient than all worlds; his inheriting all things, as ancient as all things. Than they—This denotes an immense pre-eminence. The angels do not inherit all things, but are themselves a portion of the Son's inheritance, whom they worship as their Lord.

Mark 10:6

From the beginning of the creation—Therefore Moses in the first of Genesis gives us an account of things from the beginning of the creation. Does it not clearly follow, that there was no creation previous to that which Moses describes? God made them male and female—Therefore Adam did not at first contain both sexes in himself: but God made Adam, when first created, male only; and Eve female only. And this man and woman he joined in a state of innocence, as husband and wife.

Elizabeth Quick
http://bethquick.com

Hebrews 1; 2

• Hebrews talks of Jesus as the reflection of God's glory. I think we are also reflections of God's glory, if we let ourselves be, if we let God makes us into these reflections. This is what it means to be created in God's image, isn't it?

172

- "Exact imprint of God's very being" (1:3 NRSV). Think of fingerprinting or making footprint artwork with the feet of newborns. How much are our lives imprints of God's being as we seek to imitate Christ?

- We are brothers and sisters with Christ, children of the same Parent. How intimate is that? With that intimacy comes responsibility—we are part of God's family.

Mark 10

- What kind of answer do you think the Pharisees expected Jesus to give to their questions? What answer would they have given to their own question?

- These teachings from Jesus are hard for modern-day congregations to hear because so many have experience the pain of divorce themselves or in their families. I think that, when preaching on these texts, it is important to be clear that Jesus is not saying that people belong in abusive, harmful relationships at all costs. I think Jesus' point is that the Pharisees, as ever, are interested only in the laws and details, not in the heart of God's plan for people. I think that's a better focus.

- What does it mean to welcome a child? This is the third week in a row that the Gospel lesson mentions children and welcoming them to really understand the kingdom. The repeated emphasis tells us Jesus thinks this is *really important*.

D. Mark Davis
http://leftbehindandlovingit.blogspot.com/

Mark 10

In Mark 10:2-12, some Pharisees test Jesus with a question regarding whether a man can divorce his wife. The verb that Mark uses describes this inquiry as confrontational, more like "interrogating" than "asking." The Pharisees intend a dispute over how to read the law, but two aspects of this text draw us into deeper matters.

First, the law permitting divorce (Deuteronomy 24:1-4), Jesus says, was a concession that Moses made because of the hardness of their hearts (*cardio-sclero*). In effect, not every scripture is of equal weight or import. Jesus invites readers to discern how some laws are concessions for erring persons to practice their errors with the least amount of damage. The Deuteronomic law concerning divorce concedes to human failure. It does not express God's highest ideal.

Second, the language of "two becoming one flesh" in Mark's text invites us to read the Deuteronomic text as referring to sexual intercourse. As such, it allows a man to divorce a woman because she "does not please him" sexually, but it does not allow him to remarry her after she has married another and has been divorced or widowed.

The human failure that Moses seems to be conceding is not the ongoing challenge of communication or keeping a relationship alive, but the hard-hearted nature of patriarchal desire. To divorce a woman because she does not please, then to remarry her when she is no longer one's own possession, would subject her to the kind of boredom-rejecting-recovering that marks capricious hard-heartedness based solely on a man's passion. Moses' law draws a line: It allows the divorce, but prohibits the reconquest. The creation story, on the other hand, sees sexual relations within covenantal relations, not as a matter of obtaining a prize based on desire.

October 11, 2015
20th Sunday after Pentecost, Proper 23

Job 23:1-9, 16-17; Psalm 22:1-15; Hebrews 4:12-16; Mark 10:17-31; Amos 5:6-7, 10-15; Psalm 90:12-17

David Lose

Amos 5; Mark 10

What if the religious life isn't about being good? That may not at first sound like a particularly revolutionary statement, but I bet if you suggested this to your parishioners—let alone to the typical man or woman on the street—they would be shocked. For most people, religion is *all about* being good.

Certainly there are plenty of passages in the Bible that stress the importance of leading a moral life. Hence, Amos chastises Israel for its mistreatment of the poor. But while morality is important, I'd suggest that it is not, finally, what religious life is about.

Perhaps that explains Jesus' curious reaction to the man's greeting. "Good teacher," he says, to which Jesus' replies, "No one is good except the one God" (vv. 17-18). Why would Jesus say that? Perhaps it's because he wants to stress from the beginning that the kingdom he proclaims isn't about being good. Soon enough the man will demonstrate that by all earthly stands he really is good, for he has kept the commandments since his youth. Yet he is still unhappy, still driven by some sense of lack and so seeks out Jesus with questions about eternal life.

And how does Jesus respond? By telling him to go and care for his neighbor. Notice: Jesus doesn't just tell him to give his money away, but rather to sell it and give that money to the poor.

Why? Because the religious life, and, for that matter, all of life, is about relationship. Relationship with God that comes as sheer gift—hence, no keeping of the law is sufficient to grant eternal life—and relationship with one another, which is why both Amos and Jesus direct their audiences to care for those in need. Life, now and into eternity, is something we discover and receive only together.

John Wesley
http://www.ccel.org/ccel/wesley/notes

Hebrews 4:12

The soul and spirit, joints and marrow—The inmost recesses of the mind, which the apostle beautifully and strongly expresses by this heap of figurative words. And is a discerner—Not only of the thoughts, but also of the intentions.

Mark 10:30

He shall receive a hundred fold, houses, etc.—Not in the same kind: for it will generally be with persecutions: but in value: a hundred fold more happiness than any or all of these did or could afford. But let it be observed, none is entitled to this happiness, but he that will accept it with persecutions.

Liz Crumlish

http://somethingtostandon.blogspot.co.uk/

Mark 10

You're edging your way out of the door, thinking you'll be in good time.

Against all the odds, you're ready to be on your way…then you're stopped in your tracks.

And it's never something simple that stops you. Never something that can be kept until you return.

In Mark's gospel, Jesus makes one journey—the journey to the cross. But all along the way, he stops to teach and to heal. His journey is full of interruptions.

And today's reading is yet another of those interruptions on the way to the cross.

From the subsequent conversation, this man who stops him is familiar with the laws of life—it seems likely he practices them all diligently. But there is clearly something missing from his life. He isn't fulfilled. He knows how to live—but that doesn't cut it. He wants more.

Jesus does not condemn the young man who questions him. Jesus looked on him with love. Just as he looks on us with love, today, and says: "You are lacking one thing. Go, sell what you own, and give the money to the poor" (v. 21).

How hard it is for us to follow when faced with such a demand.

Peter, the disciple, makes a good try at squirming out of it by citing all the good that he has done. And Jesus' message to him is, "Well done; now go and do more."

In the work of the kingdom, we can never feel that we've done our bit. Not while there are poor and homeless and hungry folk in the world.

The work is never done. And we have much to share. Jesus looks on us with love, not condemnation.

But his message takes no prisoners. Go and do more.

Carolyn Winfrey Gillette

http://www.carolynshymns.com/

Lord, What Must I Do? (Mark 10)

LYONS 10.10.11.11 ("O Worship the King, All Glorious Above!")

"Lord, what must I do?" A man asked one day.
The kingdom of God still seemed far away.
Christ spoke with compassion, "Just do one thing more;
Sell all your possessions, and give to the poor."

The man was upset and started to grieve;
Did he even hear what he would receive?
For Jesus continued, "Then come, follow me,
And you will have treasure in heaven! You'll see!"

O Lord, we have much and so we confess
Wealth gets in the way; possessions possess!
Our money distorts how we hear your good news;
It changes our vision, obscuring our views.

O Lord, may we have the courage today
To get rid of all that gets in your way;
And may the impossible now be found true:
By grace, we are blest and find treasure in you.

Biblical references: Matthew 19:16-30; Mark 10:17-31 and Luke 18:18-30

Tune: LYONS 10.10.11.11 ("O Worship the King, All Glorious Above!") attr. Johann Michael Haydn (1737–1806); arranged by William Gardiner, *Sacred Melodies* (London: 1815). Alternate Tune: HANOVER ("Ye Servants of God, Your Master Proclaim") attr. William Croft in *The Supplement to the New Version of Psalms*, by Nahum Tate and Nicholas Brady, 6th edition, 1708. Text: Copyright © 2013 by Carolyn Winfrey Gillette. All rights reserved. Email: bcgillette@comcast.net Website: www.carolynshymns.com

John Petty

http://progressiveinvolvement.com

Mark 10

"It will be very hard for the wealthy to enter God's kingdom!" (v. 23). Given some of the major themes of Mark—the status reversal of the kingdom, helping the poor, acts of justice—what Jesus says is perfectly plain and frankly obvious.

The disciples, however, are astonished at his words—not once, but twice (see vv. 24, 26). Jesus compounds the shock: "Children, it's difficult to enter God's kingdom! It's easier for a camel to squeeze through the eye of a needle than for a rich person to enter God's kingdom" (vv. 24-25). Sure enough, the disciples are now "greatly astounded" (CEB has "shocked even more"). It's even worse than they thought! He really means it!

The disciples worry, "Then who can be saved?" (v. 26). If this pious rich guy can't get in, who can? The disciples assume a world in which the people at the top of the social and economic ladder are specially favored. Aren't riches a sign of God's blessing? Again "looking" at them—seeing right through them, you might say—Jesus tells them flatly that it is not humanly possible.

Modern commentators, bothered by this story, have tried to fudge this saying by noting that there really was a gate in Jerusalem called "the eye of the needle," and therefore, it might—theoretically, perhaps, maybe—be possible for a camel to get his nose under it and get through.

This is special pleading of the rankest sort. The plain meaning of Jesus' words is that it is impossible for a rich person to enter into the way of the kingdom. As the disciples get a case of the vapors and head for the fainting couch, Jesus doesn't let up. It is not humanly possible, he says. It can't be done. His point made, he makes an even greater one: "All things are possible for God" (v. 27).

Two Bubbas and a Bible

http://lectionarylab.com

Mark 10

Shocked. Perplexed. Astounded. These are all pretty strong words from the Gospel for today. I can imagine that the man who knelt before the Christ was expecting—at the very least—a few brownie points for his recognition of Jesus as the Good Teacher.

So, he is shocked to receive the reprimand, "Why would you call me that? Only God is good."

That brought him up a little short—not to mention the fact that he would have to sell everything he had in order to follow this Good Teacher.

The disciples are perplexed to hear that wealth and the kingdom of God aren't exactly compatible in the Lord's book. Who wouldn't like a little extra cash now and then? Isn't that supposed to be a sign of God's blessing? Doesn't prosperity follow from obedience to the gospel?

Jesus has done "quit preaching and gone to meddling," as I used to hear the country preachers say. "What you wanna bring our pocketbooks into this for, Jesus?"

The astounding moment comes when Jesus starts talking about camels passing through needle's eyes and such. "Now, you're just getting silly, Jesus. Everybody knows that something like that is impossible!"

Ah, the absurdity of God's grace. Such feats are exactly what Jesus accomplishes in our lives in making us worthy of the kingdom.

October 18, 2015

21st Sunday after Pentecost, Proper 24

Job 38:1-7, (34-41); Psalm 104:1-9, 24, 35c; Hebrews 5:1-10; Mark 10:35-45; Isaiah 53:4-12; Psalm 91:9-16

Lowell E. Grisham

http://lowellsblog.blogspot.com/

Prayers of the People (Job 38; Psalm 104)

Presider: Gracious God, you manifest your power primarily in the service of your compassion and love for all humanity, and you are clothed with majesty and splendor: Listen to us as we call upon you in prayer, saying: O God, how excellent is your greatness; the earth is full of your creatures. Alleluia!

You have called your church to be your humble community of service, having been baptized with the baptism of Jesus: Guide your people into such faithfulness, that we may serve the world in your name and make intercession on behalf of all. O God, how excellent is your greatness;

the earth is full of your creatures. Alleluia!

In this fallen world, there are rulers who lord it over your children and great ones who are tyrants over others: Honor the sacrifice and sufferings of your lambs and take away these perversions of justice, so that the great among us will be servants, and those who wish to be first will become the slave of all. O God, how excellent is your greatness;

the earth is full of your creatures. Alleluia!

You have bound us to you in love and called us to share in your ministry of service: Empower those in our community who give their lives as servants of others that the will of the Lord may prosper. O God, how excellent is your greatness;

the earth is full of your creatures. Alleluia!

Hear our prayers and supplications through our great high priest Jesus as we intercede for all who suffer throughout the world, especially those who live under the rule of tyrants or who face violence, oppression, or poverty. O God, how excellent is your greatness;

the earth is full of your creatures. Alleluia!

We offer our prayers for those for whom we are called to pray, especially ___.
We offer our grateful thanks for your presence and deliverance, especially for ___.
Let those who have died sit with the triumphant Christ in glory, as we remember ___.
O God, how excellent is your greatness;

the earth is full of your creatures. Alleluia!

Presider: Almighty God, through your servant Jesus Christ, the righteous one, you have made many righteous, raising him from suffering into glory: Let your Resurrection power be present to all in need as you strengthen us for the leadership of service in your name, through Jesus Christ, who with you and the Holy Spirit, lives in unity and love, forever and ever. Amen

Prayers of the People (For Alternate Readings: Isaiah 53; Psalm 91)

Presider: Gracious God, you manifest your power primarily in the service of your compassion and love for all humanity: Listen to us as we call upon you in prayer, saying: Give your angels charge over us, O God, to keep us in all our ways.

You have called your church to be your humble community of service, having been baptized with the baptism of Jesus: Guide your people into such faithfulness, that we may serve the world in your name and make intercession on behalf of all. Give your angels charge over us, O God

to keep us in all our ways.

178

In this fallen world, there are rulers who lord it over your children and great ones who are tyrants over others: Honor the sacrifice and sufferings of your lambs and take away these perversions of justice, so that the great among us will be servants, and those who wish to be first will become the slave of all. Give your angels charge over us, O God

to keep us in all our ways.

You have bound us to you in love and called us to share in your ministry of service: Empower those in our community who give their lives as servants of others that the will of the Lord may prosper. Give your angels charge over us, O God

to keep us in all our ways.

Hear our prayers and supplications through our great high priest Jesus as we intercede for all who suffer throughout the world, especially those who live under the rule of tyrants or who face violence, oppression, or poverty. Give your angels charge over us, O God

to keep us in all our ways.

We offer our prayers for those for whom we are called to pray, especially ___.
We offer our grateful thanks for your presence and deliverance, especially for ___.
Let those who have died sit with the triumphant Christ in glory, as we remember ___.
Give your angels charge over us, O God

to keep us in all our ways.

Presider: Almighty God, through your servant Jesus Christ, the righteous one, you have made many righteous, raising him from suffering into glory: Let your resurrection power be present to all in need as you strengthen us for the leadership of service in your name, through Jesus Christ, who with you and the Holy Spirit, lives in unity and love, forever and ever. Amen.

Marci Auld Glass

http://www.marciglass.com

Job 38; Mark 10

Job's friends show up and sit with him as he grieves. But then they decide silence isn't enough and start being "helpful":
"Your children must have sinned—that's why they died."
"Just face it, Job. You must have done something for this to happen."

But Job won't accept that. He doesn't know about the divine wager, but he knows it is not helpful for people to explain things away. Job does not lose faith.

But Job asks God to answer, and God answers. But not, presumably, as Job would have scripted for himself. In truth, were I Job, I'm not even sure I would understand *how* God had answered my question.

People have long turned to Job to ponder the question of why bad things happen. The question of where God is in tragedy is one with which we still struggle. Yet I find comfort in the idea people were wrestling with this issue thousands of years ago too. It suggests that, if we don't have an answer to that question, it is not because we haven't put our smartest minds to the problem, but perhaps because the mystery of God is not something we understand this side of eternity.

Some things are clear, however. God doesn't mind faithful people calling for answers. God doesn't promise we'll like the answers or even understand the answers, but God doesn't critique Job for wanting to understand. It is always okay to cry out to God.

God does not, however, like it when people try to explain away the mystery of God. Their pat answers, presuming they know the mind of God, are what cause God to take offense. God tells Job's friends, "I'm angry at you...because you haven't spoken about me correctly as did my servant Job" (42:7).

Excerpted from http://marciglass.com/2012/10/21/ask-away/

John Wesley
http://www.ccel.org/ccel/wesley/notes

Hebrews 5:7

Indeed, his human nature needed the support of Omnipotence; and for this he sent up strong crying and tears: but, throughout his whole life, he showed that it was not the sufferings he was to undergo, but the dishonor that sin had done to so holy a God, that grieved his spotless soul. The consideration of its being the will of God tempered his fear, and afterwards swallowed it up; and he was heard not so that the cup should pass away, but so that he drank it without any fear.

Mark 10:38

Ye know not what ye ask—Ye know not that ye ask for sufferings, which must needs pave the way to glory. The cup—Of inward; the baptism—Of outward sufferings. Our Lord was filled with sufferings within, and covered with them without.

Suzanne Guthrie
http://www.edgeofenclosure.org

Mark 10

To be engaged with the world is to suffer. Even after the painful trauma of birth is over, a little child suffers the pains of the digestive system learning to manage itself, first teeth breaking slowly through the gums, the panic as mother incomprehensibly leaves the room even for a moment. In the best of economic and social circumstances, there is always sickness, tragedy, death, unexplainable twists of fate, love-sickness, homesickness, hurtful disagreements, mental illness, the death of loved ones. Add poverty, war, natural disasters, political oppression, and brutality, and you have life. How can I bear this suffering?

Christians, who ritually embrace the suffering of Christ and the world in worship, can nevertheless devolve into "Why did God do this to me? Why isn't God answering my prayers?" during a bout of suffering, as if God is a personal necromancer and prayer a magical incantation.

By concentrating on the exclusively personal in this way, I can avoid the questions pertaining to both theodicy and personal responsibility as a human being. If I wallow in "Why did God do this to me?" I don't have to worry about someone halfway around the world, or even down the street, for that matter.

But the moment my suffering meets your suffering, the moment our eyes meet, an alchemical change takes place. I am in you and you are in me. Suffering makes us one. Learning to suffer with you, I learn empathy for others I don't know. Suffering opens my soul to love.

And when my suffering meets God's suffering, we become one in that suffering, incarnate in the world, bearing this suffering for I-Know-Not-What. Christian practice helps me to trust living in the incomprehensible vortex of the cross. My suffering, your suffering, God's suffering, bringing forth new life. How can I bear this joy?

Karoline Lewis

Mark 10

This section of Mark is the second to last event in Jesus' public ministry. Chapter 11 is Jesus' triumphal entry into Jerusalem, and the last chapters of Mark's gospel are dedicated to the last week of Jesus' life. Perhaps it comes as no surprise that the seemingly dense disciples of Mark's gospel now ask for places of prominence in what they think Jesus' glory will be. Nonetheless, it should spark a certain sense of pathos in the hearer. Really? Now? After everything Jesus has told you, do you still not get what it means to follow him? But perhaps a more meaningful claim for this text is not that the disciples are endlessly clueless, but that the truth of what it means to be of service to the other has yet to be understood. "For the Son of Man came not to be served but to serve" (v. 45 NRSV). At the close of Jesus' public ministry, where time and time again he has revealed the nature and nearness of the kingdom of God, the question of servanthood is critical. The angels in the wilderness served Jesus. He speaks of the nature of what it means to be in service to the other. Yet when he is again in a deserted place (14:45), there will be no one to serve him. When he is on the cross, and the disciples having abandoned him, the women are there, looking on from a distance, those who had served him, provided for him, when he was in Galilee. Perhaps rather than a reprimand, Jesus' words are a reminder. In these seemingly simple and obvious words in 10:45, Jesus suggests that a critical characteristic of servanthood is that it occurs in our places of abandonment.

Rick Morley

Mark 10

The audacity of James and John is astounding. They walk up to the Savior of the World and ask for a blank check. "Give us whatever we want," they ask. You can see why these two are called the "Sons of Thunder!" I would have loved to have seen the look on Jesus' face. My guess is that it would have conveyed something akin to, "Oh, what now?"

But the problem here isn't audacity; Jesus loves audacity. It's a quality he looks for and seeks to cultivate in his disciples. In the next chapter of Mark, he'll tell his followers that if they have enough faith they will be able to command mountains to throw themselves into the sea. No, Jesus speaks in the currency of audacity.

The problem with James and John here is that they want glory for themselves. They want to be important. Prominent. They want to be high on the ladder, several rungs higher than their friends.

And that is the very opposite of how the kingdom of God works and how Christian community is supposed to work. One of the greatest stains on the church is the long litany of people who have sought to use it for power and prestige. In its history, hierarchy so often and so easily snuffs out the ethic of servitude that Jesus so fully embodies.

We are about serving others. Loving others. Lifting others up. Washing other's feet. Caring for those who need care.

The church, as the body of Christ, is not to be about itself. We are not to be about power, or survival, or riches. (Some might say, "Good thing. . . .") We are to be the people who follow Jesus to Golgotha, carrying nothing but the cross and the love of God. And that's audacious.

Teri Peterson
http://clevertitlehere.blogspot.com

Mark 10

I kinda want to go easy on James and John—after all, didn't Jesus say, "Ask and you shall receive"? Aren't we supposed to bring God the deepest desires of our hearts? Aren't we supposed to want to be the best, strive for the greater things, work toward that place of honor? What's wrong with asking for what you want? Isn't that what prayer is about?

This is the sort of partial understanding of prayer-as-magic that floats around our nominally Christian, Western culture. We ask God for what we want, and hope God will give it to us. We ask God for peace, comfort, healing, hope, sunny days, courage, understanding, justice.

In some ways, it's a little like we pray sometimes to a Jeez-O-Matic, a vending machine God. We press D-8 for Twix, and if Twix are not what come out, we try C-12 and E-4, looking for the response we want. Taken to an extreme, this can become a "What's in it for me?" approach. Sure, I'll come and follow you—what will you do for me? Yes, something needs to be done, but what good will it do me? "We want for you to do for us whatever we ask of you . . . in Jesus' name, Amen."

But, as Bishop Will Willimon says, "Jesus is not a technique for getting what we want out of God; Jesus is God's way of getting what God wants out of us" (http://day1.org/1474-good_news, accessed August 3, 2013).

Prayer isn't magic; it's a conversation. Every good conversation is a two-way street. While we're praying, asking God for things we want, talking to God about things that matter to us, God is also talking to us, praying for us to bring peace, to do justice, to have the courage to comfort hurting people, to offer hope to those in despair.

October 25, 2015

22nd Sunday after Pentecost, Proper 25

Job 42:1-6, 10-17; Psalm 34:1-8, (19-22); Hebrews 7:23-28; Mark 10:46-52; Jeremiah 31:7-9; Psalm 126

John Wesley

http://www.ccel.org/ccel/wesley/notes

Hebrews 7:25

Wherefore he is able to save to the uttermost—From all the guilt, power, root, and consequence of sin. Them who come—By faith. To God through him—As their priest. Seeing he ever liveth to make intercession—That is, he ever lives and intercedes. He died once; he intercedes perpetually.

Mark 10:50

Casting away his garment—Through joy and eagerness.

Amy Persons Parkes

Mark 10

I want peace on earth, good kids, a clean house, a trip to the Amalfi coast, and the perfect church. I want people to be kind. I want a good death when I'm old, and I don't want my car to die before I pay off the loan. I want a garden full of flowers for six months out of the year and enough time in my day to keep them free of weeds. I want to be more of a morning person and to be less addicted to the approval of others. I want to allow myself to feel the whole range of human emotion while I act and speak only from the deep wells of love, respect, and integrity.

I used to believe that wanting anything for myself was a sin. I used to believe that any desire arising from an awareness of my self was unacceptable to God. But Jesus asked, "What do you want me to do for you?" (v. 51b). Hearing this invitation, I realized that if I never have the courage to present myself before God, full of needs and wants, then I never give Jesus an opportunity to see who I really am. If I refuse to disclose my wants to God, then my desires, fueled by secrecy and shame, metastasize into resentment. But when I share, through honest and open prayer, my frivolous or grave or noble or childlike wants with a gentle and loving God, God will use even these to increase my faithfulness, to uncover my hidden wounds, and to affirm my created goodness. Maybe, even, God is doing the wanting in me and through me; and my calling is to discover what the wanting is teaching me about who God is and who I am.

John Petty

http://progressiveinvolvement.com

Mark 10

Who actually "follows" Jesus in Mark's gospel? It's not the disciples; that's for sure. For Mark, the twelve disciples never ever get it. They keep misunderstanding Jesus' message and agenda, and they keep getting the theology wrong to boot. This is true from start to finish in Mark's gospel. Not one time are the twelve disciples actually described as "following" Jesus.

Yet, occasionally, certain people do get it, and do follow. In chapter 15, an anonymous young man is described as "following." In chapter 14, an anonymous woman understands that Jesus' crucifixion will be his coronation and anoints him beforehand. In chapter 10, an anonymous and blind beggar "sees" and "follows."

It's not just any blind beggar either, but one named Bartimaeus, or "son of" Timaeus. *Timaeus* was the title of one of Plato's most popular and accessible works. In other words, one might say that the offspring of Plato now "sees." (In all four Gospels, "seeing" is the first-century equivalent of "getting it.")

"Immediately he regained his sight and followed him on the way" (v. 52 NRSV). Not only did he "follow," accomplishing something that has eluded the twelve disciples, but he also follows "on the way."

The word "way" (*hodos*) occurs seventeen times in Mark. It refers to practicing the values of the kingdom as taught by Jesus throughout the book. Its most recent usage prior to this week's text was when James and John were caught angling for position (10:32-40) in the upcoming administration of King Jesus. Self-promotion is not "following."

Ann Scull

http://seedstuff.blogspot.com

Listening Song

Bon Jovi, "It's My Life" on *Crush* (Sanctuary II Studio, N. J.: Island, 2000) CD Edition. The words of this song could easily be those of blind Bartimaeus as he stands up to the crowd and persists in calling to Jesus.

Film Clip

Mother Teresa: In the Name of God's Poor (1997). Use the conversation between Mother Teresa and her priest, where she convinces him that she must go against the conventions of her cloistered order to follow God's call to minister to the poor of India.

Discussion Questions: 1. How are Mother Teresa and blind Bartimaeus alike? 2. How is discipleship difficult for them both?

Drama

"Blind Bartimaeus" (Copyright Rosemary Broadstock and Ann Scull; permission is given to use and adapt; http://seedstuff.blogspot.com.au/2012_10_01_archive.html, accessed April, 29, 2013). This is a short drama in three parts. In Part 1, a reporter interviews Bartimaeus before he meets Jesus. In Part 2, the congregation becomes the crowd in the story. In Part 3, a reporter interviews Bartimaeus after he meets Jesus. Discussion Questions: What if Bartimaeus had not stood up to the crowd? What does Jesus tell Bartimaeus to do after he is healed? What does Bartimaeus do? Where is Jesus going?

Response Activity

Pass around ribbons and ask people to think of one aspect of following Jesus they would like to do or do better. Then pose the question, "If Jesus is asking you 'What do you want me to do for you?' what is your answer?" As they think of answers, ask them to tie knots in their pieces of ribbon. Stand together and say an affirmation of faith or creed together. Encourage people to take the ribbon home and put it somewhere significant to remind them of God's faithfulness and their determination to follow.

Mary J. Scifres

Jumping Up and Jumping In (Mark 10)

When Bartimaeus hears that Jesus is calling him, he throws his coat aside, jumps up, and goes to Jesus. This cannot have been easy for a blind man! And yet, jumping in, springing up, and bursting forth are actions that can bring new life for all who seek to follow Christ. A deep yearning resides in the human soul for something meaningful to guide and focus our lives. The rock band Snow Patrol says it this way in "Chasing Cars": "Before we get too old / Show me a garden that's bursting into life" (Polydor Records, 2006). In the Disney movie *The Incredibles*, Mr. Incredible's neighbor boy says that he is waiting for something amazing. And Mr. Incredible, bored with his life and unfulfilled in his meaningless work, says, "Me too, kid!" Bartimaeus says it in the words we use in liturgy and worship, "Show me mercy!" (v. 48b).

However we express this yearning, the answer lies within. This is why Jesus credits Bartimaeus' faith with his healing, as a reminder that our faith in God's life-giving love, our yearning for wholeness, and our sincere desire for healing and renewal can lead to the clear vision that allows us to follow God and experience the joy of Christian discipleship. But we have to throw off the cloaks that weigh us down, jump up from our familiar resting places, and commit ourselves fully and completely. When we spring forth to answer Christ's call and then jump "all in," we discover the clarity and wholeness that Bartimaeus experienced. Another rock band, Lifehouse, sings these words: "All in, I'm all in for life" ("All In," Jason Wade and Ean Mering, © Chrysalis One Music 2010). Bartimaeus lived these words as he seemingly left everything behind to follow Jesus. May Bartimaeus' experience inspire us to do the same.

Thom M. Shuman

http://lectionaryliturgies.blogspot.com/

tumbling act (Mark 10)

not by marching round and round
seven times (or more),
    but by simply
    standing still;

not in great tumult
or loud curses,
    but by a gracious,
    welcoming invitation;

not with a parable
or recounting of past
wonders and might,
    but by a gentle
    affirmation:

the meek find their voice,
    blind trust becomes the path to walk,
        futures are put at risk,
            masks are taken off,
        walls fall down
in jericho.

Martha Spong

http://marthaspong.com/

Mark 10

At clergy support group, the facilitator suggested role-playing as a discernment tool. A colleague would portray God and bounce my questions back to me. Simple enough, but when it came time to ask the question, I was afraid to say the words out loud. I was afraid of getting it wrong somehow.

In seminary, I worried about those courses where a portion of the grade was for class participation. I'm an extrovert, and sometimes I don't really know what I think until I've heard myself try saying it out loud. That's great if I agree with myself! But it's not so great if I hear the words and have second thoughts about them.

In the clergy group, I knew my colleague, who was a close friend, was not actually God; what made me so anxious? I think I might have been afraid of getting the real God's attention. I didn't want to get it wrong.

Think of standing right in front of Jesus and hearing him ask, "What do you want me to do for you?" Had I done it, I might be healed of all the afflictions of relationship, personal history, and stubbornness that then formed my comfortably uncomfortable existence. I didn't dare ask the questions aloud.

When I did, years later, God called me to travel the road to my own Jerusalem, to live through challenges for God's sake that most of us would just as soon avoid.

Yet, that way lies healing. It comes when we give up willingly the things we expect and the things we think we love and even the things we don't like in our lives. Healing can come only when we answer the question. What do you want God to do for you? God is waiting for your answer.

November 1, 2015

All Saints Sunday

Wisdom of Solomon 3:1-9 or Isaiah 25:6-9; Psalm 24; Revelation 21:1-6a;
John 11:32-44

Mark Stamm

Isaiah 25; Revelation 21; John 11

All Saints Day calls us to envision a future beyond pain and tears, yet people of faith must remain firmly grounded, and the saints with whom we live will help us in that process. Indeed, they can be a pain, and they may tempt us to tear out our hair. One is a saint by grace alone. As at funerals, then, so also on All Saints Day—we gain nothing by talking of the deceased in an unrealistic or romantic sense as if they possessed a righteousness of their own.

Isaiah 25:6-9 calls us to envision an eschatological feast in which God will wipe away all tears. Revelation 21:4 offers a similar vision. Notice, however, that the promise to wipe away tears is not the denial of crying. Along these lines, John 11 makes significant witness to the Son of God whom we proclaim is fully human and fully divine—Jesus called Lazarus from the grave, but not before he sanctified Mary's tears (and all subsequent tears) through the shedding of his own (vv. 33-35). So, tears are shed, but they are not the last word. God is at work to move us toward healing and resurrection. Such is the hope that we offer today as we remember loved ones who have died in the past year.

We are not, however, merely recipients of God's work. As people of Christian faith, we can neither deny tears nor think that God's wiping them away happens completely apart from us or only in some distant future. Who needs this ministry? Children who have been bullied or go to bed hungry? Pastors and churches in conflict? Overworked parents, especially single parents who wonder if they will ever have a few moments of sabbath? What will we do about all of this?

Two Bubbas and a Bible

http://lectionarylab.com

Revelation 21

I am an acknowledged Luddite; technology befuddles me. For instance, passenger-side rearview mirrors. For the life of me I can't figure out why they put mirrors there designed to deceive us. There you are, rushing up and down the interstate; you look in the outside mirror, plenty of room to move into the right lane. You slide over, horns blare, brakes screech, and you glance back over your right shoulder. There it is—a car—in the right lane.

Looking in the side mirror, it seemed so far back. Then you read the fine print, the fateful words. "Objects in mirror are closer than they appear." Why do they do that?

Stumped by technology I cannot come up with an answer, so I think about things I do understand, literature and philosophy and theology and such.

"The past is not dead, it is not even past." —William Faulkner's Nobel Prize speech

"The 'is-ness' of the was." —University of North Carolina Bible professor Bernard Boyd

"Objects in mirror are closer than they appear." —Anonymous auto engineer

While Christianity is a historic religion, rooted in a true story that happened at a particular time in a particular place involving a real Jesus who suffered real torment and died a real death on a real cross and rose again from a real tomb—Christianity is not just history; it is not yesterday's news.

Christ and the cross and the eternal community of the saints transcend time and place in such a way that when today's church gathers, Jesus and the disciples and all the believers from all times and all places gather with us. "Objects in mirror are closer than they appear."

John Wesley

http://www.ccel.org/ccel/wesley/notes

John 11:43

He cried with a loud voice—That all who were present might hear. Lazarus, come forth—Jesus called him out of the tomb as easily as if he had been not only alive, but awake also.

From the Sermon "The New Creation"

What a strange scene is here opened to our view! How remote from all our natural apprehensions! Not a glimpse of what is here revealed was ever seen in the heathen world. Not only the modern, barbarous, uncivilized Heathens have not the least conception of it; but it was equally unknown to the refined, polished Heathens of ancient Greece and Rome. And it is almost as little thought of or understood by the generality of Christians: I mean, not barely those that are nominally such, that have the form of godliness without the power; but even those that in a measure fear God, and study to work righteousness.

http://www.umcmission.org/Find-Resources/John-Wesley-Sermons/Sermon-64-The-New-Creation

Kwasi Kena

John 11

An acting student studying Greek tragedies learns that when an audience sees tragedy on stage, they experience catharsis. For some, the extent of catharsis is the wholesale dumping of emotions. Emotions get released, but do the people find resolution?

Today's passage thrusts in our face the seemingly preventable death of Lazarus. We witness Martha's emotional dumping, "Lord, if you had been here, my brother wouldn't have died" (v. 21). A variation of her statement echoes throughout history as a question, "How could a good God *allow* this to happen?" It is the question asked by Jews during the Holocaust, by Africans during slavery, and undoubtedly by Native Americans during their genocide and conquest. When tragedy intrudes our lives, don't we question God?

The good news is we have the opportunity to move beyond catharsis to resolution. Martha and Jesus show us how it works. As Martha spews raw emotion onto Jesus ("If you'd only been here…"), she simultaneously clings to hope: "Even now I know that whatever you ask God, God will give you" (v. 22).

Martha and Mary's brother, and Jesus' good friend, Lazarus, has been dead for four days. Common Jewish belief held that a person's spirit hovered about the body for three days in anticipation of possible reentry. But by the time Jesus arrives, Lazarus is four days' dead, laying in stinking decay. Through dialogue, Martha comes to know who Jesus is and what he is capable of doing *before* he called Lazarus back to life (see vv. 23-27):

Jesus: "Your brother will rise again."

Martha: "I know he will…in the resurrection."

Jesus: "I am the resurrection and the life....Do you believe this?"

Martha: "Yes, Lord, I believe."

Martha stays in dialogue with Jesus while in crisis and reaches resolution *before* the miracle occurs. Will we find faith to do the same?

Natalie Ann Sims

http://lectionarysong.blogspot.com

You Don't Have to Sing "When the Saints Go Marching In"

- "For All the Saints Who've Shown Your Love" (John Bell)—These are some of the best lyrics for All Saints' Day I've read. Love from Below uses ALL SAINTS; a nice new tune. Gather hymnals use a slightly different version of the lyrics to O WALY WALY (sheet music: http://www.giamusic.com/searchPDFS/G4540.pdf).

- "Sing for God's Glory That Colors the Dawn of Creation" (Kathryn Galloway)—Beautiful poetic words of creation (1st verse), release (2nd verse), justice (3rd verse), and saints (4th verse). Would be a good song to open worship. Sung to the familiar tune LOBE DEN HERREN. (lyrics: http://www.rexaehuntprogressive. com/liturgy_collection/year_a_liturgy_collection/year_a_pentecostafter/pentecost19a24a23102011.html, scroll down)

- "O Welcome All You Noble Saints of Old" / "In Christ There Is a Table Set for All" (Robert Stamps)—Radical hospitality. A song about God with us. "In Christ There Is a Table Set for All" is much more inclusive than the old version. Good for Communion, and fine without it, too. (lyrics, scroll down: http://breadan-dwine.wordpress.com/2007/09/01/radical-political-hospitality/; clunky sound sample: http://c1824532. cdn.cloudfiles.rackspacecloud.com/GC_749.midi)

- "Rejoice in God's Saints Today and All Days!" (Fred Pratt Green)—Great words about remembering all the different types of saints. Works well to PADERBORN, but would be simpler to LAUDATE DOMINUM. (lyrics and some tune options: http://www.oremus.org/hymnal/r/r020.html)

- "Song of Faith That Sings Forever" (Shirley Murray / Colin Gibson): Simple tune and beautiful image of people throughout generations, alive and dead, taking up a song together. (sheet music: http://www.hopep-ublishing.com/media/pdf/hset/hs_366.pdf)

- "We Sing for All the Unsung Saints" (Carl P Daw Jr.)—A great song. The tune is not familiar, and a little bit tricky. Could work with ELLACOMBE or KINGSFOLD. (lyrics and tune sample: http://www.oremus.org/hymnal/w/w143.html)

- "God We Thank You for Our People" (Ruth Duck)—All Saints Good words to the tune HOLY MANNA. Some really nice phrases "hardy spirits, rich in loving," and "thank you God for gentle pleasure." An excellent forward-looking final verse. (in New Century Hymnal [Cleveland: Pilgrim Press, 1995], 376)

John van de Laar

http://www.sacredise.com/

John 11

What does it mean to believe in Jesus? This question is at the heart of the "signs" that John's gospel chooses to recount, and it is asked pointedly of Martha (and of John's readers) in the turning point moment that is the raising of Lazarus. In this account, believing is not just about the ideas we hold in our heads. It's a question of life and death.

We don't know why Jesus delayed when he received the message about Lazarus' illness. Perhaps he knew what the result would be—that his healing of Lazarus would ensure his own execution—and so he needed time to prepare and consider his actions. For Jesus, giving life to Lazarus was inseparable from laying down his own life.

But what of Lazarus? Perhaps for him taking up his life again was also a kind of laying it down. Surely, knowing that his healing was the last straw that sealed Jesus' fate meant that he could not go back to business as usual? What little evidence history gives us indicates that Lazarus went on to become a bishop in the early church, so it would appear that he did choose to lay his life down for Christ.

The truth John seems to be trying to teach us is this: To believe in Jesus is to embrace his life-giving mission—and life always comes at a cost. To bring life to others costs us something of our own life. To trust another costs us something of our independence and our right to judge. To take life up costs us something of our freedom to spend it on frivolity and meaninglessness. The question is whether we can believe this and willingly pay the price.

For more detail: http://sacredise.com/blog/?p=910 (Originally written for a different setting)

Todd Weir

http://bloomingcactus.typepad.com/

John 11

The story of Lazarus confronts us with a sense that things are too late. He has been dead for four days. After that, you aren't just having a near-death experience. You are officially dead. The body has been ritually washed and prepared, the shroud is placed across the face, the corpse wrapped, the stone is rolled across to seal the tomb shut. In the King James Version, when Jesus asks that the stone be moved, Mary responds with great candor, "Lord, he stinketh!"

How do we preach about a man "who stinketh," draped as if for Halloween, but now raised to new life? We rush to our hopes for eternal life. We want to know if we too will be resurrected, if we get to go to heaven, and how great it will be. Or is it a fairy tale, nothing more than campaign promises of the church that will later disappoint? But the fact is that the resurrection of Lazarus is neither trick nor treat, it is a sign.

Jesus did not talk about heaven or eternal life in this text. No one rushes up with a microphone to ask Lazarus what it was like to be dead, or did he meet God. The most important words are spoken to a grieving and angry Martha as Jesus enters town. He asks if she believes, and then says quite simply, "I am the resurrection and the life" (v. 25). Like all great truths, there is much room for exploration and interpretation. These words set the stage for our lives, inviting us to be actors in the drama. We are not constantly stalked by the relentlessness of death, nor is life about waiting for heaven. It is a pilgrimage where we discover the way, the truth, and the life (see 14:6) in our present, smelly moment.

November 8, 2015

24th Sunday after Pentecost, Proper 27

Ruth 3:1-5; 4:13-17; Psalm 127; Hebrews 9: 24-28; Mark 12:38-44; 1 Kings 17:8-16; Psalm 146

Julia Seymour

http://lutheranjulia.blogspot.com

Ruth 3; 4

Often, something positive eventually comes from a disaster. This does not mean that the disaster was God's way of achieving the positive. The birth of David results from Ruth's union with Boaz (encouraged by Naomi), but the biblical events preceding that—Sodom and Gomorrah, Lot's incest with his daughters, the famine and death of Naomi's family—are not God's preferred method of bringing grace into the world.

The first widow I ever understood to be a widow was twenty-five years old. She was in a college class with me. Her husband died of a heart attack while playing basketball. He was twenty-nine. Suddenly, the notion of widowhood became clear to me. It was not that a woman simply outlived her husband, but that there was a blank space at the table, an empty side of the bed, a phone number that goes unanswered, conversations that become one-sided. Widows and widowers of all ages and circumstances frequently surround us. And we forget their status. We forget that they are among those considered most vulnerable and most wise in Scripture. We forget that God's heart is with them.

It is critical to remember that her beloved, deceased partner may not have been a saint, but she will still grieve. That he is still thinking of their loved one, even if you are afraid to bring up the subject. That she may grow accustomed to her new state, but never stop missing the ones who rest in light. Being widowed, being left out of partnership, should not mean being left out of community. Let not the community of God forsake those who mourn. It is not enough to say God is with them. We are to be the hands, words, and consolation of the Spirit with widows, orphans, and strangers.

John Wesley

http://www.ccel.org/ccel/wesley/notes

Hebrews 9:26

At the consummation of the ages—The sacrifice of Christ divides the whole age or duration of the world into two parts, and extends its virtue backward and forward, from this middle point wherein they meet to abolish both the guilt and power of sin.

Mark 12:43

I say to you, that this poor widow hath cast in more than they all—See what judgment is cast on the most specious, outward actions by the Judge of all! And how acceptable to him is the smallest, which springs from self-denying love!

Liz Crumlish
http://somethingtostandon.blogspot.co.uk/

Mark 12

Throughout his ministry, Jesus called to attention those on the margins of society, those who had previously gone unnoticed, the poor, the blind, the lame, the beggars, the lepers, military personnel, and widows.

These are the same folk we find on the margins of our societies today. Those who still are excluded, those whom society looks down on or simply ignores. A widow, living in poverty created by the institution charged with her care.

This gospel doesn't seem like good news: A widow giving her all to a corrupt institution, an institution that fails to care for her as it is supposed to do. But she gives anyway. And Jesus commends her giving. He commends her and condemns the system. Jesus holds her up as an example of how small but significant acts can break down a cycle of injustice and corruption.

This gospel is not a comparative giving table, steering the prosperous to give more. It is encouragement for those who go against the grain, who practice subversion in whatever way they can, even in the face of injustice. Who, by their subversion, make inroads into creating justice and fairness for all God's people.

It doesn't always take placards and a lot of shouting for trends and policies to be reversed. Persistent, simple subversion also does the trick.

D. Mark Davis
http://leftbehindandlovingit.blogspot.com/

Mark 12

One often hears the latter part of this text separated out and interpreted as the heroic, sacrificial giving of a poor widow. "The widow's mite" has even become a colloquial phrase referring to a meager contribution that has far more value than its smallness might indicate. Something far more profound happens, however. A more nuanced reading is possible when this text is retained as a whole, instead of separating verses 41 to 44 from verses 38 to 40. The widow's contribution is contextualized—she is contributing to a system that routinely oppresses her under the guise of piety (v. 40). In a profound way, she acts with nobility and self-sacrifice, *and* she contributes to an unjust system. She gives all that she has, and she abets a system that will take away all that she has. A truly tragic situation faces the widow, because her means of practicing true piety is *at the same time* a system that is devoid of justice and will, in turn, exploit her.

Telling the whole story means that this text addresses the situation of living tragically yet faithfully within oppressive systems. The context of oppression can be a place where one makes self-denying contributions toward the common good. The homiletical directions that this text can take are many—addressing those who try to work conscientiously within an exploitative economic system; those who live heroically within a militaristic system that often overreaches and destroys; those who support an imperfect candidate, but perhaps the least imperfect candidate available. Keeping Jesus' critique of the scribes, who devour widows' houses, together with his praise of the widow, who gives all she has, allows a reflection on ethical realism, the impossibility of obtaining more than "proximate goods" within sinful structures of oppression.

Carolyn Winfrey Gillette
http://www.carolynshymns.com/

Jesus Sat and Watched the Crowd (Mark 12)
HENDON 7.7.7.7.7 ("Take My Life")
Jesus sat and watched the crowd
At the temple treasury.

Some that day were rich and proud,
Making sure that all could see
Their great generosity.

Then a widow came along
Who had nothing she could spare.
Yet her faith in God was strong
And she gave as few would dare:
All she had, she chose to share.

Just a penny, nothing more,
Yet Christ said her gift was best.
What a risk, for one so poor!
What rich faith her gift expressed!
Trusting, giving, she was blest.

Lord, you see the way we live;
All within our hearts, you know.
Like that widow, may we give.
Trusting you, our gifts will grow
And our joy will overflow.

Mark 12:41-44 and Luke 21:1-4

Tune: H.A. Cesar Malan, 1827. Text: Copyright © 2000 by Carolyn Winfrey Gillette. All rights reserved. Email: bcgillette@comcast.net Web Site: www.carolynshymns.com. Copied from *Songs of Grace: New Hymns for God and Neighbor* by Carolyn Winfrey Gillette (Upper Room Books, 2009).

Matthew L. Skinner

Mark 12

Jesus' criticism of the scribes, Jewish legal experts, seems straightforward enough. They revel in their privileges and the attention they receive. They perform religious activities for show. Perhaps most serious, they prey on widows, managing to take resources from some of society's most economically vulnerable members. Jesus does not explain how the scribes do this, but the subsequent verses offer an illustration.

The "temple treasury" was funded in part by freewill offerings. When a widow donates a pair of the smallest coins in circulation, giving "everything she had," according to Jesus, he speaks up. Her sacrifice exceeds everyone else's, because it represents the totality, not a percentage, of her resources.

Often preachers turn to this passage to support stewardship, to encourage greater generosity toward the church, and to reassure those who cannot donate much that every gift counts. Sermons like those have their value, especially in present-day America where, as recent statistical studies demonstrate, poorer people give a higher percentage of their income to charity than rich people. But such sermons risk missing the sting in Jesus' criticism of the scribes. How, exactly, do these religious leaders "cheat" widows out of their resources? In part, by having them support a religious institution—the buildings themselves (see 13:1) and the scribes who benefit from the temple. If the scribes really care about the law, Jesus implies, widows in Israel would not have to endure such poverty. The sheer fact that this one has so little, and that she feels compelled to give her last little coins to support the scribes' opulence, indicates a failure of religious leadership. Wise preachers will allow this passage to help people examine what they give, why they give, and what church budgets do with those gifts to extend God's justice and mercy into a needy world.

Peter Woods

Mark 12

It is difficult in these days of human rights for all to understand the notion of nonpersonhood. As a white South African who grew up during Apartheid, it is perhaps a little easier. I remember the park bench signs, "Whites only" and the separate post-office entrance for "Non-whites" To this day, I still find it damningly easy not to notice people of color on the street despite the fact that they constitute 91 percent of the population of my country.

In the culture of Jesus, widows were nonpeople. Without a man to support or validate them in society, they were nonbeings. Vulnerable and invalid, it was easy not to see them.

Yet Jesus not only notices widows on many occasions during his ministry, in today's text, he actually uses a widow to teach trust and reliance on God.

Mark skillfully sets up the narrative to get us noticing the impressive big donors to the treasury. Just when we are impressed with the four-figure donations dropping into the bank account, he wakes us up to the jangle of the two copper coins hitting the offertory plate!

Look at her—a nonperson with an insignificant contribution. She is our teacher, not the wealthy.

I heard once of a church that takes up the offertory in bags made from fish net. The symbolism of the fish catch is very biblical, but the pastor proudly shared with me the real reason was to encourage people not to give insignificant coins. They would fall right through the offertory bag and onto the floor! Embarrassed parishioners would make that mistake only once. It's too easy not to notice the nonimpressive, nonpeople. Yet Jesus did, for to them belongs the kingdom of the heavens.

November 15, 2015

25th Sunday after Pentecost, Proper 28

1 Samuel 1:4-20; 1 Samuel 2:1-10; Hebrews 10:11-14, (15-18), 19-25; Mark 13:1-8; Daniel 12:1-3; Psalm 16

Elizabeth Quick

http://bethquick.com

1 Samuel 1

- "Because he loved her, though the Lord had closed her womb" (v. 5 NRSV). In a society that valued the fertility of women so highly, Elkanah's treatment of Hannah is particularly sweet.

- I'm amazed at Hannah's generosity. She prays for a child, but promises to give that child to God. Could you ask for and receive a gift from God, and then turn and offer that gift back to God in thanks?

- Eli accuses Hannah of being drunk because of her prayer behavior. The Bible has some interesting examples of people being touched by God and others accusing them of drinking! I guess that is the dramatic effect God's action in our lives can have.

- Eli, being set straight about what Hannah is doing, doesn't dismiss her, but acts as an agent between her and God. Do you ever act like Eli for someone seeking to connect to God?

1 Samuel 2

- This is Hannah's song of thanksgiving for giving birth to Samuel. This reading, poetry, takes the place of a psalm today.

- Hannah thanks God for being one-of-a-kind. She also recognizes that God works in particular on behalf of the poor, the low-down. Compare her song with Mary's song, which we call the Magnificat, in Luke 1. What similarities do you see in these texts? What similarities exist in the situations Hannah and Mary encountered? What other songs of women do we find in the Scriptures?

- Hannah's song is also a victory song, similar to a song one might sing after winning a great battle.

- Her song begins with the personal—what God has done for Hannah, and becomes broad—how God acts in the universe.

- How do you thank God when God answers your prayers? Do you remember to do so?

Thom M. Shuman

http://lectionaryliturgies.blogspot.com/

Shiloh (1 Samuel 1; 2)

you wait

      at shiloh,
where we can bring

our brokenness
                    and,
with the pebbles
            formed from our tears,
the rocks chiseled
            from our hardened
                        hearts,
the stones others
            have cast at us,
                    we build a
            cairn
to mark this place
        as holy ground;

            at shiloh,
where our cries
are
                plainted
with the mother
who cannot afford
medicine for her
                    child,
with the teenager
whose heart bleeds
                    first love,
with the family
whose future has been
                    foreclosed,
we whisper
        our aching loneliness
to the listening
                        One;

        at shiloh,
where our worst
        is enveloped by your
                        best,
where our emptiness
            is filled
            at your table of
                    grace,
where our despair
        is transformed by your
                    hope;

        at shiloh,
you wait . . .

John Wesley
http://www.ccel.org/ccel/wesley/notes

Hebrews 10:20

By a living way—The way of faith, whereby we live indeed. Which he hath consecrated—Prepared, dedicated, and established for us. Through the veil, that is, his flesh—As by rending the veil in the temple, the holy of holies became visible and accessible; so by wounding the body of Christ, the God of heaven was manifested, and the way to heaven opened.

Mark 13:4

Two questions are here asked; the one concerning the destruction of Jerusalem: the other concerning the end of the world.

Chuck Aaron

Hebrews 10; Mark 13

The Mark passage raises two issues that trouble the contemporary church. Some branches of the church insist on trying to predict the nearness of the *eschaton*, pointing to evidence based on contentious interpretation of scripture. The Mark passage refutes the assumption that one can determine such a time. Moreover, it reminds the church that it will do its ministry in the midst of war, violence, and natural disasters. These things remain part of the context of the church's work. This passage also warns the church of persecution. At certain times in the life of the church, and in certain countries now, the church has faced outright persecution. Even without persecution, the church faces conflict, both internally and in the wider world. The underlying admonition to the church is to "stand firm." Even when the church does not face government opposition to its ministry, it needs to stand firm in the face of all the obstacles put in its way.

The Hebrews passage gives a comprehensive understanding of salvation, through forgiveness, affected by Jesus as the priest who offers himself as the sacrifice, and genuine change, resulting in a heart "sprinkled clean." Because of these offers of forgiveness and inner transformation, the church should endure.

Even if the contemporary church does not face persecution, the background for both passages (Hebrews 12:4), it nevertheless faces the temptation of losing faith. The contemporary church faces distractions and competition for time and effort. Both passages affirm the uniqueness of the church and issue calls for enduring faith. In the midst of violence and natural disasters, the church continues its witness, persevering because it knows the value of its message of hope. Despite the struggle with sin, we trust that God can cleanse us.

Julie Craig
http://winsomelearnsome.com

Mark 13

As a child, I didn't want Jesus to come back. I wanted my life to stay my life, and no amount of fire and brimstone from the pulpits of my childhood, no vivid promises of bejeweled crowns to wear or walking on streets of gold so pure they will seem like they are glass, or mansions just over the hilltop, or of all eternity to spend with Jesus could keep me from wanting to see how my earthly life would turn out. An eleven- or twelve-year-old girl doesn't want Jesus to come back before she gets a chance to go to high school, or drive a car, or kiss a boy, or grow up. So when the preachers of my childhood would loudly, insistently, and fervently pray, "Come quickly, Lord!" I, ever the rebel, would be sitting in my pew, or kneeling at the front altar railing, quietly but just as fervently praying, "Not, just yet, Lord. Not just yet."

Not just yet. We're not quite ready just yet, are we?

An entire generation has passed between the death and resurrection of Jesus, and the writing of Mark's gospel. Even though the eyewitnesses are long gone, the Christ's promised return remains uppermost in people's minds—a promise of redemption to a people living under an oppressive government—the promised return of the Savior. Each generation has interpreted this promise within its own context, through its own lens.

My adolescent self could not imagine what she would miss out on if Jesus returned before her life was accomplished, finished, achieved somehow. Sometimes today when I think about Jesus' return, it is tempting to think of all the things I would get out of if it happened today. "Well, there are eight loads of laundry I wouldn't have to do." Somehow, I think Jesus is probably more pleased with the attitude I had when I was a young girl than the idea of "rapture" as a way to avoid housework—or the difficult work of being the church.

David Lose

Mark 13

These verses will likely sound rather odd, even peculiar, to your hearers. And that's for good reason—they are odd and peculiar! Apocalyptic literature—which characterizes this passage—is highly symbolic, operates out of a dualistic worldview, and is usually written to comfort people experiencing severe disruption and confusion. For all these reasons it is open to misinterpretation (think *Left Behind*) or easily dismissed as having little relevance for our life today.

Yet I think it is entirely possible to address this passage to our immediate circumstances. For I suspect that each of us, at one time or another, has asked the question the disciples ask Jesus: "Tell us, when will these things happen? What sign will show that all these things are about to come to an end?" (v. 4). Peter and company are talking about the destruction of the temple. But we may wonder about any number of the multiple prophecies and predictions that occur in Scripture.

Jesus gives no clear answer, only bidding his comrades not to be led astray by those who pretend to be him (perhaps by claiming to know the times and dates that, as Jesus elsewhere says, are known only to the Father). This leads me to wonder if we are called, not to prepare simply for the end times, but *for all times*. Might we, that is, be called to live now, allowing the promises of God about the future to infuse our every present moment? And might we be called to see God at work in ordinary places such as an act of kindness, an opportunity to help another, or the outreach ministry of a congregation? God shows up in all kinds of places, working with us, for us, through us, and in us. You just have to look. Now.

Editor's Insights

Living in Apocalypse (Daniel 12)

I live near Detroit. We understand about apocalypses. I know we're not the only ones. As I write this, people I love in Moore, Oklahoma, are understanding about apocalypses. Between this day and the day you read this, more people will understand about apocalypses caused by all sorts of things we wish we could control but cannot.

How do we control a hurricane? How do we control forces of evil in our society? And how are we the church in the midst of apocalypse—in the midst of an upside-down world where nothing is as it should be?

I wonder not only what it means to have faith within these situations but also what it means to be faithful. Is it living as we always have, carrying on traditions, being faithful to what we know is God in the midst of great chaos? Yes, I think. And is it being ready to experience the Spirit speaking to us through uncomfortable situations, uncomfortable people, within the reality of danger to ourselves and our own power structures and "certainties" that keep us safe? Yes, I think it is.

How do we respond in the midst of such chaos, as individuals? As communities? How do we, to go back to epiphany, find God when it has all been thrown up in the air and things are not as they were, and we are not as we were? How do we understand ourselves? How do we keep watching and waiting when it's difficult to open our eyes to what is around us and among us? Is this what it means to be the church, to be faithful? Merely to listen and to see when all around us are pronouncing the end and the beginning and everything in between? What does it mean to do that within our own lives and within our congregations? How do we prepare to prepare? How do we get ready for the Advent of God?

John Petty

http://progressiveinvolvement.com

Mark 13

The Roman-Jewish War began in 66 CE. In the beginning, the tide of war seemed to favor the rebels, and they had several early successes. In Jerusalem, a provisional government was set up, but never achieved any real stability because of contention between the rebels and zealots on the one side and the clerics and remnants of the aristocracy on the other.

When the rebels eventually gained control of Jerusalem, they did two things. First, they burned the temple archives that contained the records of debt. (Foreclosure had rendered many citizens destitute.) Second, they overthrew the high priest and elected a commoner in his place. The high priest and his retinue were seen as blatant collaborators with Rome.

By late 68 CE and all through 69 CE, the rebels maintained an often-brutal control inside Jerusalem, accompanied by increasing religious fanaticism. The rebels expected the intervention of God and the arrival of the Messiah. In the meantime, they expected all Jews to fight with them against Rome.

This apocalyptic fanaticism received a boost when the Emperor Nero was "removed" from office in 68 CE. General Vespasian, who was conducting the military campaign against the rebels, broke off his attack and returned to Rome. Eventually, Vespasian himself emerged as emperor.

The rebels considered this Roman political crisis to be an intervention from God. Their enemy was in disarray! God really was on their side! Victory was near!

The rebels were delusional. The Romans eventually broke through the Jerusalem defenses, and the bloodbath that followed was horrific. During the course of this bloody melee, the temple caught on fire and was destroyed.

It is just such an environment that tends to generate apocalyptic literature such as that found in Mark 13.

November 22, 2015

Reign of Christ/Christ the King, Proper 29

2 Samuel 23:1-7; Psalm 132:1-12, (13-18); Revelation 1:4b-8; John 18:33-37; Daniel 7:9-10, 13-14; Psalm 93

John Wesley

http://www.ccel.org/ccel/wesley/notes

Revelation 1:5

And from Jesus Christ, the faithful witness, the first begotten from the dead, and the prince of the kings of the earth—Three glorious appellations are here given him, and in their proper order. He was the faithful witness of the whole will of God before his death, and in death, and remains such in glory. He rose from the dead, as "the first fruits of them that slept"; and now hath all power both in heaven and earth. He is here styled a prince: but by and by he hears his title of king; yea, King of kings, and Lord of lords." This phrase, the kings of the earth, signifies their power and multitude, and also the nature of their kingdom. It became the Divine Majesty to call them kings with a limitation; especially in this manifesto from his heavenly kingdom; for no creature, much less a sinful man, can bear the title of king in an absolute sense before the eyes of God.

Dan R. Dick

Revelation 1; John 18

The kingdom language from scripture doesn't translate well in the twenty-first century. Very few people in the Western world have experience with a ruling monarchy. For those whose reality has been modern democracy, the analogy of a kingdom has virtually no meaning. A single ruling individual or family, wielding unlimited power and absolute authority, is rarely viewed as a good thing. We live under the "power corrupts, absolute power corrupts absolutely" cloud. We love our rugged individualism and our personal freedoms. Those who dislike "big government" would absolutely hate having a king, yet as Christians, we acknowledge that this is God's will for our lives.

Today we recognize Christ the King. We hope and pray for the return of the Christ to establish a kingdom of truth and love. We view Christ as the ultimate benevolent dictator, knowing that this king will rule with absolute wisdom, mercy, and justice. This is why the qualities of humility, obedience, and community are so vitally important throughout the Hebrew and Christian Scriptures. The harder we fight for our individual rights, our own autonomy, our personal entitlements, the less prepared and accepting we will be of a ruling monarch in our lives. To envision the heart as a throne, it is challenging and humbling to ask who sits upon it. If we place ourselves on the throne, there is no room for Christ. If Christ is king—not of this world, but definitely of our hearts—then everything changes. Our faith—our core beliefs and practices—ceases to be simply personal and private. We don't get to call the shots. Many people bristle at the very idea of being "ruled." Yet, to become who God calls us to be, there is room for only one monarch—Christ the King.

Marci Auld Glass

http://www.marciglass.com

John 18

Power and authority are often conflated, but the two are not necessarily the same. Pilate has the power to determine if Jesus lives or dies. But he seems a little confused about his authority. The religious leaders come to visit Pilate so he will do their dirty work and kill Jesus. But they won't enter his quarters because it would religiously defile them. Pilate goes out to see them, and his authority begins to evaporate. Why didn't he just tell them, "Right. I'm a busy man. I'll be in my office whenever you're ready to talk"?

Instead, he runs back and forth, seemingly at their whim.

Jesus is summoned to Pilate's office with no concern for his defilement. You wonder if the religious leaders are outside, smirking, "Not only is Jesus guilty, now he's defiled!"

But Jesus doesn't seem concerned about defilement, about the religious leaders and their plans, or about Pilate and his power.

When Pilate asks if Jesus is king of the Jews, Jesus doesn't answer the question, but says, "Did you come up with that question all by yourself? Or did others tell you what to ask me?" (see v. 34). Who's got the authority now, Pilate?

Jesus' words, his calm presence, and his actions constantly remind us that worldly authority has no power in the kingdom of Heaven. Yet we continue to seek, value, and lift up worldly power.

We want to trust in the power of guns or the power of might. We seek political power and prestige. And Jesus stands there calmly, reminding us to ask our own questions, to let the allure of worldly power walk on by.

http://marciglass.com/2013/12/01/for-this-i-was-born/

Suzanne Guthrie

http://www.edgeofenclosure.org

John 18

The sacred cycle of the church year ends with apocalypse in the last Sundays of Pentecost. And the sacred cycle of the church year begins with apocalypse on the first Sunday of Advent. Between apocalypse and apocalypse is the Feast of the Reign of Christ.

To begin and end the year with apocalypse reveals a profound and loving psychology. The church says face your deepest fears. Unless you undertake the journey through your deepest fears, the shadows of the things you depend upon, the questions of existence and annihilation, you won't approach the Real at the heart of reality.

Apocalypse (*apokalypsis*), although associated with the sun darkening, the moon not giving its light, the stars falling, earthquakes, fire and destruction, literally means "unveiling." The lifting of the veil, opening the curtain. Revealing. Revelation. (Ah, but there are so many veils to cling to!)

At the heart of the apocalyptic season, Jesus reigns from a cross. It is the end. It is the beginning. His death is the catastrophic end that begets new life. Jesus is the high priest of the temple. A temple not made with human hands but through the spaciousness of his self-sacrifice. Through the curtain of his flesh, he opens a new and living way (see Hebrews 10:20).

On either side of this revelation is Christ enthroned, not in suffering, not in glory, but in the human heart. To realize this, every person must undergo great upheaval. The church helps us practice year by year for the unveiling of the Real at the heart of the heart.

Karoline Lewis

John 18

This is the second scene of seven narrating Jesus' trial before Pilate. Pilate's question, "Are you the king of the Jews?" is familiar, but its location is different in John. For John, Jesus as king is the major theme of the trial narrative and not of the crucifixion (unlike the Synoptic Gospels). Instead of responding to Pilate, "You say so" (Matthew 27:11; Mark 15:2; Luke 23:3), Jesus answers with a question, "Do you say this on your own or have others spoken to you about me?" essentially putting Pilate on the defensive. Now, who's on trial is the question posed to the reader as well. The reader cannot evade the question any more than Pilate can. How will you answer? What does it mean to call Jesus your king? In Jesus' response to Pilate, it is important to understand the meaning of "kingdom" in the context of larger themes in the fourth Gospel. The term for "kingdom" can also be translated "kingship" and this better captures Jesus' sense here. In John, there is no "the kingdom of heaven is like" because Jesus himself is the very revelation of God to the world in the Word made flesh. There can be no metaphorical answer to what the kingdom of heaven is like because in Jesus, the kingdom of God has been from the beginning, is now, and forever will be. Christ's reign, Christ's kingship is never in doubt. This Jesus is in absolute control, has initiated his own arrest, trial, and crucifixion, and knows exactly what will happen and when. At the same time, Jesus' reign is signaled by love for the world and an intimacy with God that is as close as it gets. A sermon might somehow locate us in this precarious yet poignant place between control and vulnerability.

Todd Weir

http://bloomingcactus.typepad.com/

John 18

This passage begins with Pilate engaging in shuttle diplomacy to defuse the angry mob outside his headquarters. He speaks with Jesus to find out his version of the events, and says, "Look, I'm not one of you, what is this all about?" All he gets is that Jesus sees himself as some kind of king, but not of this world. Jesus says that he is telling the truth and at this point, Pilate scoffs his most famous words, "What is truth?"

Pilate goes back and forth between Jesus and the mob, trying to resolve this without bloodshed. He travels back and forth seven times. First, he has Jesus beaten and tells the mob, "Look, I had my guards rough him up. See his black eye. I think he learned his lesson. Let's just call it a night." He tries to pardon Jesus and release him, but the crowd won't have it. They want a crucifixion and nothing less before their big feast. So Pilate washes his hand of the whole deal, and says that Jesus's blood is on their hands.

Like Pilate, I navigate seven times a day between church and world, and sometimes wearily ask, "What is truth?" But better that for me than to be with Peter swearing, "I do not know that man, Jesus!" I cannot objectively say what truth is. I can only confess I'm challenged and brokenhearted at the injustice of the world's crosses that still crucify the innocent, but still filled with the hope of Resurrection. I confess I am blessed by the love of God, called out of the waters of baptism to serve, and Jesus strangely warms my heart. Advent comes next week, with the promise of new birth and a light shining in the darkness.

November 26, 2015

Thanksgiving Day

Joel 2:21-27; Psalm 126; 1 Timothy 2:1-7; Matthew 6:25-33

Lowell E. Grisham

http://lowellsblog.blogspot.com/

Prayers of the People

Presider: We give thanks to you, Gracious God, for the abundance of creation, for the gifts of the earth, and for your benevolent care for all life: Hear our grateful prayers as we come to you, saying: "God has done great things for us, and we are glad indeed."

Litanist: Our good and generous God, you have given yourself to the church through your Son, Jesus Christ our Savior: Free us from worry or anxiety that we may be your thankful and Eucharistic people, sharing your abundant love for all creation. God has done great thing for us,

and we are glad indeed.

Almighty One, hear our supplications, prayers, intercessions, and thanksgivings for all who are in high positions: Guide them with your wisdom, that we may lead quiet and peaceable lives in all goodness and dignity. God has done great thing for us,

and we are glad indeed.

Loving One, bless this community: Feed us with your abundance like the birds of the air and clothe us in beauty like the grass of the field. God has done great things for us,

and we are glad indeed.

Compassionate One, listen to those throughout the world who sow with tears or who live with any form of anxiety or threat: Comfort them with your gracious generosity, restore their fortunes, and establish them securely so they may never again be put to shame. God has done great things for us,

and we are glad indeed.

Gracious One, we bring to your loving presence all who suffer or who need our intercession, especially ___.
On this day of thanksgiving and praise, we offer our prayers of deep gratitude, especially for ___.
Bring into the feast of your heavenly banquet all who have died, especially ___.
God has done great things for us,

and we are glad indeed.

Presider: With thankful hearts, we offer our prayers to you, O God, the source of all that is: Grant us grace to strive first for your kingdom and your righteousness, and give us all things necessary for our flourishing and service, through your Son Jesus Christ, who with you and the Holy Spirit, lives and reigns, forever and ever. Amen.

John Wesley

http://www.ccel.org/ccel/wesley/notes

1 Timothy 2:2

For all that are in authority—Seeing even the lowest country magistrates frequently do much good or much harm. God supports the power of magistracy for the sake of his own people, when, in the present state of men, it could not otherwise be kept up in any nation whatever. Godliness—Inward religion; the true worship of God. Honesty—A comprehensive word taking in the whole duty we owe to our neighbor.

Matthew 6:30

If God so clothe—The word properly implies, the putting on a complete dress, that surrounds the body on all sides; and beautifully expresses that external membrane, which (like the skin in a human body) at once adorns the tender fabric of the vegetable, and guards it from the injuries of the weather. Every microscope in which a flower is viewed gives a lively comment on this text.

Amy Persons Parkes

Matthew 6

Forget the grain that never grew or the olives that were never harvested or the grapes that never matured into fine wine. I don't care if I swim in olive oil in the near future, or if everyone I know will be fat from threshing floors full of grain. I want to know about the years that passed in devastation and despair. I want to know about the days and the weeks and the months that stretched into year after year of surviving suffering—and not just one suffering, layered suffering, one after another. I want to know how you will repay those years, God. Exactly, how do you propose to do that? Is it possible?

At nine years old, I was enamored with Superman's ability to turn back time when he furiously flew to change the rotation of the Earth; but I'm guessing this is not what you have in mind. At this point, I don't care whether or not I have suffered because of some failure on my part or some unknown, indecipherable intention on yours. I don't have the strength of heart or the foundation of faith to accept or deny either one.

What I want to know is how you intend to repay me for those years? Because I'm not sure you can repay me, not like you can repay me for the money you took or the car you wrecked. Not even like you can repay me for the cookies I baked or the love I have shown.

Unlike the pine trees I planted, time is not a renewable resource. These years may hopefully be redeemed; but they will not be replaced. The years you pledge to repay me may be reinterpreted; but they cannot, they will not be reinstated—just so we are clear.

Teri Peterson

http://clevertitlehere.blogspot.com

Matthew 6

Don't worry about what you'll eat? A foolish exhortation for this day—if we don't worry, will dinner be ready on time? Will the turkey be finished, the mashed potatoes warm and smooth, the pie just right? If we don't worry about it, who will?

Somehow, I doubt this was Jesus passing off responsibility for the big dinner.

Worry, in this text, is the opposite of gratitude. Worry takes our minds off the blessings around us. Worry leads us down rabbit holes so overwhelming that we're oblivious to what God is doing. When we're busy worrying about dinner, we're not enjoying one another's company, we forget that this abundance is not our doing; we rush right past the beauty of an autumn day.

The same is true of other days. Just as gratitude is not reserved for one day (whatever the calendar may say), the admonition to avoid the worry trap is for every day.

Gratitude doesn't require its own holiday—it is a part of the fabric of our being, a natural response to all that has been given to us. Sometimes gratitude is hard—it's difficult to give thanks in all circumstances. *All* circumstances seem as much of a stretch as turning off worry. However, given that Scripture often portrays Jesus as concerned about what we do, not just what we feel. Could it be that worry and gratitude are best known by their actions? What would happen if we acted gratefully in all circumstances?

I suspect we would share more. That old story of stone soup is a great example—the villagers were so worried, they were blind to abundance in their midst. When the traveler shifted their gaze, suddenly they were able to give thanks in ways they never could before. Do not worry, indeed.

John van de Laar

http://www.sacredise.com/

Matthew 6

Jesus sounds pretty naïve when he says, "Do not worry." These words can be understood only if we keep them firmly in context—alongside these other often misunderstood words: "Seek the Kingdom of God above all else, and live righteously, and he will give you everything you need" (v. 33 NLT). This verse is the key to worry-free living.

The Sermon on the Mount is Jesus' manifesto of God's reign. Luke's gospel frames God's reign in terms of the Jubilee instruction to mutual care and protection (see Luke 4:14-21; Leviticus 25:10-19). Both passages offer a vision of a society in which no one would ever have to worry about tomorrow, because the whole community would recognize their connectedness and their dependence on one another, and, like birds and flowers trusting a healthy ecosystem for sustenance, would support, protect, and provide for one another.

This is why Jesus calls his followers to seek first God's reign and righteousness. It's an invitation to change our priorities from trust in our own resources to participation in a community of those who are willing to embrace a new, interconnected way of living. If we do this, all things will be added to us, because we will know the freedom of strong and secure networks of mutual care and support. In such networks, victims of violence and war will discover that protective peacemakers surround them, the hungry and the homeless will find that they are welcomed into the hospitality of caring brothers and sisters, and everyone will know the security of shared resources and mutual generosity. Is it possible to live a worry-free life? Jesus certainly believed it was. But we won't know if he was right until we've actually tried it.

For more detail: http://sacredise.com/blog/?p=696

November 29, 2015

1st Sunday of Advent, Year C

Jeremiah 33:14-16; Psalm 25:1-10; 1 Thessalonians 3:9-13; Luke 21:25-36

Elizabeth Quick

http://bethquick.com

Jeremiah 33

- "Surely." Check out the Advents texts for this whole season. The word *surely* appears almost every week. Maybe that's nothing, but I like it—it's a word of promise, a word of sure fulfillment. Definite.

- A promise being fulfilled. What promises have you made? Broken? Kept? Which have others made/broken/ kept with you? What promise is Jeremiah referencing here? Do you believe God fulfills promises made to you? The world? How?

- A name: "the Lord is our righteousness" (v. 16). That is a powerful name. What does your name mean? What would you like God to call you?

Luke 21

- Advent always begins with surprising "end times" texts that probably catch parishioners, who are ready to sing Christmas carols, off-guard. How do we refocus them and us? This text is about time and expectations and waiting. So is Advent. What we do while we wait is important.

- In our world today, we're often told to be on guard: against terrorists, suspicious activities and packages, and so on. Being on guard *always* can be exhausting. Is this what Jesus means? I don't think so. In fact, he says almost the opposite. We're to be on guard against being weighed down with the "worries of this life" so that Christ's coming doesn't catch us not ready.

- Too often I put things off, procrastinate: I will start giving more…when I'm out of debt. I will take risks *for* God…after I get my DMin. I will speak out about what I really believe . . . when? God arrives unexpectedly. I should stop acting like I have something to wait for before I get to work the way God wants me to. The time is *now*.

Matthew L. Skinner

Jeremiah 33; 1 Thessalonians 3; Luke 21

The beginning of Advent rarely makes a preacher's job easier. Because the assigned texts always direct sermons to grapple with difficult questions concerning living in light of God's yet-to-be-fulfilled promises. We hear older texts' anticipations of God's deliverance alongside newer passages looking toward Jesus Christ's return. We find ourselves asking, "How much of God's work remains undone?" and "How should we therefore live?"

Jeremiah describes God as a promise keeper, determined to send a deliverer as a new "branch" in King David's family tree. Justice, righteousness, salvation, and security will flourish for Israel and Judah. Christians recognize Jesus

Christ as God's means of accomplishing these things on a wider scale, but the daily news reminds us that we still wait for their full fruition.

Paul desires the Thessalonians to grow in holiness as they stay ready to see Jesus come again. In Luke, Jesus speaks of his coming as a manifestation of his future glory (or "splendor"). The passage's conventional imagery describes a cosmic event, something that reorders creation and reveals Jesus as Lord above any possible rival. Nothing indicates "rapture" or our departure to another place. Nothing threatens punishment. Rather, Jesus comes to complete our redemption, finally bringing God's salvation to fulfillment.

Advent's purpose is not to transport us back to the days before Jesus' birth. Advent situates us in an interim, to understand ourselves wedged between promise and fulfillment. Advent prods us to expect more from God. Faith sustains us in such places as we dare to trust that God will be proven right, that promises will be kept, and that God's intentions for our complete wholeness are never far off. It is a season when preachers help us see things we forget are possible. Thus we believe; thus we live as if our redemption is truly near.

Ann Scull

http://seedstuff.blogspot.com

Film Clips

"The Man in the Egg" Found on *Leunig Animated, Madman* (2001). This clip, one of numerous, brilliant, two- or three-minute films. Goes well with both the Gospel and the Thessalonians reading.

"Paperless Christmas": The site, http://www.paperlesschristmas.org.uk (accessed April 29, 2013), has the greatest set of short films based on a modern look at the Christmas story, which will last you from Advent 1 until Christmas 1. A brilliant effort!

Children's Time

Hope: Ask the kids if they have ever planned something that didn't work out the way they intended it to. Share a story from your own life that will illustrate this (mine is a quilt that went horribly wrong between the planning and the completing!) Tell them that Advent is the time when we remember all of God's terrific promises to us that everything will work out because Jesus is the one who brings us… Have huge letters, H-O-P-E, stuck up in random order around the worship space. Ask the kids to help you sort them into a word they know. Discuss with them what the word means and how it relates to Christmas.

Prayer/Poem

"The Coming Bushman" in Pro Hart and Norman Habel, *Outback Christmas* (Adelaide: Lutheran Publishing House, 1981). This fits in well with the Gospel reading.

Response Activity

Fridge magnets: Give everyone a small, laminated card attached to a small fridge magnet with the words of Psalm 25:4-5 on it.

Meditation

"And This Shall Be a Sign to You" by Robert A Raines in Kenneth T Lawrence, Jann Cather Weaver and Roger Wedell (eds.), *Imaging the Word* Volume 1 (Cleveland: United Church Press, 1994), 78. I put this with multiple images of babies and backed it with Ben Harper and the Blind Boys from Alabama, "11th Commandment" on *There Will Be Light* (Hollywood, Calif.: Virgin, 2004) CD Edition.

John Wesley

http://www.ccel.org/ccel/wesley/notes

Psalm 25:8

Upright—Holy and true, in all his declarations and offers of mercy to sinners. Therefore—He will not be wanting to such poor sinners as I am, but will guide them into the way of life and peace.

Luke 21:34

Take heed, lest at any time your hearts be overloaded with gluttony and drunkenness—And was there need to warn the apostles themselves against such sins as these? Then surely there is reason to warn even strong Christians against the very grossest sins. Neither are we wise, if we think ourselves out of the reach of any sin: and so that day—Of judgment or of death, come upon you, even you that are not of this world-Unawares.

Julia Seymour

http://lutheranjulia.blogspot.com

Luke 21

The life of faith is one of anticipation. We long to see the end of the world as we know it. We look for the signs that Christ is coming. The brokenness of the world—wars, poverty, injustice, hunger, nakedness, imprisonment, sickness—are signs of our shortcomings, the presence of sin in the world. We dare not attribute these things as signs to Christ's return, because we then ignore our culpability in the brokenness.

Jesus says that the signs will be as obvious as when spring comes and leaves appear. There will be celestial and earthly signs, and all that occurs will overwhelm people. We, however, cannot allow ourselves to be mired in dread and fear for that time, to be drawn into speculation of when it might be, what it will be like or what will happen afterwards.

Christ tells us to raise our heads, for our redemption will draw near. Christ has promised to be with us, whatever may come. Until that time, we live fully and completely in this life, but in so doing to anticipate with joy in the life of the world to come. The Holy Spirit remains in and among us, nurturing our faith and opening our eyes to the work of God in the world, work that has been done and still needs doing. Until that time, of which we know neither day nor hour, we have work to do.

Assured of our salvation and with the help of the Spirit, the love of Christ compels us into the world. Both Christ's love for us and our love for Christ are compelling, turning us toward our neighbors. In that unfailing light, we take strength and courage that there is still time to change the world.

Peter Woods

Luke 21

The quirky Jesuit-psychotherapist Anthony de Mello (1931–1987) wrote in *One Minute Nonsense* (Loyola Press, 1992) of an interview between an enquirer and a spiritual master.

"What is the secret of your serenity?" asked the enquirer

Said the Master, "Wholehearted cooperation with the inevitable."

If I contemplate the apocalyptic teachings of Jesus, I am confronted with the truth of what Tony de Mello was saying.

So much of the preaching I hear about the coming of the kingdom suggests that we have to implement and successfully execute some program to bring about the coming of the kingdom. Lord knows, there are even some radical Christian groups who believe their role is to hasten global conflict so that the metaphors of the book of the Revelation may literally take place!

This is certainly not what Jesus is saying in this gospel passage. The person of faith, the follower of Christ, is urged to take a far more contemplative and organic stance to these eschatological manifestations. The "coming of the Son of Man" will no doubt be dramatic. When is the breaking in of God into human reality not dramatic?

Yet the signs will be as organic as the sprouting of trees after winter. Stand up and see the coming salvation. That is all that is required.

Simply offer your complete cooperation to what God is doing in the world. After all, this is not your project. It is the work of God. All we have to do is be alert to the fact that it is happening right in front of our eyes.

December 6, 2015
2nd Sunday of Advent

Baruch 5:1-9 or Malachi 3:1-4; Luke 1:68-79; Philippians 1:3-11; Luke 3:1-6

Teri Peterson

http://clevertitlehere.blogspot.com

Malachi 3

There are lots of ways to get ready for Christmas. Some get ready by decorating, wrapping, and baking. Others prepare by reading Advent e-votionals, serving the hungry, shopping from the Heifer Project catalog. However we prepare, I think what the prophet Malachi wants us to consider is that we have absolutely no idea what we are doing.

Intellectually, we know we're getting ready to welcome the Christ child, to see what new thing God will do among us. And there are time-honored ways of preparing and welcoming and looking. But, Malachi says, we've forgotten something important. Our whitewashed vision of "God with us" is really a fantasy. It's not going to be Christmas-card perfection, it's not going to be the beauty of one small candle burning in the dark; this is way more than a candle. We are talking about the light of the world. This fire burns so hot that injustice can't stand it. This is messy and sometimes difficult. Our Christmas cards and nativity scenes and Macy's windows don't even begin to get at the reality of God-with-us. And, in spite of our best intentions, we can't possibly begin to prepare for something like this.

There is a sort of motto of the Presbyterian church—*Reformata, Semper Reformanda,* or "Reformed and always being reformed"—being reformed, re-created, by the Spirit of God who is continually at work. I wonder if that motto might also apply to our Advent season. We prepare the best we can, but what's really important is that we are *being* prepared. God's messenger is coming: the messenger who prepares us to be the living temple so that God can enter and be brought to life again and again, right here among us and within us.

Eric D. Barreto

Malachi 3; Luke 1; Luke 3

Prophetic voices dot the opening chapters of the gospel of Luke. In this way, Luke anchors the story of Jesus in the ancient tradition of the prophets of Israel, who pointed out the subtle but powerful ways that God was reshaping the world. This week we see father and son together proclaim the advent of Israel's Messiah. First, Zechariah sings about a "mighty savior" (Luke 1:69) whom God has sent. His *Benedictus* turns to the many prophets who have professed that God would care for God's children and defeat their enemies. He sings with confidence about a promise God made to Abraham ages ago. Time may have passed, but God's trustworthiness is not diminished. Zechariah also sings about his newly born son, whose call is to "go before the Lord to prepare his way" (v. 76).

His son John does precisely this. His ministry is introduced by a litany of historical markers. This eccentric preacher in the wilderness stands with the supposedly great of his time. In his prophetic words, John echoes Malachi and starts readying the paths upon which the Lord will walk. At the close of the proclamation of both John and Zechariah is a confession that stands at the center of Lukan theology. "All humanity will see God's salvation" (3:6). There is no corner too dark to see the dawning light of God's "tender mercy" (1:78 NRSV).

We don't always welcome prophets. Prophets are assigned to point out when our actions are not in line with our faith in a loving God. They call us back to faithfulness and forgiveness. The question for us today is how we can join the chorus that rings from Malachi to Zechariah and John. We can start where they all did. God's light of love and judgment will shine upon us all.

John Wesley

http://www.ccel.org/ccel/wesley/notes

Malachi 3:2

Abide—Who shall be able to stand under the weight of those crosses which in that day, will fall on all sorts of men?

Luke 3:1

The dominions of Herod the Great were, after his death, divided into four parts or tetrarchies. This Herod his son was tetrarch of Galilee, reigning over that fourth part of his dominions. His brother reigned over two other fourth parts, the region of Iturea, and that of Trachonitis (that tract of land on the other side Jordan, which had formerly belonged to the tribe of Manasseh). And Lysanias (probably descended from a prince of that name, who was some years before governor of that country) was tetrarch of the remaining part of Abilene, which was a large city of Syria, whose territories reached to Lebanon and Damascus, and contained great numbers of Jews.

Cameron Howard

Malachi 3; Luke 3

It is traditional in Christian interpretation to read this passage from Malachi during Advent and to think of the messenger described here as John the Baptist: the one who prepares the way for the coming of God. Yet it is important to acknowledge that the book of Malachi imagines the coming of the Lord centered on the Jerusalem temple. That is, the messenger will have a very particular mission to purify the priests and restore correct worship practices in the sanctuary. Even so, the intense imagery of the "refiner's fire" (v. 2) remains an appealing description of the work of John the Baptist, whose wild appearance and menacing words contrast with the docile ideas of the infant Jesus or the Holy Spirit as dove in the surrounding narratives.

The Gospel writers associate John with a different prophetic text, also prominent in Advent liturgies: Isaiah 40. Reading Luke with that passage, John becomes the voice crying in the wilderness. The texts from Malachi and Isaiah both articulate a longing to be in the presence of God. Both prophesy that the Lord is on the way to us, and both acknowledge that preparations are necessary for such an encounter. The way must be made straight, worship must be purified. John, too, makes such preparations by "proclaiming a baptism of repentance for the forgiveness of sins" (3:3 NRSV). While the themes of *waiting* and *hope* rightly dominate Advent, cultivating an accompanying sense of preparation also lays a foundation for the encounter with God we experience in the incarnation. Advent preparation is an active hope, hope forged in the refiner's fire. This preparation may be something we participate in, but it is rooted in something God begins.

Martha Spong

http://marthaspong.com/

Malachi 3; Luke 3

We can imagine what the refiner's fire might be like. Terrific heat melts away impurities in metal. But fuller's soap, how many of us know what that means? It wasn't a gentle soak in a tepid-water bath, such as the ones I use when I block a pair of hand-knit socks. Fullers didn't gently squeeze the fabric without twisting or stretching it. They didn't baby the cloth. They beat the fibers. A fuller put some arm into it.

Have you ever been worked over by someone who told you the truth about yourself? We know, if we have even a little maturity, that like a deep tissue massage or a flow yoga class, the truth can both hurt and heal. When the massage therapist or the teacher sends you home with a bottle of water, you had best drink it. Your muscles will need it. But the ache of the moment gives way to increased flexibility and strength. It allows us to move differently in the world.

The coming of Christ we consider in Advent is not just the birth of a sweet little baby. The texts proclaim an apocalyptic message, pointing to world-changing events that will also change hearts. We still hope God will make things the way we want them to be, while we sit quietly by. We still hope God will change those "other" people. But God's messenger, John, prepares the way and gives warning: We are the metal; we are the cloth. The Savior comes to change us. The arrival of Jesus will change us. He is the refiner. He is the fuller. He refines the metal. He *fulls* the cloth. Are we prepared for the day of God's coming? Can we endure it? Jesus Christ will surely put some arm into us.

D. Mark Davis

http://leftbehindandlovingit.blogspot.com/

Luke 3

Luke uses the word *hegemon* to describe the reign of Tiberius Caesar as well as of Pontius Pilate, inviting the interpreter to appreciate the insightful work of Marxist social analyst Antonio Gramsci. For Gramsci, *hegemony* denotes not only leadership but also a thorough form of domination that requires subjected peoples to adopt value systems that are historically and culturally alien to them. The fact that Luke begins his story with reference to names that have nothing to do with the biblical Hebrew tradition is an example of the hegemony at work. It shows that Luke's audience would understand immediately how this hierarchical system of "Caesar-to-Caesar appointees-to-local rulers-even to religious leadership" works. Many Bible dictionaries and lexicons treat this imperial chain of command as the *background* of the story that follows. For Luke, it is in the *foreground*, stated from the outset. The fact that Luke includes the religious temple leadership in this chain of command is jarring. One is tempted to ask, "What has Rome to do with Jerusalem?" For faithful Jews, the answer should be "nothing." Under the power of hegemony, the answer is "a lot."

Into this structure of power and obeisance, the word of God comes to John. He is in neither the palace nor the temple, but in the desert, going to the Jordan, calling those who live under the arch of the empire to repentance—literally, to turning around. John, as Luke points out, is the voice, crying in the wilderness, "Prepare the way of the Lord." Isaiah's message and John's message merge in this story. What one proclaims, the other also proclaims, both pointing to radical changes in the landscape and ending with the stirring words, "All flesh shall see the salvation of God" (v. 6 NRSV).

December 13, 2015

3rd Sunday of Advent

Zephaniah 3:14-20; Isaiah 12:2-6; Philippians 4:4-7; Luke 3:7-18

John Wesley

http://www.ccel.org/ccel/wesley/notes

Zephaniah 3:20

A praise—So the universal church of the firstborn will be, in the great day. And then the Israel of God be made a name and a praise to all eternity.

Luke 3:8

Say not within yourselves, We have Abraham to our father—That is, trust not in your being members of the visible church, or in any external privileges whatsoever: for God now requires a change of heart; and that without delay.

Two Bubbas and a Bible

http://lectionarylab.com

Zephaniah 3; Luke 3

Celebrating a warrior God for Advent is more than a bit jangling to our nerves, and perhaps to our sensibilities. This is not the "gentle Jesus, meek and mild" (with a tip of the hat to theologian/hymnist Charles Wesley, of course!).

Yet, it *is* God's strength that we celebrate; it is precisely this God who is mighty enough to conquer every enemy—even death.

We do well to remember that Advent is a season for upsetting the tidy apple cart of our worship—at least just a bit.

John the Baptizer gives some pretty practical direction here when asked about the kind of repentance that would stave off being cut down by the root and thrown into the fire.

Apparently, repentance is not just feeling bad about what you did. John wants to see some action.

"Got two coats? Give one of them away to somebody who doesn't have one. Got more food than you can (or should) eat? Why not dollop a bit out to those who would otherwise be hungry today?"

With similar aplomb, he speaks to the tax collectors and the soldiers about fairness, equity, and the like. But actually, John is speaking to us all. Be honest; be open. Don't be arrogant, don't take undue advantage.

This is just good, plain, sensible living. This is doing what's right. We ought to "get it" and be willing to "do it." More often than not, we don't.

The bad news is there's always the Lord's winnowing fork and that unfortunate, unquenchable fire! The good news is Christ is coming—it is he who will save us, and not we ourselves.

Thom M. Shuman
http://lectionaryliturgies.blogspot.com/

come again? (Zephaniah 3; Luke 3)

if what
          the novelists portray,
    the moviemakers show,
       the radio hosts talk,
    the tv preachers yell
    is all true,
           then why would
      i want you to
          return? but

if you come
      so

those thirsting for hope
    will find it gushing
       out of the taps,

those cursed by the world
    will be embraced
       in your arms of love,

that the despair which overwhelms
         so many
    will be gathered with the
      chaff
    and used to warm the
      homeless,

those who have lived
         on the scraps
    we toss into the trash
    will be at the
      head table
    of your feast,

and every one, every last one
         of us
    will find our way
      home;
well then,
      i will wait,
    and while waiting,
      i will rejoice,
    and while rejoicing,
      i will make this
    great news
known.

Editor's Insights

The Question of Salvation (Isaiah 12: 2–6)

What does it mean to say, "God is my salvation?"

If we read verse 1 in this chapter, we find the writer admitting that God was angry with the writer and the writer's community; then God's anger turned away, and God comforted the writer and the community. These are difficult texts, I think, when we consider the historical, critical realities surrounding them. When people in our contemporary world claim that things have gone badly because God is angry with us, our communities, or "them" and "their behavior," we wince. Our contemporary sensibilities are offended. We don't believe in that God.

And yet, is there a way in which it is true? By turning away from what is obviously bad theology, do we miss a point, namely that there are consequences for our actions? Often, consequences are major and complex, and they don't always come immediately, and they don't always come directly; but is there a sense in which we reap what we sow? Is there a sense in which all of what is "God" actually *angers* at injustice, whether it is "ours" or "theirs"?

At the same time, is it true that there is grace—a wider grace way, beyond good consequences—for when we do good? This grace is larger and wider than "forgiveness of sins" or the reward or punishment paradigm. It permeates the entire world and, like a well, the entire world can draw from the salvation found there, not because of our actions but because of God's.

Sharron Blezard

Luke 3

"What should we do?" the people ask John the Baptizer upon hearing his fiery condemnation. The answer is not now, and it reflects the great commandment Jesus will later put forth. To love God, self, and neighbor, we must be willing to share, to give unselfishly, to be fair, and to have the chaff of the world and its siren song burned away from our souls.

At this time of year, people are anticipating Christmas and are primed for generosity. What might you need to do to help them shift their focus from the commercial holiday cheer of the marketplace to the joy, generosity, and mutuality found in today's lessons? How can you help people look for the Advent of the Son of God in new and fresh ways?

Real joy, true gentleness, and peace do not come by frantically rushing around looking for the perfect presents to ensure the best-yet celebration of Christmas. Nor can happiness and fulfillment happen on the heels of guilt and shame. Real, lasting joy springs from an authentic relationship with God in Christ Jesus, who is coming again into our midst, and who loves us madly and completely. Give thanks and praise to God because all of us—lame and outcast, oppressed or lost, imperfect yet beloved—all are being gathered into the body of Christ to celebrate the gift of life abundant.

This most precious gift comes unwrapped, unearned, and unbidden. It is a gift of pure mercy and grace. Make room for the babe of Bethlehem in the humble, hopeful, and hurtful recesses of your heart. What should we do? Prepare a place to nurture the child, to share the good news, to serve in love, and to be surprised anew by joy at the advent of God.

Liz Crumlish

http://somethingtostandon.blogspot.co.uk/

Luke 3

Crashing into our Advent season comes John the Baptist to tear our attention away from the distractions that assail us at this time of year, away from the glitter and tinsel, the shiny trappings that take us away from the heart of our faith.

These distractions provide for us a way out of being challenged by the gospel, help us remain in our cozy complacency, make us feel busy with important things and thus avoid the uncomfortable challenge contained in the gospel. That is the challenge to repent, to share the good news in a way that speaks to and reaches out to those who need to hear it most and, in so doing, be convicted ourselves to change our ways to accommodate God who came among us.

John proclaimed the gospel in a time of change. He proclaimed a way forward in the uncertainty of the world of those who flocked to hear him. And the message he preached speaks into our changed landscape.

We are challenged, today, to find ways to proclaim good news in our changing scene. That involves embracing the hope that is one of the themes of Advent. The hope that the one for whom John was sent to prepare the way is still able to bring light into the darkness.

So, instead of lamenting how difficult it is to see God—instead of harking back to the way things were—what if we start to look for God in unexpected places? What if we prepare to hear the good news from unexpected people? What if we prepare to open ourselves to change so that God can transform us? It's time to wake up to the fact that God lives at the margins of life today and waits to meet us there.

Marci Auld Glass

http://www.marciglass.com

Luke 3

People are coming from everywhere to be baptized by John. Every church dreams of people coming to be baptized, right? And what would we say to those who join us?

"You brood of vipers! Who warned you to flee from the wrath to come?" (v. 7 NRSV).

How's that for an evangelistic message?

"Welcome! We're so glad you're here, children of poisonous snakes!"

John, by calling the crowds a brood of vipers, as opposed to a passel of vipers, or a crowd, or a gaggle, is claiming that they are children, offspring, of these vipers. And surely, the snakes from whom they are descended didn't lead them to repentance. John has not much nice to say about the religious leaders of his community.

So John asks them, "Who warned you to flee from the wrath to come?" Who, he wants to know, called them to repentance?

I imagine the crowd on the riverbanks started to reconsider following this guy. "Umm...you did, John. You're the one who called us here. Remember? Voice crying out in the wilderness and all that?"

But what were they expecting when they came to the riverbanks, one event that would magically change their lives so that nothing bad would ever happen to them? An easy "presto!" moment of salvation that doesn't require any change in your life?

John calls them to something much deeper. Sure, he can baptize large crowds, but if they are just going to go home and live as if everything is the same, then it is a waste of everyone's time.

To the crowd's credit, they seem to get it. At the end of this long lecture about vipers, axes leaning against trees, and everlasting fire, instead of fleeing back to the comfort of their homes, they ask him "What, then, should we do?" (v. 10).

Excerpted from http://marciglass.com/2009/12/17/december-13-2009-brood-of-vipers/

December 20, 2015

4th Sunday of Advent

Micah 5:2-5a; Luke 1:47-55 or Psalm 80:1-7; Hebrews 10:5-10; Luke 1:39-45, (46-55)

Paul Bellan-Boyer

He Shall Be the One of Peace (Micah 5; Luke 1)

Followers of Jesus have looked to the Hebrew Scriptures to understand his mission and his place in God's kingdom. They have stressed its predictions of Jesus' coming. We might also focus on their consistency, not in precision forecasting, but in witnessing to the kind of future God envisions.

God has always been on the side of justice. God wants a world where the hungry are fed, where the lowly are lifted up, where the oppressor's rod is broken, and swords are reforged into plowshares.

The one who is to rule, the coming Messiah, comes clothed in exactly the same cloth the Lord has been weaving from of old. "He shall stand and feed his flock.../ and they shall live secure" (Micah 5:4 NRSV). God's majesty is revealed in God's active role in bringing peace to God's people.

The Song of Mary comes straight out of this tradition. It is a prophetic witness to God's liberative power. And it is more. Coming from the mouth of a young girl in danger, it is testimony that God takes sides.

God lifts up the lowly. But the proud and powerful do not abandon their thrones to the humble poor. Those in command do not invite their servants to the banquet table to be served by princes and potentates. God is going to intervene to see that the hungry are fed. Mary sings what she hopes and knows, that God's mercy is with her and with all her kindred on the margins.

But in this world we live in, the poor are not the only ones who need deliverance. We may cringe at the thought that the rich are sent away empty. Do we also cringe that *every day* the poor are sent away empty? If you are so high you cannot touch the lowly, if you are so full you cannot feel your neighbor's hunger, a role reversal is God's prescription for *your healing*. God looks with favor on the lowliness of his servants. Get "down" with God, and be blessed.

John Wesley

http://www.ccel.org/ccel/wesley/notes

Psalm 80:2

Before Ephraim—Here is an allusion to the ancient situation of the tabernacle in the wilderness, where these tribes were placed on the west-side of the tabernacle, in which the ark was, which consequently was before them.

Luke 1:47

My spirit hath rejoiced in God my savior—She seems to turn her thoughts here to Christ himself, who was to be born of her, as the angel had told her, he should be the Son of the Highest, whose name should be Jesus, the savior. And she rejoiced in hope of salvation through faith in him, which is a blessing common to all true believers, more than in being his mother after the flesh, which was an honor peculiar to her. And certainly she had the same reason to rejoice in God her savior hat we have: because he had regarded the low estate of his handmaid, in like manner as he regarded our low estate; and vouchsafed to come and save her and us, when we were reduced to the lowest estate of sin and misery.

Ann Scull

http://seedstuff.blogspot.com

Listening Song

4Him, "A Strange Way to Save the World" on *The Season of Love* (Nashville, Tenn.: Benson Records, 1993) CD Edition. This is a Christmas song from Joseph's perspective. It is a rarer take than most on the Christmas story and all the more important because of that. Make sure people hear or see the words clearly.

Children's Stories

Ruth Brown, *One Little Angel* (London: Red Fox, 1998): This is a delightful Christmas story with an unexpected ending.

Hilary Robinson and Anthony Lewis, *email: Jesus@Bethlehem (*East Essex: MacDonald Young Books, 1999): This is an unexpected take on the Christmas story.

Prayer/Poem

"The Joy of Elizabeth" in Pro Hart and Norman Habel, *Outback Christmas* (Adelaide: Lutheran Publishing House, 1981). This fits in well with the Gospel reading.

Meditation

"I Sang for Him" in Wild Goose Worship Group, *Present on Earth* (Wild Goose Publications, 2002, 78): This is based on the Gospel reading.

"The Magnificat" Drama: "Mary and Lizzie" Response Activity: "Cloth for the Cradle": all found in The Wild Goose Worship Group, *Cloth for the Cradle* (Glasgow: Wild Goose Publications, 1997), 45, 48, 74. They are all based on the Gospel reading.

Response Activity

"The Promise": List all the promises out of Mary's song, ask people to choose the one that gives them the most hope and to share that hope with someone sitting near them. (Source unknown but probably me)

Safiyah Fosua

Luke 1

Luke describes prophetic words uttered while Mary was pregnant! Mary's pregnancy was so much more than a hideaway, throwaway time, full of discomfort and sickness not talked about in polite company; it was a time of hearing God and speaking words that come from God. Here, Mary is not self-absorbed. Mary sings that God has "scattered the proud.../...brought down the powerful . . . / and sent the rich away empty" (vv. 51-53 NRSV), while the poor will have enough to eat and receive good things in the soon promised future. These are the words of a young revolutionary with a baby bump!

While our ears fill with promises of a new era that upends the old, the future portends coming danger for both Mary and her child. Mary's imminent danger lies in being able to bring this child of heavenly origin into the world. She is an unwed mother, and Matthew (1:19) tells us that it at least crossed Joseph's mind to put her away. Her child's danger lies in his work. There will be a high price paid for scattering the proud. Resist the pressure to turn a messy situation into tidings of comfort and joy too quickly. Much of the splendor of the story lives in the parts that do not look like a popular greeting card.

Mary was young and unexplainably pregnant. In spite of this, she had the spiritual maturity to look beyond herself to the blessings that her child was destined to usher into the world. *This* is one of the lessons to learn from the story of Mary's pregnancy. Which of us is able, when under pressure, to look beyond personal discomfort, loss of relationships or reputation, fear of life, or similar factors to the good that our temporary distress will bring for God and God's people?

Lowell E. Grisham
http://lowellsblog.blogspot.com/

Prayers of the People

Presider: Our souls proclaim the greatness of the Lord and our spirits rejoice in God our Savior. Look with favor upon your children who come to you in prayer and expectation, O God, as we say: The Almighty has done great things for us; and holy is his Name.

Litanist: Merciful God, in the obedience of your servant Mary you have given to the church a model and example of service: Inspire our witness to your presence, that we may be Christ-bearers who manifest your love to all the world. The Almighty has done great things for us;

and holy is his Name.

Almighty God, from modest upbringings you have raised up a Ruler whose origin is from old; you have cast down the mighty from their thrones, and lifted up the lowly: Come to the help of our leaders and all in authority, that they may be instruments of justice and peace. The Almighty has done great things for us;

and holy is his Name.

Gracious God, you hear the voice of all who cry out in suffering or despair throughout the world: Visit all in need with the comfort of your presence, that they shall live secure to the ends of the earth and know the comfort of your abiding peace. The Almighty has done great things for us;

and holy is his Name.

Benevolent God, your Holy Spirit fills the meeting places between friends and relatives: Grant to this community, cordial relationships of support and trust, that we may bring to birth your creative hope for all people. The Almighty has done great things for us;

and holy is his Name.

Loving God, you fill the hungry with good things and come to the help of your servants: We remember your promise of mercy as we offer our prayers of intercession, especially for ___.
You bless us with new life and hope: Hear our gratefulness as we offer our thanks, especially for ___.
You hold our lives within the majesty of your Name: Receive into your eternal life those who have died, especially ___.
The Almighty has done great things for us;

and holy is his Name.

Presider: In your great might you have come to the help of your servants, for we remember your promise of mercy made to our ancestors, to Abraham and his children forever: Fulfill what you have spoken to us and sanctify your people, through the offering of our Savior Jesus Christ once for all, in the power of the Holy Spirit. Amen.

Suzanne Guthrie
http://www.edgeofenclosure.org

Luke 1

The image of an unborn child leaping for joy in the presence of the Holy Spirit calls you and me to that same wild and primal instinct. Emulating the babe in Elizabeth's womb, bounded by water and taut flesh, nearly deaf and blind and without reference to meaning, time, or fate, quickens in us the possibilities of holy recognition.

As the women approach each other, Elizabeth's son leaps in her womb. The future John the Baptist recognizes womb to womb One Who Is to Come: The Christ.

When I visit our cows, something happens that makes me think of Mary and Elizabeth. I'm not involved with the care of the cows. I've never milked them. I've never given them hay or treats. I only bottle-fed Mercy once. I don't even visit them every day. And yet, Silmarill, Jiffy, and Mercy respond to my visits with full attention. I feel a connection that evokes a strong sense of Presence that reminds me of deep prayer. An interior shift happens when I am with them, which moves the same part of the soul that quickens in meditation. We recognize one another.

Recognition implies knowing, acknowledging, perceiving truth. What truth emotes from those huge, warm, graceful creatures and fills me with a sense of calm and connection? What sacred thread unites us in that silent and tender mutual acknowledgment? What do we know together that makes me feel at one with them in so short a time?

The answer is probably as complex as the Milky Way and as simple as prayer. No matter. Something in me leaps for joy, and I leave the pasture full of grace, as the cows return to grazing.

John van de Laar

http://www.sacredise.com/

Luke 1

Our world is addicted to the extraordinary. But in spite of what we may think, Christmas is not about extraordinariness. Neither Mary nor Elizabeth was chosen because of some inherent specialness. They were chosen because they were the epitome of the ordinary. This is what makes the Christmas story extraordinary. How could commoners give birth to children that would be God's Son and his forerunner? How could these children of promise grow up in such ordinary circumstances under such ordinary parents? The answer is this: God's reign does not come through extraordinary people; it stands or falls on ordinary people embracing it and living it out in their daily lives.

The significance of Mary and Elizabeth is based only and completely on the reign of God birthed through them. This is why Elizabeth proclaims Mary blessed—because she believes—and why Mary's song praises God for the justice, grace, love, and peace that God brings into the world through her and through the ordinary, often overlooked, people of the world.

This means that Mary and Elizabeth are us. God *visits all of us*. God's Spirit overshadows *all of us*. We are *all* parents of God's reign. It is time for us to accept the "calledness" of our ordinariness and to give birth to God's reign in our own small ways. Whenever we reject the broken values of Empire and use our wealth to foster simplicity and generosity; whenever we stop waiting for "leaders" to fix things and begin to act in new, restorative ways; whenever we refuse to perpetuate violence in our lives and homes, we proclaim our own *Magnificat* of God's justice and liberation. And, in this way, we become an ordinary part of God's extraordinary, saving mission.

For more detail: http://sacredise.com/blog/?p=1096

December 24 or 25, 2015

Christmas Eve/Day, Proper 1

Isaiah 9:2-7; Psalm 96; Titus 2:11-14; Luke 2:1-14, (15-20)

Carolyn Winfrey Gillette

http://www.carolynshymns.com/

All of You Who Walked in Darkness (Isaiah 9)

MENDELSSOHN 8.7.8.7.8.7.7.7 with refrain ("Hark! The Herald Angels Sing")

All of you who walked in darkness who have known the fear of night—
Now rejoice and sing with gladness; come and see the wondrous light!
God has turned your tears to songs, lifting burdens, righting wrongs.
God sent us a tiny boy bringing hope and peace and joy.
In one little baby's birth, God knelt down to love the earth.

Still Christ comes to save God's people; still he comes to those oppressed.
To the folks who toil and struggle, God has sent the very best.
To the young and to the old, to the homeless, tired and cold,
To the lost, to those who mourn, to the world, a child is born.
In one little baby's birth, God knelt down to love the earth.

In this time of celebration, may we show what life can be,
As we care for God's creation, as we serve the Prince of Peace.
Seeking justice everywhere, lifting burdens others bear,
May we gladly serve and pray—knowing why we live this way:
In one little baby's birth, God knelt down to love the earth.

Biblical reference: Isaiah 9:2-7

Tune: Felix Mendelssohn, Festgesang an die Künstler, 1840. Arrangement by William H. Cummings, 1856. Text: Copyright © 2012 by Carolyn Winfrey Gillette. All rights reserved. Email: bcgillette@comcast.net Web site: ww.carolynshymns.com

Mary J. Scifres

Light in the Darkness (Isaiah 9)

Why is the candlelight service such a powerful image of Christmas Eve? Singing "Silent Night" and sharing the light together is a highlight for many. From ancient times, people have sought ways to find light in the midst of darkness. Humans created fire, then candles, then oil lamps, then electric lights to disperse the darkness. Isaiah proclaimed that God's light shines even in the deepest darkness, and Luke speaks of the glory of the Lord shining around the shepherds. Light is a powerful gift and a vivid portrayal of God's miraculous presence amongst us.

221

In the dark days of winter, light can warm a house and transform a mood. In the story of God's people, God's light warms our cold hearts and transforms our world with new possibilities. At Christmas, we are reminded that the time has come for God to dwell among us (Luke 2:6). Yet Jesus' birth was only the beginning of this indwelling. After Christ's death and resurrection, the Spirit came in order that God's presence might dwell among and within us in new and life-giving ways. Glory to God in the highest, for the peace that passes all understanding now lives in our very being!

John Wesley

http://www.ccel.org/ccel/wesley/notes

Psalm 96:10

Reigneth—God hath now set up his kingdom in the world. Established—The nations of the world shall by the means of it enjoy an established and lasting peace.

Luke 2:6

And while they were there, the days were fulfilled that she should be delivered—Mary seems not to have known that the child must have been born in Bethlehem, agreeably to the prophecy. But the providence of God took care for it.

Elizabeth Quick

http://bethquick.com

Titus 2

• Christmas Eve/Day is the only time Titus appears in the lectionary, and I'm guessing people usually don't use the Titus text when we have so much to talk about in Isaiah and Luke. Poor Titus! But there's some good stuff in this short selection.

• "The grace of God has appeared" (v. 11 NRSV). Grace, something we think of as intangible and invisible, has become tangible, literally touchable, certainly visible, in the coming of the Christ child.

• What are the worldly passions you need to announce? Instead of a season of joy and abundance, it seems we often make the season one of gluttony and selfishness. But in Titus we are called to lives that are "self-controlled, upright, and godly" (v. 12 NRSV). What would you have to change to make that true for yourself?

• "Zealous for good deeds" (v. 14 NRSV). Could you describe yourself as one who is *zealous* for good deeds?

Luke 2

• What does Mary feel in these words? Is she stressed? Exasperated? Scared out of her mind? We don't know the details, but from the text we can't see that there's anyone there to help her through the birthing process except Joseph.

- Why do you think God speaks to the shepherds? Why are they included in the birth? Why not the innkeeper? A priest? Other townsfolk? What do you think the shepherds felt about what they saw? What did they do after the nativity? Did they still wonder about these events years later?

- "Mary treasured all these words and pondered them in her heart" (v. 19 NRSV). One of my favorite verses in the Bible. Could you keep so calm and cool in Mary's situation? What moments have you simply pondered and treasured in your heart because they were so sacred?

Natalie Ann Sims
http://lectionarysong.blogspot.com

Luke 2

- "Child of Joy and Peace" (Shirley Murray)—Excellent words for Christmas and Epiphany; recognizes the poverty of Christ and contrasts it with the greed of Christmas—without being too heavy-handed. I like the Ian Render tune (JENNIFER'S GIFT) best even though it's a little tricky.

- "Dark Is the Night" / "Sing Alleluia" (Francis Patrick O'Brien)—Excellent and simple Christmas song that reflects the Magnificat and the happiness of Jesus' parents. I especially like the last verse: "Word that brings life, embracing humanity, / Jesus, companion be born into our lives." It would be particularly good for a Christmas Eve service. (lyrics and sheet music sample: http://c1824532.cdn.cloudfiles.rackspacecloud.com/GC2_362-1.jpg)

- "Dream a Dream" (Shirley Murray)—Broad words of hope for the future of creation and the world's people. There are many possible tunes! (sheet music sample: http://c1824532.cdn.cloudfiles.rackspacecloud.com/G6653rebox.jpg)

- "Her Baby Newly Breathing" (Brian Wren)—Realistic words of Mary's motherhood of a real-life type of infant, to the familiar tune MERLE'S TUNE. (lyrics: http://campus.udayton.edu/mary/resources/music/mus_words/christma.htm, scroll down)

- "Star-Child" (Shirley Murray)—A lovely, lovely carol. Very easy to sing. A big favorite! (lyrics and midi: http://www.hymnary.org/text/starchild_earthchild_gobetween_of_god)

- "The Tiny Child to Bethlehem Came" (Marty Haugen)—Good words of hope for peace sung to a Celtic-style tune that is not too hard. (sheet music sample: http://c1824532.cdn.cloudfiles.rackspacecloud.com/GC_355-1.jpg; sound sample: http://c1824532.cdn.cloudfiles.rackspacecloud.com/GC_355.midi)

- "The Wind Blew Keen" (Colin Gibson)—A beautiful carol, with simple, straightforward Celtic-type tune. I hope this becomes popular, because it's really lovely.

- "Who Is the Baby an Hour or Two Old" / "The Aye Carol" (John Bell)—Very simple flowing tune and good challenging words "Will you come with me, e'en though I feel shy?" seems perfect for those who rarely step into a church. (sheet music sample: http://c1824532.cdn.cloudfiles.rackspacecloud.com/GC_371-1.jpg)

- "Within a Stall a Baby Lies Cradled" (David Wood)—Inspiring words for Christmas Eve full of hope for a better world. (free sheet music: http://singingthesacred.wordpress.com/2012/12/13/within-a-stall-a-baby-lies-cradled-but-on-this-night/)

- "He Came Down" (traditional from Cameroon)—A simple, repetitive song. Great for kids and for drumming; some translations have "Jesus came bringing us love." (sheet music and sound sample: https://www.onelicense.net/index.cfm?go=main.preview, enter "He Came Down" in search window)

Two Bubbas and a Bible

http://lectionarylab.com

Luke 2

I grew up in a four-room house: living room, kitchen, parent's bedroom, children's bedroom. Well, five if you count the outhouse in the woods.

On Christmas Eve, the children went to bed by nine, the four of us in one room, all under age ten. Daddy reminded us every Christmas Eve that if we heard noise in the night we should stay in bed, because Santa would take our presents back if he caught us peeking.

Early Christmas morning, we slipped into the living room. As we opened our presents and filled our mouths with candy, we became aware of a presence in the room. We turned and saw a large man with white hair and a beard sleeping on the couch, his huge belly going up and down with every snore. We were, to use a biblical phrase, "sore afraid." We were sure we knew who this visitor was.

We did the only thing we could; we gathered all the toys and candy and hid in our beds, cowering in the dark and cold, waiting for him to leave. Mid-morning, our parents came to see why we were not up. "Is he gone?" we asked. "Is who gone?" they responded. "Santa," we whispered. They laughed so hard the house shook.

Our visitor was my mother's uncle, who had shown up around midnight, on foot and a bit tipsy, with nowhere to go. And my parents put him to bed in the only place they had, the living room couch in front of the Christmas tree. No sermon or story ever taught me more about the true meaning of Christmas.

Rick Morley

Luke 2

Luke's account of the nativity opens like a grand, epic movie. It's so wondrously regal that one can almost hear James Earl Jones's narration.

The emperor issues a command to the whole world, and the whole world hears and responds. The impressive name of the governor of Syria is invoked, and a certain man whose lineage includes David, king of Israel, rises and goes to his ancestral home to fulfill the wish of the emperor. The woman to whom this man is engaged makes the journey with him, and when they arrive she bears their child.

Oh, it's just so wonderful! So dramatic! A fairy-tale beginning.

But then the action shifts, and all of a sudden we're brought to...a manger. A manger? How incongruous after all the talk of emperors and governors and kings and such.

Then, just to add insult to injury, the scene moves to a field brimming with smelly sheep and smelly shepherds doing their work on the third shift. Couldn't those angels have sung their "Glorias!" to a more august audience and in a more proper setting?

Luke writes the story of Jesus' nativity with whiplash built in. The shift from emperors and angelic choirs to mangers and shepherds is abrupt to say the least. "Majestic" becomes "homely" very quickly.

Jesus did not come to hang out with royalty issuing their decrees from the splendor of marble palaces. The austerity of the manger and the shepherd's field wondrously shows how Jesus came to live among all God's people: the meek and the lowly, the poor and the lame, the sinners and the saints. Us.

Todd Weir

http://bloomingcactus.typepad.com/

Luke 2

Preaching challenges me in Advent because of the sharp contrast between the texts I am given to preach and the peculiar gift-giving, office-party holiday that stole the name "Christmas." I am tempted to stick with the benign words "Be not afraid," but to avoid the source of fear. The text has more to say to us than that the presence of angels is startling, and life sometimes requires unexpected journeys, even during pregnancy. Luke 1 announces the birth of prophets who will live out the great reversal of wealth and power proclaimed in Mary's Magnificat. Luke 2 brings the birth of Jesus under the shadow of Quirinius, a warrior favored by Augustus to subdue the provinces. The Jewish historian Josephus recorded that a census was forbidden under Jewish law, and the province of Judea was near revolt (http://jewishency-clopedia.com/articles/12463-quirinius-p-sulpicius, accessed August 3, 2013). Luke's birth narrative is the hope of an occupied people frustrated by injustice.

"Be not afraid" is a crucial message to preach, but we must first exegete the empires and occupations of our time. Will we tell our congregations that the toys and gadgets they buy might be made by other peoples' children or in servile, unsafe working conditions? Do we have the courage to preach a "fair trade" Christmas? How will we be in solidarity with those who have no room at the inn, born at a disadvantage from their first breath? Or will we celebrate the good news while keeping Jesus outside our merry, candlelit sanctuaries, worshiping like the innkeeper who will give him only a manger? To celebrate fully the great joy and the message "Be not be afraid," we must welcome the oppressed and suffering into our Christmas season.

December 27, 2015

1st Sunday after Christmas

1 Samuel 2:18-20, 26; Psalm 148; Colossians 3:12-17; Luke 2:41-52

Mark Stamm

1 Samuel 2; Luke 2

When preaching Luke 2:41-52 and other texts within Luke's infancy narrative, one must push beyond sentimentality, although the greeting-card images are difficult to resist. In this case, we see the stresses of a family pilgrimage along with the devastating parental anxiety over a missing child. We find Jesus—still a boy—actively engaged in the temple, "sitting among the teachers" (v. 46) who were amazed at his understanding. Imagine not simply a precocious child, but real debate.

The infancy narratives are not simply interesting stories from a family album; they point to the vocation and mission of the "adult Christ" (for elaboration of this idea, see *An Adult Christ at Christmas* by Raymond E. Brown [Collegeville, Minnesota: The Liturgical Press, 1978]). Although a child, he stands among the rabbis, and he does so in Jerusalem, to which he will return for confrontation and suffering, and resurrection.

We do, however, see him here as a child, and the childhood of Jesus sanctifies all childhood. That assertion is both scandalous fact and challenge. Young children and youth are our brothers and sisters in Christ, and the Holy Spirit abides in them as in us. How shall we receive their perceptions and affirm their baptismal dignity while continuing our work of shaping them?

Luke echoes some of what we hear in 1 Samuel 2, including the summary statement, "Samuel continued to grow both in stature and in favor" (v. 26 NRSV; compare Luke 2:52). The boy Samuel stands before the Lord, given to God by his mother. The idea that one could give a child to someone, even God, may seem repulsive. Nevertheless, we give our children deep exposure to a particular vision of life, our own. Therefore, we should choose wisely, both in the fear of God and in love for these our young neighbors.

Julia Seymour

http://lutheranjulia.blogspot.com

Psalm 148

My son has a plastic nativity set that he uses as part of his regular toys, and I do not know where most of the set is. I once said to my husband, "I have not seen Jesus since March." The most popular parts of the set at our house are in regular play rotation: the donkey, the cow, the dog, and the sheep.

Thus, the animals that witnessed the birth of the Savior of the world are bus passengers, log house residents, and obstacles for trains and cars to pass just in time. They are considered "everyday." This is the opposite of what happens in most congregations, where the animals are trotted out to be sure everyone gets a part in the Christmas pageant, and then we do not think of them again for eleven months. What is the role that animals play in our theology and in the lives of our congregations?

Psalm 148 confronts the problem of humancentric theology with the very real notion that all creation rejoices in salvation. Animals are literally among those who sacrifice for our way of life.

People will dismiss charity to animals or broadening our understanding of theology to include salvation *to all creation* by saying that animals do not have reasoning ability (not true), do not have feelings (not true), or are not as important as people (not true). If we ignore the most vulnerable around us (arguably animals), we can easily make the leap from ignoring animals to ignoring people who are somehow less functioning members of society (however that's determined). As Christians, either every aspect of our lives connects to our faith or none of it does. What's it going to be with regard to animals? Let us read Psalm 148 again.

John Wesley

http://www.ccel.org/ccel/wesley/notes

Psalm 148:14

The horn—In scripture commonly denotes strength, victory, glory, and felicity.

Luke 2:46

After three days—The first day was spent in their journey, the second, in their return to Jerusalem: and the third, in searching for him there: they found him in the temple—In an apartment of it: sitting in the midst of the doctors—Not one word is said of his disputing with them, but only of his asking and answering questions, which was a very usual thing in these assemblies, and indeed the very end of them. And if he was, with others, at the feet of these teachers (where learners generally sat) he might be said to be in the midst of them, as they sat on benches of a semicircular form, raised above their hearers and disciples.

Julie Craig

http://winsomelearnsome.com

Luke 2

We lost track of our youngest child once at the happiest place on earth. It was only a few moments, but they were the longest, scariest moments of my life.

We were at Disney World, and our daughter was about to turn three years old. We'd gone into one of those indoor stand-up screenings, the ones with the Very Large Screens. The subject was space walking or something like that. My fear of heights kicked in and I closed my eyes, just for a moment. When I opened them, she was gone. She'd been standing right in front of me, but suddenly she was gone!

I admit it; I panicked. I stood there, frantically shouting her name, holding onto my son's hand for dear life as the lights came on and the dark room started to empty. My husband found her a minute later, walking toward the exit, perfectly fine, as if nothing had happened. As if my heart hadn't stopped beating. As if my world hadn't begun to end.

So I understand Mary and Joseph's point of view here. I know the frantic feeling of losing track of a child for a moment. I cannot imagine three sleepless nights and three terror-filled days of not knowing where my child was.

(And, as a mother, I have to say I find Jesus' response here to be not very Godlike, but that of a sulky tween. Good heavens, child!)

How much more must God feel when we wander away? How much more must God long for us to be close, to trust, to seek God's face, to never be out of God's sight? I can't even imagine.

Kwasi Kena

Luke 2

Christmas, the season of gift giving, is over. Gifts receive varying treatment: Some are cherished and some get exchanged, while others get tucked away to be forgotten or rediscovered.

Mary and Joseph received the gift of God's son, Jesus. This gift, birthed with great fanfare, with a bright star and visitation by wise men, is now twelve years old and stirring his parents' consternation. After a frantic three-day search, Mary and Joseph find Jesus in the temple, calmly speaking with teachers. Mary, understandably upset, demands an explanation from Jesus saying, "Child, why have you treated us like this?" (v. 48). Equally dismayed, Jesus responds, "Why were you looking for me? Didn't you know that it was necessary for me to be in my Father's house?" (v. 49).

Mary and Joseph aren't ready for the boy Jesus to begin acting in unpredictable, Spirit-led ways. But Jesus, God's gift, won't stay boxed up. His divine destiny won't stay out of sight and out of mind.

The reading from 1 Samuel records another experience of parents and their God-given gift, Samuel. Hannah dedicated her son to God's service and left him in the care of Eli for training in priestly ministry. Despite his constant exposure to Eli's corrupt, womanizing sons, Samuel remains faithful to God. Why? We can only speculate. Each year Hannah sews a new robe for Samuel and she and husband Elkanah deliver it to him. Who knows what is said during those visits. Maybe Hannah reminds Samuel of God's call on his life. Maybe she speaks about her love for God. Maybe the robe becomes a yearlong reminder of who he is to become. Hopefully, his parents' conversations contribute to Samuel's faithfulness to God.

God still sends gifts to us—children singled out for divine service. What can we do to encourage them to love and serve God?

John Petty

http://progressiveinvolvement.com

Luke 2

This story completes the early identification of Jesus in Luke's gospel. Gabriel had told Mary that her child would be "holy," and would be "God's Son" (1:35). He was identified as "dedicated to the Lord" in 2:23. Now, in this episode, he self identifies as God's Son.

"His mother cherished every word in her heart. Jesus matured in wisdom and years, and in favor with God and with people" (vv. 51a-52). The verse forms a bookend with verse 40: "The child grew and became strong. He was filled with wisdom, and God's favor was on him," which refers to the years between Jesus' birth and this episode. Verse 51 refers to the years between this episode and his public ministry. In each case, Jesus grows in wisdom, and, in each case, the favor of God was upon him.

Note that Joseph and Mary search for Jesus for "three days." When an early Christian heard the phrase "for three days," one of their first associations would have been to think "resurrection." Jesus rose from the dead after "three days." Virtually every first-century Christian would have made this association automatically. This would indicate that the story should be understood and seen in light of the Resurrection.

In the Resurrection, Jesus' conversation and dialog "among" of the teachers in the temple is a portrayal of life in the new world of God wherein the hallowed place of tradition—the temple—is transformed into a place where Jesus is now in the center. From that position, he is in dialog with the tradition, yet with new and astonishing understanding, so much so that the teachers of the tradition look upon him with respect and astonishment.

Martha Spong
http://marthaspong.com/

Luke 2

The whole family has been to Jerusalem, to the temple, traveling with friends and neighbors. They made the journey together. Everyone keeps an eye on the children. One of the mothers counts repeatedly. It takes pressure off the others.

She hates to tell Mary. A good boy missing could mean a boy in real trouble. Time matters. Has someone taken Jesus? She calls to his mother. "I'm sure we can find him," she says, but she can hear the sharp edge in a voice usually so soft, when Mary calls, "Joseph! Come quickly!"

That's when people tell the mother to breathe, but she can't get a breath at all.

Word spreads. Some go ahead, in case he ran that way. Boys do run off, she says to Mary. Boys will be boys. Don't worry. Not yet.

Not yet. That's what they say. Boys will be boys.

Some go back, retracing steps. Some look on the side of the road, just in case he fell, or worse.

Mary's heart beats fast. How can a heart beat so fast?

Joseph and Mary run back to Jerusalem. After three days, they find him at the temple, talking to the elders as if he knows what he's doing.

He didn't know how they had worried. He lost track of the time. He has work to do, his Father's business. He is an unusual boy.

Boys will be boys. Jesus will be Jesus.

You want to yell at them, when they finally come home. You want to yell and cry, but you don't. You hug them, if they'll let you.

Mary is unusual, too. She takes these things and keeps them. She keeps them in her heart.

Online Media and Other Helpful Resources

(PLEASE CHECK AT SITE FOR COPYRIGHT RESTRICTIONS)

Activity Sheets for Children

http://www.ucc.org/children/fun-page/activity-sheets-for-children.html—Weekly activity sheets from the United Church of Christ.

Agnus Day

http://www.agnusday.org/—The weekly lectionary cartoon by Pastor James Wetzstein, with archives and indexes.

Art in the Christian Tradition, Vanderbilt University's Jean and Alexander Heard Divinity Library

http://diglib.library.vanderbilt.edu/act-search.pl—Classical and contemporary images with attributions.

Bulletin Covers

http://www.scholia.net/bulletins.htm—.doc file bulletin covers using line drawings and scripture readings from Our Redeemer Lutheran Church in Emmett, Idaho.

Christian Reflection from Baylor University, The Center for Christian Ethics

http://www.baylor.edu/christianethics/index.php?id=14715—A site that includes excellent adult study resources, articles, and media resources based on theme.; issues indexed into the lectionary cycle at www.textweek.com

Faith Element

http://www.faithelement.com/—A Bible study curriculum for youth and adults which includes images and movie clips.

Faith Formation Journeys

http://faithformationjourneys.org/—Children's resources for church and home.

Faith Lens

http://blogs.elca.org/faithlens/—From the Evangelical Lutheran Church in America, Faith Lens contains weekly conversations with youth about contemporary issues, including videos and images; available from September to May.

Hermano León Clipart

http://www.cruzblanca.org/hermanoleon/—Free clip art for church bulletins, etc.

Hymnary.org

http://www.hymnary.org/—A comprehensive index of 1,181,339 hymns from 5,465 hymnals; includes scores, media and information.

Lectionary Planning Helps

http://www.gbod.org/lead-your-church/lectionary-planning-helps/—Commentary, worship resources, hymn suggestions, and prayers from the General Board of Discipleship (GBOD), The United Methodist Church.

ON Scripture, Odyssey Networks

http://odysseynetworks.org/on-scripture—Weekly commentaries by various authors relate contemporary issues and scriptural themes; articles include videos of contemporary events.

Oremus Hymnal

http://oremus.org/hymnal/—Traditional and original hymns based on the weekly lectionary texts; includes sound files.

Pitts Theological Library Digital Image Archive Lectionary Index

http://pitts.emory.edu/dia/elca_lectionary.html—Many images from the Kessler Reformation Collection.

Samuel

http://www.ucc.org/worship/samuel/—Commentary and other resources from the United Church of Christ.

Scripture Pics

http://www.scripturepics.org/—Free PowerPoint backgrounds.

Sermon Brainwave

http://www.workingpreacher.org/brainwave.aspx—Excellent podcast discussion of weekly scriptures by faculty at Luther Seminary; an excellent resource for preaching.

Sermons 4 Kids

http://www.sermons4kids.com/—Weekly coloring pages, puzzles, games, song, and children's ideas in English and Spanish by Charles Kirkpatrick.

Sing for Joy

http://www.stolaf.edu/singforjoy/—Radio broadcasts of lectionary-related music from St. Olaf College in Northfield, Minnesota.

Storypath

http://storypath.upsem.edu—"Connecting Children's Literature with Our Faith Story."

The Sunday Website of Saint Louis University

http://liturgy.slu.edu/index.html—Commentary, exegesis, spirituality, history, prayers, and musical suggestions specifically for the mass, but useful to all preachers.

Together to Celebrate

http://www.togethertocelebrate.com.au/—A resource for contemporary worship music by David MacGregor; here you'll find original material plus information for finding contemporary music resources for each lectionary week.

Visual Theology by Dave Perry

http://visualtheology.blogspot.com/—Lectionary-themed photography.

Working Preacher

http://www.workingpreacher.org—Commentaries, articles on the craft of preaching, discussions, and more; Working Preacher has a scripture index and commentary indexed according to the Narrative Lectionary for those not using the *RCL*.

Worshiping with Children

http://worshipingwithchildren.blogspot.com/2013/07/year-c-proper-14-19th-sunday-in.html—Suggestions for including children in congregational worship by Carolyn C. Brown.

You Call That Church Music?

http://youcallthatchurchmusic.blogspot.com/—Contemporary secular music suggestions for worship, Ann Strickland.

Commercial Sites

Church Galleries

http://www.churchgalleries.com/—PowerPoint backgrounds and other images by/from Dorothy Okray; images for purchase along with free weekly samples.

Jan Richardson Images

http://www.janrichardsonimages.com/—My favorite contemporary art site. Jan creates new images each week. Images and subscriptions available for purchase.

Ministry Matters

http://www.ministrymatters.com/—An excellent resource for preaching, teaching, worship, evangelism, and leadership

The Work of the People

http://www.theworkofthepeople.com/—Excellent scripture-based videos, available for purchase individually or by subscription.

Conversation Partners
Index

Chuck Aaron

Charles Aaron serves as pastor of Whaley UMC in Gainesville, Texas. He tries to balance parish ministry with scholarship, writing, and participating actively in the Society of Biblical Literature. He has pastored churches in Texas, Tennessee, North Carolina, and Virginia. He has written or edited four books, and published several articles and sermons. He has taught courses in Bible and preaching at Duke, SMU, Austin Seminary, and Union Presbyterian Seminary.
Find Chuck's contributions in January 4, March 1, April 19, July 5, September 13, November 15

Eric D. Barreto

Eric D. Barreto is Assistant Professor of New Testament at Luther Seminary in St. Paul, Minnesota. and an ordained Baptist minister. The author of *Ethnic Negotiations: The Function of Race and Ethnicity in Acts 16* (Mohr Siebeck, 2010) and co-author *New Proclamation*, Series C, Easter through Christ the King, 2013 (Fortress, 2012), he is also a regular contributor to ONScripture.org, the Huffington Post, WorkingPreacher.org, and EntertheBible.org.
Find Eric's contributions in January 4, March 8, May 17, July 12, September 20, December 6

Paul Bellan-Boyer

Paul Bellan-Boyer is a member of St. Matthew's Lutheran Church (ELCA) in Jersey City, New Jersey, where he runs a special-needs housing program for Garden State Episcopal Community Development Corporation. Paul is actively involved in community organizing locally and statewide, leading successful campaigns in housing reform and community health care. Paul blogs at http://citycalledheaven.org/.
Find Paul's contributions in January 11, March 1, May 31, July 19, September 13, December 20

Sharron Blezard

The Rev. Sharron Blezard is an ELCA pastor who serves Trinity Evangelical Lutheran Church in Rouzerville, Pennsylvania. Also a freelance writer, editor, and college writing instructor, Sharron is married to the Rev. Robert Blezard. Between them, they have four children ages fourteen to twenty-five. Sharron's interests include film, fiction, poetry, and the interplay of spirituality and the arts. She blogs at www.adventuresinthanksliving.com and writes a weekly lectionary reflection for stewardshipoflife.org.
Find Sharron's contributions in January 11, March 8, May 24, July 19, September 20, December 13

Julie Craig

http://winsomelearnsome.com

Julie Craig is a writer, speaker, and pastor living in Wisconsin. She is an ordained minister in the Presbyterian Church (USA) and has served in the local and synod level. She currently lives in the suburbs with her spouse while their adult children manage just fine without them in far-flung places. A reluctant dog walker, failed knitter, and capricious reader, Julie is fueled by strong coffee, deep laughter, and really cute shoes.

Find Julie's contributions in January 4, February 1, March 8, April 2, May 31, June 28, July 5, July 19, September 13, October 4, November 15, December 27

Liz Crumlish

http://somethingtostandon.blogspot.co.uk/

Liz Crumlish is a Church of Scotland minister, working in Ayr, on the west coast of Scotland. Married, with two children and a border collie, Liz finds renewal by walking on the beach or along the riverside. She *love*s the *Vicar of Dibley* (BBC) and aspires to be like her, teaching the gospel while having fun—challenges for a Scottish Presbyterian! (See Liz's personal blog http://liz-vicarofdibley.blogspot.co.uk/.) Liz's passion in life is to discern the presence of God in everything and, along the way, to reveal that presence for others.

Find Liz's contributions in January 25, February 8, March 1, March 15, April 2, May 31, June 21, July 26, September 27, October 11, November 8, December 13

D. Mark Davis

http://leftbehindandlovingit.blogspot.com/

Mark Davis frequently writes about theology and biblical interpretation. He is the author of *Talking about Evangelism* (2006, The Pilgrim Press), *Left Behind and Loving It* (2011, Wipf and Stock) and blogs weekly at leftbehindandlovingit. blogspot.com. Currently serving as the pastor of Heartland Presbyterian Church in Clive, Iowa, Mark holds a PhD in Theology, Ethics, and Culture from the University of Iowa, as well as a D.Min. from Union Presbyterian Seminary in Virginia.

Find Mark's contributions in February 1, February 18, March 1, April 3, May 17, June 21, July 12, August 2, September 6, October 4, November 8, December 6

Dan R. Dick

Dan Dick is a pastor serving as the director of Connectional Ministries in the Wisconsin Annual Conference (of The United Methodist Church). Dan has a passion and love for the church, working for over thirty years in spiritual formation, leadership development, spiritual giftedness, stewardship, planning, evangelism, and outreach. He has authored (or co-authored) fifteen books and hundreds of articles. Read Dan's thoughts on the church and other topics in his blog, United Methodeviations (http://doroteos2.com/).

Find Dan's contributions in January 18, March 22, April 26, July 26, October 4, November 22

Safiyah Fosua

Dr. Safiyah Fosua is the assistant professor of Congregational Worship at Wesley Seminary of Indiana Wesleyan University. She is a former director of transformational preaching at the General Board of Discipleship (The United Methodist Church). Safiyah has written several Bible study and devotional books, served as associate editor for Discipleship Resources' *Africana Worship Book series*, contributed to several commentaries and preaching anthologies, and is a columnist for WorkingPreacher.org. Safiyah is married to Kwasi Kena, who also teaches at Wesley Seminary at IWU.

Find Safiyah's contributions in January 25, March 22, May 31, August 2, October 4, December 20

Carolyn Winfrey Gillette

http://www.carolynshymns.com/

Carolyn Winfrey Gillette is the author of *Songs of Grace: New Hymns for God and Neighbor* (Upper Room Books) and *Gifts of Love: New Hymns for Today's Worship* (Geneva Press). She and her husband Bruce are the co-pastors of Limestone Presbyterian Church in Wilmington, Delaware. She is the mother of John, Catherine, and Sarah.

Find Carolyn's contributions in January 4, February 1, March 8, March 29, April 19, May 31, June 21, July 5, September 6, October 11, November 8, December 24

Marci Auld Glass

http://www.marciglass.com

The Rev. Marci Auld Glass is the pastor of Southminster Presbyterian Church in Boise, Idaho, and a graduate of Columbia Theological Seminary in Decatur, Georgia. She and her husband, Justin, have two teenaged sons, Alden and Elliott. She also serves on the board of the Covenant Network. In her free time, she rides her bike (primarily to coffee shops) and hikes in the Boise foothills.

Find Marci's contributions in January 4, March 15, April 5, May 3, May 17, June 14, July 5, August 16, September 20, October 18, November 22, December 13

Lowell E. Grisham

http://lowellsblog.blogspot.com/

The Rev. Lowell Grisham is rector of St. Paul's Episcopal Church in Fayetteville, Arkansas. He is working to complete a three-year cycle of Prayers of the People. Lowell is involved in several social-justice ministries and writes a local newspaper column. He has special interests in congregational development and contemplative prayer. Lowell's blog is also picked up four days a week by EpiscopalCafe.com on their Speaking to the Soul blog. He's a native of Mississippi. He and his wife, Kathy, have two children and three grandchildren.

Find Lowell's contributions in January 11, February 15, March 15, April 3, May 31, June 14, July 5, August 16, September 6, October 18, November 26, December 20

Suzanne Guthrie

http://www.edgeofenclosure.org

Suzanne Guthrie is an Episcopal priest, writer, and retreat leader. Suzanne has served the church as a pastor, children's priest, and college and university chaplain. She creates Soulwork Toward Sunday: a weekly self-guided retreat based upon the coming Sunday's Gospel at http://www.edgeofenclosure.org.

Find Suzanne's contributions in January 11, February 15, March 1, April 3, May 3, June 7, July 12, August 9, September 20, October 18, November 22, December 20

Cameron Howard

Cameron B. R. Howard is assistant professor of Old Testament at Luther Seminary in St. Paul, Minnesota, and a member of the Presbyterian Church (U.S.A.). Among her publications are contributions to *The New Interpreter's Bible One-Volume Commentary* (Abingdon Press) and the twentieth-anniversary edition of the *Women's Bible Commentary* (Westminster John Knox Press).

Find Cameron's contributions in January 18, March 15, May 17, June 28, September 27, December 6

Kwasi Kena

Kwasi Kena is an assistant professor of Christian ministry at Wesley Seminary at Indiana Wesleyan University. Prior to that, he served on the staffs of three United Methodist agencies and was a missionary to Ghana West Africa with his wife, The Rev. Dr. Safiyah Fosua. Kwasi is an ordained elder and member of the Greater New Jersey Annual Conference. His hobbies include playing and arranging jazz versions of popular hymns and Christian songs and creative writing.

Find Kwasi's contributions in February 22, April 5, June 21, August 23, November 1, December 27

Linda Lee

Linda Lee (retired) serves as bishop-in-residence at Garrett Theological Seminary in Evanston, Illinois. She resides in the Madison area with her husband, Lamarr Gibson, a United Methodist elder serving as a member of the Wisconsin Conference. They have three children and twelve grandchildren. Bishop Lee has been a contributing writer to several books and is editor of *A New Dawn in Beloved Community: Stories with the Power to Transform Us* (Abingdon Press). She is also a graduate of the Upper Room Two-Year Academy of Spiritual Formation.

Find Linda's contributions in January 25, March 15, May 24, August 2, September 27

Karoline Lewis

Karoline M. Lewis (www.karolinelewis.com) is the Alvin N. Rogness Chair of Homiletics at Luther Seminary in St. Paul, Minnesota, and is an ordained pastor in the Evangelical Lutheran Church of America. She holds degrees from Northwestern University and Luther Seminary, and a PhD in New Testament Studies from Emory University, Atlanta. A contributing writer for www.workingpreacher.org, she is also co-host of the site's weekly podcast, "Sermon Brainwave."

Find Karoline's contributions in February 1, April 2, April 26, August 9, October 18, November 22

David Lose

David Lose is the author of the popular books *Making Sense of Scripture, Making Sense of the Christian Faith, and Making Sense of the Cross*, all from Augsburg Fortress. You can find his writing on faith and life at his blog "… in the Meantime" (http://www.davidlose.net). David is the director of the Center for Biblical Preaching at Luther Seminary, where he led the creative team that developed WorkingPreacher.org.
Find David's contributions in February 1, March 29, April 19, August 9, October 11, November 15

Rick Morley

A graduate of Saint Joseph's University and the Candler School of Theology, Rick Morley has been a priest in the Episcopal Church for over a decade. Rick currently serves as rector of St. Mark's Episcopal Church in Basking Ridge, New Jersey, and maintains a lectionary reflection blog, http://www.rickmorley.com/, which features some of his writing, prayers, and art.
Find Rick's contributions in February 15, April 2, June 7, August 16, October 18, December 24

Amy Persons Parkes

Amy Persons Parkes, an ordained elder in The United Methodist Church, serves as a minister in the Alabama-West Florida Conference, and she writes a blog called "An Everyday Mystic" (www.aneverydaymystic.wordpress.com). Her passion is in the area of faith development and spiritual formation. With some bits of intentionality and much grace, Amy tries to grow beautiful flowers, to keep clean clothes in the closets, and to be open to God's Spirit.
Find Amy's contributions in February 15, April 3, May 3, August 23, October 25, November 26

Teri Peterson

http://clevertitlehere.blogspot.com

Teri Peterson is a Presbyterian pastor in the suburbs. She holds a degree in clarinet performance from DePaul University and an MDiv from Columbia Theological Seminary. She enjoys exploring new cities, being a bit of a music snob, writing, and coming up with creative ideas for worship. Teri co-authored *Who's Got Time? Spirituality for a Busy Generation* (Chalice, 2013), and founded and contributes to www.liturgylink.net as well as her own blog, clevertitlehere.blogspot.com. Teri is a great lover of farmer's markets, reading, *Doctor Who*, snuggling with kitties, and any TV show made by Joss Whedon.
Find Teri's contributions in January 11, February 8, March 1, March 29, April 5, May 24, June 14, August 30, September 20, October 18, November 26, December 6

John Petty

http://progressiveinvolvement.com

John Petty has been a Lutheran pastor for twenty-five years. He is a graduate of Wartburg Theological Seminary in Dubuque, Iowa, and serves as pastor of All Saints Lutheran Church in Aurora, Colorado. John has been active in

Habitat for Humanity since the early 1980s and currently serves on the board of Habitat Metro Denver. He serves as ecumenical representative for the Rocky Mountain Synod of the Evangelical Lutheran Church in America, and chair of the Unity Commission of the Colorado Council of Churches.

Find John's contributions in January 11, April 2, April 26, May 24, June 28, July 19, August 30, October 11, October 25, November 15, December 27

Elizabeth "Beth" Quick

http://bethquick.com

Beth is a United Methodist pastor serving Liverpool First United Methodist Church, near Syracuse, New York. By the time of publication, she hopes to have completed her DMin at the Methodist Theological School in Ohio, focusing on Leadership for Transformational Change. Beth is passionate about social-justice issues, particularly in the areas of environment, economy, and racial justice.

Find Beth's contributions in January 18, February 22, March 29, April 19, May 24, June 21, July 12, August 23, October 4, November 15, November 29, December 24

Mary J. Scifres

A graduate of Boston University and the University of Indianapolis, Mary is a United Methodist pastor and church leadership consultant in Laguna Beach, California. Mary's writings include *The Abingdon Worship Annual, The United Methodist Music and Worship Planner, Prepare, Searching for Seekers*, and *Spirituality for Just in Time Special Services*, all from Abingdon Press. As a consultant and teacher in leadership and worship, Mary hosts workshops at her Top of the World Retreat, with her UCC clergy-spouse, B. J. Beu. Learn more at www.maryscifres.com.

Find Mary's contributions in February 18, April 3, June 7, August 30, October 25, December 24

Ann Scull

http://seedstuff.blogspot.com

Ann is married to Joe and they have two great adult kids—Jared and Kate. Ann is an ordained Minister of the Word in parish ministry in the Uniting Church in Australia. She has a passion for contemporary worship (whatever that means) and has set up her blog to share resources that she finds interesting and exciting.

Find Ann's contributions in January 18, February 15, March 22, April 5, May 10, June 14, July 19, August 30, September 27, October 25, November 29, December 20

Julie Seymour

http://lutheranjulia.blogspot.com

Julia Seymour currently serves as pastor of the Lutheran Church of Hope (ELCA) in Anchorage, Alaska. She lives with her husband, two children, and one much put-upon Labrador retriever. Seymour enjoys reading, gardening, and

hiking—alone and with her family. Regarding living in and loving Alaska, Seymour says winter is never as bad as you expect and summer is never as long as you hope.
Find Julia's contributions in January 18, February 1, February 22, March 29, April 5, June 28, July 12, August 30, September 13, November 8, November 29, December 27

Thom M. Shuman

http://lectionaryliturgies.blogspot.com/

Thom M. Shuman is a Presbyterian Church (USA) pastor and poet whose lectionary-based liturgies are used throughout the world. These include the Advent devotionals, *The Jesse Tree* and *Gobsmacked* (Wild Goose Publications), and his contributions to worship resources of the Iona Community. Thom is currently involved in transitional (interim) ministry and always on the lookout for new challenges and positions, especially in or near Columbus, Ohio.
Find Thom's contributions in February 15, February 22, March 15, April 3, April 19, May 24, July 19, August 9, September 13, October 25, November 15, December 13

Natalie Ann Sims

http://lectionarysong.blogspot.com

Natalie Sims is a laywoman and one of a number of volunteer musicians and liturgists at Brunswick Uniting Church in Melbourne, Australia. Reading, playing, and singing church music provide respite from her work as a medical research scientist. Her blog began as a weekly email to three Uniting Church ministers who wanted help choosing songs for their congregations.
Find Natalie's contributions in January 18, February 18, March 22, April 12, April 26, May 10, August 2, August 16, September 27, November 1, December 24

Matthew L. Skinner

http://mathewskinner.org

Matthew L. Skinner is associate professor of New Testament at Luther Seminary (Saint Paul, Minn.). Ordained as a teaching elder in the Presbyterian Church (USA): Matt co-hosts the weekly *Sermon Brainwave* podcasts on WorkingPreacher.org; is a contributing editor of the resource *ON Scripture—The Bible*, published online each Wednesday by Odyssey Networks; and blogs occasionally for the Huffington Post's religion page.
Find Matthew's contributions in February 18, April 12, May 10, August 30, November 8, November 29

Martha Spong

http://marthaspong.com/

Martha is a United Church of Christ pastor, writing about faith, family, and coming out as a middle-aged mom and minister. She lives in South Central Pennsylvania with her Presbyterian pastor wife and her young son; they all keep an interested eye on Martha's three grown children. In 2013, Martha became director of RevGalBlogPals (http://revgalblogpals.org/), an ecumenical nonprofit created to support women called to ordained Christian ministry; her work includes development, volunteer coordination, and social media ministry.

Find Martha's contributions in January 25, February 8, February 22, April 2, April 12, May 17, August 2, August 9, October 4, October 25, December 6, December 27

Mark Stamm

Mark W. Stamm is professor of Christian Worship at Perkins School of Theology, Southern Methodist University in Dallas, Texas, and a graduate (ThD) of the Boston University School of Theology. He came to Perkins in July 2000 after serving seventeen years as a pastor of United Methodist congregations in Pennsylvania and Kentucky. As director of Community Worship for Perkins, he gives oversight to the school's chapel program. He is also known for organizing trips to baseball games.

Find Mark's contributions in February 22, April 5, June 14, September 6, November 1, December 27

Two Bubbas and a Bible:
Delmer L. Chilton and John Fairless

http://lectionarylab.com

Delmer Chilton is a North Carolina native and a graduate of the University of North Carolina and Duke Divinity School. An Evangelical Lutheran Church in America pastor, he is serving as priest-in-charge of the Episcopal Church of the Messiah in Murphy, North Carolina. He has served parishes in North Carolina, Georgia, and Tennessee, on staff at the Hinton Rural Life Center, and as an assistant to the bishop in the ELCA's Southeastern Synod.

John Fairless is a Tennessee native and serves as senior pastor of the First Baptist Church in Gainesville, Florida. With his wife, Sheila, he is the proud parent of three adult children, and is an even prouder grandparent of one beautiful granddaughter. John has served churches in Tennessee, Alabama, Michigan, Kentucky, and Florida. His loyalty to the University of Tennessee Volunteers remains unabated.

Find the Two Bubbas' contributions in January 4, March 8, March 22, April 19, June 7, June 28, July 26, September 27, October 11, November 1, December 13, December 24

John van de Laar

http://www.sacredise.com/

John van de Laar is a Methodist minister and the founding director of Sacredise.com, a liturgical training and publishing ministry. He holds a Master's degree in Theology and is the author of *The Hour That Changes Everything* and *Learning to Belong*, both from CreateSpace Independent Publishing. John lives in Cape Town, South Africa, with his wife, Debbie (also a minister); they have two sons.

Find John's contributions in January 25, February 8, March 22, April 12, May 3, June 7, July 26, August 23, September 20, November 1, November 26, December 20

Cynthia Weems

Dr. Cynthia D. Weems is pastor of First United Methodist Church in Miami, Florida. A Phi Beta Kappa graduate of Millsaps College, she received her Master of Divinity degree from Yale Divinity School. She has served in mission in Cochabamba, Bolivia, and pastored urban and suburban congregations around the United States. Her current ministry setting has an extensive outreach to the diverse homeless population in Miami.

Find Cynthia's contributions in June 14, June 21, June 28, July 5, July 12, July 26

Todd Weir

http://bloomingcactus.typepad.com/

Todd Weir is the pastor at First Churches (UCC/ABC) in Northampton, Mass., where Jonathan Edwards preached during the Great Awakening (see www.firstchurches.org). Todd operated an emergency shelter and transitional housing for homeless people for eight years in Poughkeepsie, New York. He has a Master's degree in psychology, focusing on mindfulness-based therapies. Todd is interested spiritual practices, socially responsible investing, and ballroom and Latin dancing.

Find Todd's contributions in January 25, February 18, March 8, April 26, May 10, June 7, July 26, August 23, September 13, November 1, November 22, December 24

John Wesley

http://www.ccel.org/ccel/wesley/notes

An Anglican priest and theologian (1703–1791), John Wesley is one of the founders of the Methodist movement. His *Explanatory Notes on the Bible, Journals,* and published *Sermons* all offer rich insights into his evolving theology of grace. Wesley drew from a broad array of theological sources and thinking, encouraging an active life of intentional faith development through both devotion and action for individuals and communities.

Find John Wesley's contributions, most of them excerpted from his Notes, throughout the Annual

Jenee Woodard (editor)

http://www.textweek.com/

Jenee is the creator and curator of the major lectionary study website "The Text This Week." She is a 1984 graduate of Saint Paul School of Theology in Kansas City and a 1980 graduate of Augustana College (ELCA) in Sioux Falls, South Dakota. Jenee is Mama to two children. Jaie is a PhD student in biophysics at Harvard. Phil, diagnosed with severe autism when he was two years old, works part-time at Michigan Public Schools and the Geek Squad at Best Buy. The financial, physical, and emotional energy required for Phil's care precluded further career plans for Jenee. She started "The Text This Week" in 1998 as a means of observing diverse and informed voices in conversation about the lectionary, linking scholars and storytellers from across the theological and ecumenical spectrum.

Find Jenee's "Jottings" in January 4, January 25, February 15, February 22, March 29, April 12, May 31, June 14, October 4, November 15

Peter Woods

Peter Woods is a pastoral therapist who spent thirty years in pastoral ministry. As a healer, he is passionate about making the gospel understandable to people inside and outside the church. Peter pursues this as a lectionary blogger at "The Listening Hermit" (http://thelisten_inghermit.wordpress.com/), and as spirituality columnist for the *Weekend Post*. He lives in the Eastern Cape Province of South Africa.

Find Peter's contributions in February 8, April 12, May 10, September 6, November 8, November 29

Scripture Index

Theme Index

Visit cokesbury.com to download a free PDF of *The Abingdon Creative Preaching Annual 2015*. Password: A2C0P1A3

2015 Lectionary Calendar

Lectionary readings in the Abingdon Creative Preaching Annual 2015 relate to Lectionary Year B (January 4–November 22) and Lectionary Year C (November 29–December 27). Bolded dates below correspond to Sundays and other liturgical events in the calendar year.

2015

JANUARY 2015						
S	M	T	W	T	F	S
				1	2	3
4	5	6	7	8	9	10
11	12	13	14	15	16	17
18	19	20	21	22	23	24
25	26	27	28	29	30	31

FEBRUARY 2015						
S	M	T	W	T	F	S
1	2	3	4	5	6	7
8	9	10	11	12	13	14
15	16	17	**18**	19	20	21
22	23	24	25	26	27	28

MARCH 2015						
S	M	T	W	T	F	S
1	2	3	4	5	6	7
8	9	10	11	12	13	14
15	16	17	18	19	20	21
22	23	24	25	26	27	28
29	30	31				

APRIL 2015						
S	M	T	W	T	F	S
			1	**2**	**3**	4
5	6	7	8	9	10	11
12	13	14	15	16	17	18
19	20	21	22	23	24	25
26	27	28	29	30		

MAY 2015						
S	M	T	W	T	F	S
					1	2
3	4	5	6	7	8	9
10	11	12	13	14	15	16
17	18	19	20	21	22	23
24	25	26	27	28	29	30
31						

JUNE 2015						
S	M	T	W	T	F	S
	1	2	3	4	5	6
7	8	9	10	11	12	13
14	15	16	17	18	19	20
21	22	23	24	25	26	27
28	29	30				

JULY 2015						
S	M	T	W	T	F	S
			1	2	3	4
5	6	7	8	9	10	11
12	13	14	15	16	17	18
19	20	21	22	23	24	25
26	27	28	29	30	31	

AUGUST 2015						
S	M	T	W	T	F	S
						1
2	3	4	5	6	7	8
9	10	11	12	13	14	15
16	17	18	19	20	21	22
23	24	25	26	27	28	29
30	31					

SEPTEMBER 2015						
S	M	T	W	T	F	S
		1	2	3	4	5
6	7	8	9	10	11	12
13	14	15	16	17	18	19
20	21	22	23	24	25	26
27	28	29	30			

OCTOBER 2015						
S	M	T	W	T	F	S
				1	2	3
4	5	6	7	8	9	10
11	12	13	14	15	16	17
18	19	20	21	22	23	24
25	26	27	28	29	30	31

NOVEMBER 2015						
S	M	T	W	T	F	S
1	2	3	4	5	6	7
8	9	10	11	12	13	14
15	16	17	18	19	20	21
22	23	24	25	**26**	27	28
29	30					

DECEMBER 2015						
S	M	T	W	T	F	S
		1	2	3	4	5
6	7	8	9	10	11	12
13	14	15	16	17	18	19
20	21	22	23	**24**	25	26
27	28	29	30	31		